The Revolting Body of Poetry

Chiasma

General Editor

Michael Bishop

Editorial Committee

Adelaide Russo
Michael Sheringham[†]
Steven Winspur[†]
Sonya Stephens
Michael Brophy
Anja Pearre

VOLUME 36

The titles published in this series are listed at *brill.com/chia*

The Revolting Body of Poetry

By

Scott Shinabargar

BRILL
RODOPI

LEIDEN | BOSTON

Cover illustration: Victor Hugo, *Le Serpent*, 1866, © RMN-Grand Palais / Art Resource, NY.

Library of Congress Cataloging-in-Publication Data

Names: Shinabargar, Scott, author.
Title: The revolting body of poetry / by Scott Shinabargar.
Description: Leiden ; Boston : Brill, 2016. | Series: Chiasma ; 36 | Includes bibliographical references and index.
Identifiers: LCCN 2016021887 (print) | LCCN 2016025883 (ebook) | ISBN 9789004324473 (hardback : acid-free paper) | ISBN 9789004324572 (E-book)
Subjects: LCSH: French poetry--History and criticism. | Poetics.
Classification: LCC PQ401 .S56 2016 (print) | LCC PQ401 (ebook) | DDC 841.009--dc23
LC record available at https://lccn.loc.gov/2016021887

Want or need Open Access? Brill Open offers you the choice to make your research freely accessible online in exchange for a publication charge. Review your various options on brill.com/brillopen.

Typeface for the Latin, Greek, and Cyrillic scripts: "Brill". See and download: brill.com/brill-typeface.

ISSN 1380-7811
ISBN 978-90-04-32447-3 (hardback)
ISBN 978-90-04-32457-2 (e-book)

Copyright 2016 by Koninklijke Brill NV, Leiden, The Netherlands.
Koninklijke Brill NV incorporates the imprints Brill, Brill Hes & De Graaf, Brill Nijhoff, Brill Rodopi and Hotei Publishing.
All rights reserved. No part of this publication may be reproduced, translated, stored in a retrieval system, or transmitted in any form or by any means, electronic, mechanical, photocopying, recording or otherwise, without prior written permission from the publisher.
Authorization to photocopy items for internal or personal use is granted by Koninklijke Brill NV provided that the appropriate fees are paid directly to The Copyright Clearance Center, 222 Rosewood Drive, Suite 910, Danvers, MA 01923, USA. Fees are subject to change.

This book is printed on acid-free paper and produced in a sustainable manner.

Dedicated to the Memory of Philippe Bonnefis

Contents

Foreword IX
Acknowledgements X
Overview XI

Introduction 1

PART 1
Revolutions

1 *La diction du mal*: Baudelaire 33

2 An Exaggerated Scale of Evil: Lautréamont 75

PART 2
Revolitions

3 Grounding Force: Césaire 127

4 The Wind's Gold: Char 151

Conclusion 169

Bibliography 187
Index 196

Foreword

Chiasma seeks to foster urgent critical assessments focussing upon joinings and criss-crossings, single, triangular, multiple, in the realm of modern French literature. Studies may be of an interdisciplinary nature, developing connections with art, philosophy, linguistics and beyond, or display intertextual or other plurivocal concerns of varying order.

∴

The 'revolting poetry' of which Scott Shinabargar will write in this important study of major work by Baudelaire and Lautréamont, Césaire and Char, and, indeed, to a lesser degree, though in conclusion, of elements of the poetry of Dupin, Bonnefoy, Frénaud, Roche and Prigent, is not essentially concerned with the significant historical breaks from earlier traditions such as those brought about by Baudelaire, by Mallarmé, by Rimbaud and by Breton. The revolt of which he speaks, eloquently and compellingly, entails a more radical and visceral gesture embedded in the very body of language's phonetic expressivity. A fine critical contextualisation of our understanding of such a 'revolution' is offered and melds with the textually focussed defence and illustration of Shinabargar's thesis. To read aloud the work at issue is essential, as it always has been in that revelatory passage from written text to speech and voice and presence, and allows for a full appreciation of the pulsional articulatory violence at play. We are beyond the study of mere lexical fields and imagery taken to be a sufficient indication of modern anguish or horror, refusal or revolt, beyond, in effect, poetry's self-reflexive discourse and argument as normally conceived. Enactment of the latter via their enfoldment within the physiology of language and its powerful sound symbolism is what is at stake and what is eloquently demonstrated in a book I am delighted to welcome to the *Chiasma* series.

Michael Bishop
Bedford, Nova Scotia
July, 2015

Acknowledgements

I would first like to express my gratitude to those who saw potential in the initial proposal for this book—the late Steven Winspur, and especially Michael Bishop, who felt it was worthy of publication in Rodopi's innovative *Chiasma* series. I would also like to thank the College of Arts and Sciences at Winthrop for support of this project, Christa Stevens, who patiently helped me through the final stages of manuscript preparation, and Brill, for publishing the work. In the area of patience, I must also thank my wife Anna, for abiding my cloistered hours during weekends and vacations, and for her continuous expression of confidence in my work. Finally, it is unlikely this book would ever have come into being without the mentoring and friendship of Philippe Bonnefis—an incomparable inspiration to me, through the singular content and expression of his thought, and a faithful advocate and source of encouragement over the years. Deprived of the experience of *hearing* his lectures, while at Emory – which a silent reading of his work, however rewarding, can never entirely capture – I might never have come to truly listen to poetry. Whatever I have been able to reveal in the language of the great works approached here, he is in large part responsible.

Overview

French poetry was indelibly altered in the modern era, at both the thematic and formal levels, through the sudden appearance of a *revolting* aesthetic. I have chosen this particular formulation in order to designate both the gesture of active revolt and the grotesque subject matter that, introduced into the lyric by Romanticism, become increasingly central to the work of succeeding poets. Such an observation, in and of itself, is hardly a revelation of course. I am proposing, however, that while this aesthetic is initially highly self-conscious and controlled, by the Romantics, it should be recognized in later manifestations as an ultimately anarchic, if not autonomous source of textual creation; an engine for the production of expressive force that *takes form*, in the most literal sense of this expression, in language. The celebrated "crisis of verse" identified by Mallarmé is further aggravated in the very body of the read poem, as these poets assault not only the eyes (through "revolting" content), and ears (through infractions against conventional prosody), but a much more immediate, visceral level of the reader's being, through the extreme phonetic articulations that force themselves into the reading act.

The Introduction first situates the development of this new poetics historically, as a product of sociopolitical and epistemological shifts in the mid 19th century. I draw on the reflections of Vivès and Galibert, who remind us that such upheavals in the arts are often the result of larger existential crises. In this instance, the encroaching nihilism that will dominate the following century is clearly already experienced and expressed with a heightened level of intensity within the poetic genre, despite the blasé attitude of the *poète maudit*. I then transition, through a concept of Hugo Friedrich – that *dissonance* is the distinctive, defining feature of modern poetry – into an explanation of the methodology utilized in my own treatment of this phenomenon. While most textual analysis of French poetry remains oriented by the highly codified formal structures of the tradition (David Evans' insightful work on rhythmic innovation, for instance), I propose that the psychosomatic forces brought into play in both the composition and active reading of poetry's phonetic structures constitute the most salient form of dissonance in this literary genre. That this level of the text is largely neglected is due, as a survey of work dealing with "sound symbolism" demonstrates, to a certain polemical atmosphere that has come to limit the scope of inquiry. The burden of proof – in the debate, for instance, whether light/dark connotations of vowels are universal – has prevented most linguists and critics from attending to more complex phonetic textures bearing on the communicative act; effects that would be validated if readers recognized their own, unformulated perceptions during reading—a recognition that the following formal analyses are intended to facilitate, by bringing forth these textures.

With the first section – studies of two key 19th-century poets in the revolting tradition, Baudelaire and Lautréamont – one of the primary objectives is to simply demonstrate how these textures are actually deployed, constituting a new resource for expressivity that will be accessed by future poets. In the first study, of *Les Fleurs du mal*, I am not identifying a use of phonetic effects that ends with Baudelaire, but, by correlating various points along the spectrum of articulation with the thematic motifs and distinct tonalities he introduces into the lyric (putrefaction, biting sarcasm, etc.), I am calibrating the reader's perception of the reading act to textures that will resurface in those works treated in the succeeding studies. After establishing the primacy of aggressive, sadistic drives in Baudelaire's creative process (despite the classical formal ideals that are so often valorized, by the poet and critics alike), I propose that, like the positively valorized "sorcellerie évocatoire" associated with "Correspondances," the forces of *le mal* are *physically* present in the text, in the materiality of the poetic enunciation. I then proceed to identify a number of the phoneme groups privileged throughout *Les Fleurs*, demonstrating how they are utilized to different ends. Juxtaposed in contrasting categories – dental -vs- velar consonants, front -vs- back vowels – I gradually reveal how these should not be limited, in formal analysis, to individual alliterative series, corresponding to single effects, but must be recognized as interrelated, synchronized textual components utilized in a complex amplification of meaning and affect.

I conclude the first study with a proposition that arises in the course of these analyses, and which will be borne out in readings of Baudelaire's successor, Lautréamont. If the author of *Les Fleurs* has brought a new, more visceral expressive force into the poetic medium, he has also introduced a sort of virus into the latter: the sound and physical gesture of disruption in the poetic enunciation come to replace, as a new source of redundancy and reification, the very generic conventions they were intended to leave behind. Increasingly sought for its own sake, the "irreparable" must be continually reproduced for the revolting poetics to retain the sense of force that validates it, paradoxically.[1] Hence, the designation chosen for this first section. Like the title, explained above, this term is meant to lead in several directions, corresponding to the multiple – and contradictory – aspects of the new poetics developed (if not programmatically, or even consciously, perhaps) by the poets in question. If

---

1 Thus further substantiating, at the phonetic level, Marder's claim: "Instead of being the last lyric poet, Baudelaire becomes lyric poetry's first simulacrum—its first stuttering ghost" (78).

the dramatic, and indeed violent undermining of literary and societal conventions articulated in their work clearly correlates with actual revolution, it is also found to be a gesture that is potentially circular (*revolvere* in the original Latin), doomed to endless reiteration—hence the plural: Revolution*s*.

This phenomenon becomes more fully apparent in the second study, of *Les Chants de Maldoror*.[2] This seminal work of poetic revolt has most often been lauded by modern writers and critics for expanding the breach in moral and aesthetic literary conventions undertaken by Baudelaire. And the mode of analysis developed for the present project contributes significantly to our appreciation of this event, I believe, in revealing for the first time an immense network of *textural* forces utilized effectively by Lautréamont. It also, however, leads us to identify a mode of discourse that is in fact *limited* by the seemingly unregulated source generating it. While similar readings have been put forth, admittedly (psychoanalytical hypotheses regarding the historical writer, Ducasse, for the most part, which it remains impossible to confirm), my own perspective reveals a truly "vicious" cycle at the most concrete, accessible level of the text. As we progress through the cantos, identifying more elaborate, extended variations of the revolting textures first witnessed in the relatively restrictive verse forms still utilized by Baudelaire, we find that Lautréamont's language of force increasingly appears *forced*, itself; not only in its abrupt dislocations of narrative and absurd imagery, but in the textures communicating them—"coagulations" of verbal matter with which the poet would assault the reader.

I conclude the second chapter with a new reading of the famous sixth canto, in which the final apotheosis of Maldoror's favorite, recurring mode of violence – the human sling – provides a way of regulating (at least in appearance) the preceding excesses of liberated expression. The absurd sound-images that surge into the otherwise coherent *roman feuilleton* narrative are progressively invested with significance, and seemingly resolved, through a sort of literary sleight of hand, in the controlled circling of this gesture—the description of which, significantly enough, is devoid of all poetic flourish in its Zen-like precision of consciousness. Like the centrifugal force it produces in the world of the text, this final act would seem to master the volatile, heteroclite verbal matter constituting this extended work as a whole. And yet, while the confidence and finality with which this conclusion is "executed" imparts a certain sense of closure, the revolting body of *Les Chants* is not so easily immobilized in the

---

2 Some portions of this chapter were previously published in *Dalhousie French Studies*, in my comparative study of the work of Lautréamont and Michaux, "Disarming Transgressions: Maldoror, Michaux and Beyond." See the Bibliography of the present work.

mind of the reader, I suggest, who has just traversed the "abrupt and savage" course of the preceding cantos.

In the second section, *Revolitions*, I demonstrate how two 20th-century writers in this poetic lineage develop strategies for negotiating the tendencies toward excess and repetition inherent in such a mode of expression. For Aimé Césaire, who attempts nothing less than coming to terms with the history of oppression undergone by an entire people, in his celebrated *Cahier d'un retour au pays natal*, *le mal* is a more immediate and brutal reality than the psychological torments of the Parisian bohemian; the need to develop a voice in the service of large-scale social and spiritual regeneration is experienced as an imperative. And indeed, without relinquishing any of the anger and rejection of hypocrisy that he shares with his poetic predecessors, Césaire is able, in his own deployment of similar themes and articulatory structures, to redirect the forces of revolt to serve a convincing expression of awakened consciousness.

As observed in the language of Baudelaire and Lautréamont, the moral corruption of society is given a physical presence in the text, not only through the pathological discourse used to figure it ("un vieux silence crevant de pustules tièdes," *Cahier* 8), but in the active, physical presence of these terms. I am also able to show, however, how the Martinican poet utilizes such language to different ends. Series of percussive consonants, for instance, are deployed early in the poem, not to attack the oppressive culture of colonization, but to re-enact its violent effects on the oppressed, allowing the poet to reclaim the forces involved. And where we observed recurring phonetic condensations as a problematic phenomenon in the preceding studies, we progressively discover that this embodiment of a negative reality allows the poet to then utilize such matter to express – inciting, if not literally enacting – the effective revolt of his people against that reality. The accumulated "mud" of enslavement is transformed in the final pages of the text, firmly rooting the speaking subject in both the past and present, and allowing him to rise above them ("<u>d</u>e <u>b</u>o<u>u</u>e" => "<u>d</u>e<u>b</u>o<u>u</u>t").

In the fourth and final study, I focus even more closely on this evolving and transformative use of the revolting poetics, exploring a major turning point in the writing of René Char who, during the last half of the 1930's, is transitioning out of his active participation in the Surrealist group and crafting the distinctive voice of his later work.[3] As the intellectual militantism of the Surrealists is about to be replaced by a very real form of combat in Char's life (as a soldier at the beginning of the Second World War, and later, as a captain in the

---

3 An earlier version of this study, "René Char and the Matter of Language," was previously published in *French Forum*. See the Bibliography of the present work.

Resistance), there is a distinct change in the themes and tone of his writing. Whereas a number of poems in *Dehors la nuit est gouvernée* continue in directions established by his early work, revealing a writing subject at odds with the world and himself, those of the following collection, *Seuls demeurent*, stand out for their lyrical affirmation of lived experience, celebrating chance glimpses of beauty, and quasi-mystical insight.

In the first section of this study, I identify what I term "the economy of *crasse*." This *champ lexical* of terms related to filth and physical corruption is deployed throughout the earlier work to express – through the materiality of the signifier as well as its signified – those forces oppressing the poet—whether the capitalist scions challenged by the *Front Populaire*, or the gnawing of the poet's own consciousness, constrained by illness. After observing how a number of these poems in fact reveal the poet's own dissatisfaction with this inflated, repetitive expressive economy – a self-critique that is indeed central to the texts in question (in contrast to the denial of *Maldoror*'s author, for instance) – I turn to the poems of the following collection. Whatever biographical factors might be at their source (a return to health, an unprecedented amorous relationship), they clearly reveal a significant transition in the poet's creative process. While demonstrating an awareness of his own participation in the forces of entropy undermining the evolution of self and work, Char is now able to detach himself, finding access to a benevolent presence, "a loyal meaning" that is discovered within a previously chaotic and tragic experience of reality. By reading poems from both collections in succession, we observe the poet mastering a sort of alchemical *Œuvre*—not simply at a thematic or symbolic level, but at the most immediate, *poïetic* level of creation. At the same time we witness a major shift in the themes of his writing, the continual revolt against stasis and corruption making room for an experience and affirmation of presence, we observe a corresponding change in its texture: the "crass" matter of language is transmuted, carefully channeled through phonetic patterns, into a resonant force.

In my concluding remarks, I attempt to assess the effectiveness of this transformation of poetic revolt, by looking at the work of poets writing in the second half of the 20th century and beyond. Just as Baudelaire found ways to utilize the decaying corpse of high Romanticism that he could not help mourning as he dissected it, succeeding poets – for whom the elevated, oracular voice of a Césaire or a Char cannot be reduplicated, any more than the self-conscious transgressions of the *poète maudit* – must find ways to utilize and transform these innovations, in the matter, as well as the meanings of poetry. And indeed, looking at the work of major poets – Bonnefoy and Dupin – who directly follow the 20th-century poets treated in the second section, we observe a similar containment of both lyrical *and* anti-lyrical effusion, when reading them in the perspective of the preceding analyses—an austerity imposed on the proliferation of the signifier itself, while the forces of violence and decomposition – the revolting poetics they have inherited – remain central to the poem. Other, more recent contributions lead us to question what such revolutions have in fact accomplished for poetry. An evaluation that depends, ultimately, on the palate of its readers…

Introduction

> Je ne m'oppose pas moins que Hegel au mysticisme poétique. L'esthétique, la littérature (la malhonnêteté littéraire) me dépriment. [...] Je me détourne de l'esprit vague, idéaliste, élevé, allant à l'encontre du terre à terre et des vérités humiliantes.
>
> BATAILLE, OC (345).

∵

With this personal credo, Bataille could be articulating the motivating principles of modern poetry itself—and the work, in particular, of those poets treated in the present study: Baudelaire, Lautréamont, Césaire, Char.[1] Indeed, such ideas have become so familiar to readers of literature that they approach the status of cliché in the postmodern era. At the major turning point in the French (if not the *world*) poetic tradition that is conventionally marked by the publication of Baudelaire's *Les Fleurs du mal*, a number of ideals that had come to define this genre are overturned, through a revolution that is now taken for granted. The conflation of traditional aesthetic, epistemological, and ethical values (crystallized in Keats' dictum, "Beauty is truth, truth beauty," 360) is put into question, and found "dishonest"; the spiritual "elevation" afforded by Romantic *enthousiasme* is contained, as poetry must inhabit the lower, as well as the sublime spheres of existence ("les vérités humiliantes"); and perhaps most importantly, all of this is undertaken, insisted upon, with the gesture and tone of disdainful revolt ("la malhonnêteté littéraire [...] me déprim[e]"; "Je [...] m'oppose [...] au mysticisme poétique"; "allant à l'*encontre* du terre à terre"). Without revisiting all of the factors involved in this significant historical development – an event with which the reader is most probably

---

1 If Baudelaire is still orientated at times by the "vague, idealistic and elevated" states of mind valorized by his predecessors, he of course also embraces the "humiliating truths" of human existence—not initiating a clean break with the tradition denounced by Bataille, but inhabiting the threshold between Romantic and Modern, old and new. I will continue to refer to the author of *Les Chants de Maldoror* by his *nom de plume*, Lautréamont (instead of his historical name, Isidore Ducasse, often used by contemporary critics), based on the particular perspective of the present study. For it is through the agency of this fantasized persona that the suppressed, pulsional language of the text is allowed expression (a persona that will be abandoned, significantly enough, when Ducasse signs his next work, *Poésies*, after breaking with the dark aesthetic of *Maldoror*).

already familiar, and which is extensively treated in a number of available literary anthologies and critical studies[2] – I would call attention to two of the predominant causes, central to the perspective of the following study.

The first of these takes place in the sociopolitical sphere. As the *Ancien Régime* is gradually laid to rest, with brief uprisings punctuating the otherwise assured bourgeoisification of post-revolutionary France, the artist's "job" is no longer clearly designated within the social order. With the ascendancy of science, and the burgeoning technocracy it makes possible, utility increasingly becomes the standard of value in the 19th century (inciting the Parnassians' famous credo of *l'art pour l'art*, which posits artistic worth, precisely, as the *absence* of such usefulness: "Il n'y a de vraiment beau que ce qui ne peut servir à rien ; tout ce qui est utile est laid").[3] Furthermore, where the Romantic poets – particularly Hugo – had taken the poethical to a new level, expressing solidarity with the oppressed of society, the succeeding generation of poets is often disillusioned with a democratization that, in enforcing complete equality, ends up levelling public taste in all things artistic and intellectual:

> Contrairement à la génération des *grands* romantiques qui s'orientent vers une implication politique toujours plus forte, les *petits* sont à ce point marqués par la désillusion que l'on assiste à une sorte de désolidarisation d'avec la masse [...]. [...] si la liberté de chacun passe par l'égalité de tous, fi donc de l'égalité et proclamation des différences (Galibert 17).

This alienation of the poet is even more profound, however, as it takes place during a metaphysical crisis. Long before Nietzsche's pronouncement of God's death, European thought had begun to register a de-centering of the intellectual and spiritual universe it had occupied since the beginning of the Christian era.[4] And however much artists and poets may have aligned themselves, in their subject matter and technique, with the traditions of pagan antiquity, the progressive secularization of the post-Renaissance era has a destabilizing

---

2   See the work of Depierris and Merlin, for instance.
3   Gauthier 23.
4   Friedrich Heinrich Jacobi (1743–1819) is generally recognized as the first to identify the presence of nihilistic thought within Western philosophical discourse, if the term (nihilism) was most widely broadcast through Turgenev's *Fathers and Sons*. Kierkegaard is also well known for his prognostications in this regard—writing, incidentally, on the process of *levelling* discussed above: "The abstract levelling process, that self-combustion of the human race, produced by the friction which arises when the individual ceases to exist as singled out by religion, is bound to continue, like a trade wind, and consume everything" (*The Present Age* 55–56).

effect on the language of poetic expression: "Le lyrisme et le mysticisme qui magnifiaient l'homme et Dieu sont remis en cause [...]. [Le monde] est un objet déceptif, d'autant plus qu'il ruine l'assise ontologique du discours esthétique" (Vivès 9). As Guermès suggests in this regard, the death of Victor Hugo, famously identified by Mallarmé as the event that detonates the "crisis of verse" in France, resonates at a much more profound level of consciousness in the French reading public than we perhaps realize:

> la 'crise de vers', qui est celle de toute la seconde partie du dix-neuvième siècle, [...] est la conséquence de la crise religieuse qui mine la période. Hugo, qui représentait à lui seul le vers, avait contribué à maintenir une unité factice. Aussi sa mort semble-t-elle, dans notre littérature, comme une répétition de celle de Dieu (13).

These twin events bearing on poetic activity – displacements of the poet and the divine, essentially – thus have a significant impact on the formation of modern poetics: for the *poète maudit*, the imperative to create a new form of discourse depends, in the absence of any grounding ideological principle, on a negative, *reactionary* relation to the very entities that he rejects.[5] The modern poet will define himself and his language in large part, that is to say, *against*— whether the object is his fellow man (and woman, in the case of Baudelaire), the divine, or the discourses that continue to validate them. Lautréamont's infamous declaration of absolute revolt – against both humanity and the Creator – is simply an overt articulation of the crisis undermining the poetic tradition more generally.

As a result of this major shift in the telos of lyric poetry, there is a correspondingly dramatic change in the effect produced by such writing. Whereas in the initial phase of this transition the poet had volunteered to function as a self-appointed prophet, replacing past intermediaries of divine truth, illuminating a wandering humanity (Vigny's "Moïse" and "La Maison du berger," for instance, and Hugo's poetry in general), succeeding poets will seek, on the contrary, to disrupt the "dishonest" harmony of the consoling discourse, alienating the reader in turn. As Friedrich observes:

---

[5] I am echoing Friedrich's definition of modern poetry as a genre constituted by predominantly *negative* categories, which are "[...] definitional, not pejorative. They are, in fact, applied as a result of the historical process by which modern poetry has departed from older literature" (7).

> Definitions based on German romanticism (and employing improper generalizations) claim that poetry is the language of the heart, the emotions, the individual soul. This concept of *Gemüt* points to an easing of tension through self-communion in a psychical habitat which even the loneliest of men can share with anyone capable of sentiment. Such communicative coziness is exactly what the modern poem eschews (4).

And the modern poem not only refuses to ease an existing psychical tension on the part of the reader, but actively seeks to *increase* such a sensation—what Friedrich identifies as "dissonance": "We may call this combination of incomprehensibility and fascination a dissonance, because the result is a tension that creates agitation rather than calm. Dissonant tension is an aim of the modern arts in general" (3). It is interesting to note here that Friedrich highlights the literal, aural sense of this term, citing the great modernist composer Igor Stravinsky, who identified a corresponding transition in the aesthetic of western music: "Nothing forces us to be constantly looking for satisfaction that resides only in repose. [...] dissonance has emancipated itself" (cited in Friedrich, 3). While Friedrich does not call further attention to the analogy between linguistic and musical forms of expression, it is worth pausing for a moment here, where the relevance of the perspective and methodology of the present study begins to become apparent. For indeed, no significant study has yet been undertaken of the *sound* units structuring the major "dissonant" poetic works of this period – not simply in the rhyme schemes or alliterative series of these texts, but throughout their entire phonetic texture. And yet, by what means could one more effectively approximate the dissonance of musical expression – augmenting what can otherwise only take place on the conceptual, semantic level of language – in a *substantial* manner?

Before surveying the groundwork that *has* been accomplished, regarding the expressive function of phonemes in language, I would call attention to one more element of this new, intentional dissonance. Whatever claims to unsentimental detachment many artists of the post-Romantic era profess, there is a very particular emotive charge underlying much of their work. Whether or not it is explicitly manifested in the text in question (and indeed, it is sometimes all the more effective for not being so, as we shall see), there is often a highly aggressive, and even sadistic element in the writer's stance during this period— whether in relation to the mass of society, as observed above, to other artists, to the reader, or even to the text itself. Flaubert, for instance, defines his method of "dissecting" the humanity surrounding him as a form of "vengeance": "Il me semble que le mieux est de les peindre, tout bonnement, ces choses qui vous exaspèrent. Disséquer est une vengeance" (cited in Vivès, 64); a statement that the critic then elaborates:

> La vengeance de quoi ? De la société et de sa propre imbécilité. Le complexe se retourne facilement. La supériorité du poète vient de ce qu'il est capable de maîtriser, de surplomber la bêtise de ses contemporains comme un juge. Il deviendra donc asocial, il habitera les hauteurs glacées, dans la mesure où cette *a-topie* réalisée lui permettra de parler d'ailleurs et de plus haut (Ibid.).

And yet, if the post-Romantic writer would appear to exact this calculated revenge through an act of mastery, his apparent self-containment and control is betrayed by a smoldering intensity within the voice—a sort of inverted alchemy, whereby the aesthetic purity of the Parnassian *Übermensch* is converted into "haine et mal"; a process that Vivès defines, interestingly enough, as a form of *discordance*:

> la beauté devient le discordentiel qui tient lieu de subjectivité [...]; [...] une « négation » sans emploi « face au monde ». Mais elle cache derrière cette négativité des rêves inassouvis : ceux de resacraliser le statut de l'écrivain à travers la littérature [...] et laisse résiduellement émerger un discours refoulé, conversion de l'ascétisme en haine et mal, transvaluation psychique de l'impersonnalité, du désinvestissement du moi en sado-masochisme. [...] plus la forme est travaillée, plus elle est contraignante et plus la violence s'expulse comme un *cri* longtemps contraint, appel de la chair, érotisme dissous sous le glacis froid du rythme – l'orchestration des désirs muselés laisse sourdre de nouveaux chants (Ibid. 13–14).

The first goal of the present study is, precisely, to demonstrate how this violent "cry" is actually produced in the language of the most prominent revolting poets who appear during this period. For if it remains largely suppressed and muted under the "glacial rhythms" of the writers treated by Vivès, it is unmistakably present, fully articulated – in the most physical sense of this term – in the language of Baudelaire and his successors.

Sound Symbolism: From Contest to Context

That this aspect of poetic expression has been generally neglected – briefly utilized in support of formal analysis, while never employed as an effective means to any thorough, large-scale study of a poet's work – is hardly surprising.

Linguistic "sound symbolism" has remained more of a battlefield for debate than a stable working concept, beginning with Plato's *Cratylus*. And arguments asserting the existence of such a phenomenon have become even more difficult to sustain following the popularization of Saussure's ruling on the nature of signification, with its insistence on the arbitrary relation of signifier and signified, and the consequent tendency to limit authentic examples of sound symbolization to onomatopoeia.[6] Tom Barney has even utilized a sociological perspective to localize the persistent problem of establishing an accepted methodology for the treatment of phonetics in literature, highlighting a divide within the academic community between literary stylisticians and actual linguists.[7] Whatever degree of validation has been attained in the last century for the role of phonetics in literary expression, it has been hard fought.[8]

And despite such advances, the often polemical nature of this discourse has had lasting, negative effects on phonetic analysis, continuing to restrict the development and potential application of such a methodology. Whereas it has been necessary, admittedly, to bring a certain degree of scrutiny and rigor (through trans-linguistic case studies and radiographic testing of speaking subjects, for instance) to what have often been highly subjective, if not "poetic" interpretations of how sound might function in literary language, approaches on both sides of the divide have been heavy-handed in many cases. As Hrushovski has noted: "structuralist methods of analysis were often taken – by adherents and by adversaries alike – for ontological assumptions, and seemed therefore to fail (or to be 'forced') where such assumptions could not be held in any rigorous sense" (40). One example of this phenomenon can be found in an ongoing discussion of the various connotations attributed to opposing vowel categories—the perception that back vowels are lower, darker and larger, while front vowels are higher, brighter and smaller. Beyond the fact that the near universality of such associations has been objectively proven by a number of linguists, through the testing of numerous subjects (Newman, for instance, 75), the very fact that they *have* been the subject of debate and testing for so long points to a certain myopia in the wider enterprise of sound symbolism analysis. Even those studies that take as a given some symbolic function of linguistic sound are most often constrained, through a fundamental imperative to *prove* this function, by a relatively rigid, empirical approach—Fisher's skeptical

---

6 See p. 11 of the present work.
7 "This attitude of regarding phonetics as slightly foreign, however useful, to literary study still exists today" (310).
8 Jakobson provides a useful overview of this effort in chapter four of *The Sound Shape of Language*, beginning with Jespersen's critical rereading of Saussure (186).

nuancing of the small/large opposition theory of vowel sound, for instance, and Coates' use of "Z-score" statistical analysis of phoneme recurrence in the work of Rimbaud and other poets.

If the lucidity required by scientific method has helped to eliminate the type of subjective, ungrounded observations that have contributed to the discrediting of sound symbolism, it is nevertheless only when phonemes are no longer studied in the isolation of the laboratory that we can begin to perceive how they actually function in literary language—in the *text* itself. As Delbouille insisted: "Ce n'est pas l'addition de sons isolés, doués chacun de certains pouvoirs, qui constituent l'imitation, mais l'ensemble lui-même, l'assemblage des sons et leurs rapports" (31); or Kayser: "C'est seulement lorsqu'un son acquiert un sens par son accumulation ou par sa position spéciale qu'il peut produire des effets de symbolisme phonétique. Plus encore que dans les onomatopées, ce sont d'abord les significations qui nous mettent sur la voie de ce qui est symbolisé" (104).[9] This does not eliminate altogether the need for empirical grounding when positing instances of sound symbolism. Putting us "on the way" toward this symbolic function, however, as Kayser phrases it, undertaking the process of understanding within the context of actual chains of signification helps to resolve the absolutist, essentially binary structure limiting many investigations.

As Tsur, one of the most important thinkers at present regarding these questions has observed, it is not in fact obligatory that an individual phoneme can be identified as producing one invariable effect in each instance of its articulation (light, to the exclusion of dark, for example). Indeed, he asserts that all sounds are in fact "double-edged," "'expressive' of vastly different, or even opposite qualities" (*CP* 210).[10] Far from hindering the establishment of a coherent basis for interpreting linguistic sound, this element of multiple potential qualities ceases to become problematic, apparently arbitrary, when it is situated in relation to the signifying function of the language in which it appears: "in different contexts, different potentials of the various features of the same sounds may be realized" (Ibid. 211). Furthermore – a fact that will be particularly relevant for the analyses undertaken in the following chapters – the

---

9   "Statistical methods in poetics do not seem to be very successful in handling [...] multidimensional contrasts and correlations between moods and qualities" (Tsur, *CP* 213).
10 My varying annotations of the front/central [a] in the following analyses, for example, is based on a related principle: when appearing in series of back, enclosed articulations, it seems to participate in their distinct connotations of darkness and heaviness, while in series of predominantly open, front articulations it takes on lighter, more expansive qualities.

symbolic function of these sounds is not necessarily determined by the particular semantic content with which they coincide; indeed, such sounds can in turn determine which elements at the semantic level will be valorized in the ongoing act of reading: "in a part of a text in which a sound pattern coexists with a number of semantic elements, the sound pattern may contribute to shifting the center of gravity from one direction of meaning to another" (Ibid. 211).

When, then, given this repeated insistence on the need for a contextual reading of phonetic expressivity, will the actual analyses begin?, the present reader might ask. And indeed, the preceding observations may not seem to have gotten us very far from the abstract, polemical discourse I have been problematizing. Before moving on to the poetic works treated in the following studies, however, it is important that we again consider the very particular needs imposed upon such writing by the aesthet-historical situation in which it was produced (outlined in the first section of this chapter), and that the relevant "potentials" of specific phonemes are introduced in this context. It is hardly coincidental – if not indeed a further justification of the present study – that the very distinct expressive gestures employed by the revolting poets are in fact *constituted*, as we will discover, by those sounds that most stand out in language production in general, rendering skepticism in this regard all the more tenuous. The aggressive tendency that comes to predominate in much of the poetry of this period, and would rupture the existing fabric of the lyric discourse, that is to say, will draw primarily on the most salient sounds in the chain of *signifiants*—those which inherently call attention to themselves as such (i.e. sound), irrespective of their function as linguistic code.

In Text: Sounding Revolt

Once again, Tsur provides a pragmatic approach to the issue at hand, presenting a continuum on which categories of phonemes are arranged in a progression between two extremes. These defining qualities can be understood, in layman's terms, as *tonal* or *percussive* sounds, essentially—qualities, interestingly enough, that correspond to the basic opposition at play in the texts treated in the present work:

> the sequence **vowels, liquids & nasals, voiced fricatives, voiced stops, voiceless fricatives, voiceless stops** constitutes a scale of decreasing periodicity or sonority in this order. The feature [+/−PERIODIC] is responsible for the opposition tone ~ noise, which is analogous, in a sense, to the opposition harmonious

~ not harmonious, or soft ~ hard. [...] The optimally tender sounds are periodic (voiced), continuous, and relatively unencoded; the optimally aggressive sounds are aperiodic (voiceless), abrupt, and highly encoded (*CP* 215).

While each category is not absolutely fixed in its position here, as Tsur himself notes (due to the "double-edged" quality, mentioned above, and the variable of encoded-/unencodedness), this chart provides a useful template for the mode of analysis employed in the following studies.[11] While vowels can of course lend their particular qualities to the expression of anger (we will see that front vowels, for instance, can be particularly effective in this regard), I would first call attention to those phonemes on the "high" end of this spectrum, beginning with the stops or *plosives*—those sounds that, when accumulated and arranged in prosodic structures, provide the most recurring and clearly perceived expression of aggressive force in the texts I will be analyzing.

The effect of these consonants is fairly self-evident, and hardly needs justification through any authoritative, researched perspective of the specialist.[12] Identifying them as "consonnes momentanées" ("p, t, c (*dur*), b, d, g (*dur*)," *PTV* 134) in his pioneering work, Grammont provides a definition which, intuitive, and not overly analytical, captures an effect that is immediately recognizable for most readers: "frappant l'air d'un coup sec, [elles] sont aptes à saccader le style par leur accumulation" (Ibid.). And the choice of terms here, while it might be called into question by the more rigorous, contemporary linguist, is entirely appropriate when we observe how this predominant "potential" of such phonemes is employed by poets who could most benefit from its effect—by someone as undeniably aggressive and attuned to properties of the voice as Lautréamont, for example:

---

[11] I won't elaborate further the concepts *encoded/unencoded* here, letting those readers who wish to acquire a more in-depth understanding of these statements consult the work in question. I would only propose one significant alteration to the order of the above chart, based on the conclusions of the following textual analyses. One finds that in the conscious *application* of these phonemes, the *stop* quality tends to override the *voiceless* quality, in the poet's search for more disruptive textures—thus inverting the *voiced stops* and *voiceless fricatives*, on the above scale. The velar [k], for instance, is "harder" than [f]; [d] more percussive (similar to its voiceless equivalent, [t]) than [s]. One other exception, to which Tsur himself calls attention, will be addressed below: the rhotic [R].

[12] In my undergraduate courses in which methods of textual analysis are introduced, there are always students – a number of whom are not specializing in literature, or even language majors – who immediately identify such series as contributing to a certain disruptive effect in the text.

> il enleva le sa<u>c</u>,\ ainsi <u>q</u>u'un <u>p</u>a<u>q</u>uet de linges,\ et en fra<u>pp</u>a,\ à <u>p</u>lusieurs re<u>p</u>rises,\ le <u>p</u>ara<u>p</u>et du <u>p</u>ont.\ Alors,\ le <u>p</u>atient,\ s'é<u>t</u>an<u>t</u> a<u>p</u>erçu <u>d</u>u <u>c</u>raquemen<u>t</u> <u>d</u>e\ses\os,\se\<u>t</u>ut\ (310).[13]

Indeed, two of the specific emotive categories connoted by these phonemes, according to Grammont, are defining qualities in the work of the first two poets in the present study: "l'ironie âpre et sarcastique" and "le halètement de la colère" (135).

The establishment of this correlation is not entirely dependent on intuition, furthermore. Data based studies have arrived at similar conclusions—such as Fónagy's sampling of poetic texts from numerous languages:

> L'analyse de la distribution de fréquences des sons dans des textes (poétiques) d'ambiances différentes suggère [...] que les consonnes réputées *dures* sont plus fréquentes dans des poèmes agressifs que dans des poèmes tendres où dominent les liquides, les nasales surtout le *l*, le *m* (*VV* 64).

Tsur has gone so far as to hypothesize the source of this phenomenon, based on data obtained in the mapping of sound-wave structures—beginning here with the "soft," periodic phonemes:

> The recurring signal portions with similar structures may arouse in the perceiver a relatively relaxed kind of attentiveness (there will be no surprises, one may expect the same waveform to recur). Thus, periodic sounds are experienced as smoothly flowing. The randomly changing waveforms of aperiodic sounds, with their 'idiosyncratic features', are experienced as disorder, as a disruption of the 'relaxed kind of attentiveness'. Thus aperiodic sounds are experienced as harsh, strident, turbulent, and the like (*CP* 222).

While empirical evidence is certainly helpful in substantiating such correlations, it is once again Grammont who provides one of the most convincing, if simple examples to further support his own claim for these effects. A number of words that are undeniably onomatopoeic in origin, he observes, and which communicate "un bruit sec et répété," are constituted, in large part, of plosives: "tinter, tintamarre, clapotis, cliquetis, tic-tac, cric-crac, claquet, crépiter" (*PTV*

---

13 The backward slashes here, which will be utilized throughout the following textual analyses, are intended to indicate interruptions or other forms of awkwardness in the prosodic flow—most often due to punctuation, but through other elements of the text as well (such as the monosyllabic series in the above citation).

134). The manner in which this observation both supports Grammont's interpretation of these phonemes, and simultaneously moves us beyond yet another binary opposition maintained by critics of sound symbolism, is significant. If not all of these terms communicate a decidedly violent event, as examples of the most common and effective type of onomatopoeia (those based not only on the distinct sound of a stop consonant, but on repeated, multiple phonemes from this category of articulation), they demonstrate how these phonemes are particularly useful for calling attention to the sound of these units of signification *as sound*. That is to say that their disruptive expressivity is twofold: not only is their aggressive "potential" ideal for reinforcing any corresponding semantic content, but, on a more profound level, these sounds have the potential effect – particularly when accumulated in such dense clusters – of disrupting the normative dominance of the signifiers' function in the linguistic act (i.e. to signify)—they *sound out of* language, so to speak. Furthermore, while those who police the domain of stylistic phonetics have utilized the unquestionable sound symbolism of onomatopoeic terms as a way of delimiting the arbitrary nature of all other phonetic structures, by opposition, in the manner of Saussure,[14] the above demonstration of these sounds' *over-determined* symbolic function (purely as sound) helps to reveal how such a distinction itself becomes arbitrary as soon the very units constituting the imitative terms are spread throughout a chain of signification—as demonstrated in the above citation of Lautréamont: the inert *object* of the act – the bridge ("le para̱p̱et du p̱ont") – and indeed all of the surrounding texture, are equally, if not more important than the source of agency here – the verb ("frap̱p̱a") – in the communication of impact. Whether or not such sounds even appear in the individual term denoting the phenomenon signified is irrelevant for the poet, in any case, as Mallarmé established long ago: "A côté d'*ombre*, opaque, *ténèbres* se fonce peu ; quelle déception [...]. [le vers] rémunère le défaut des langues, complément supérieur ("Crise" 203).

There is one additional consonant that, along with the plosives, is universally recognized for its connotations of aggressivity; a phoneme that, not unsurprisingly, we will find to be a predominant component of the textures analyzed in the following studies. While the rhotic *r*–sounds in no way benefit from the ex*plosive* quality produced by the stop consonants at the high end of Tsur's chart (they are generally recognized as *trills*), their effect is quite similar, if not greater, as he himself acknowledges ("<u>outstanding</u> aggressive potentials"): "it should be noted, that /r/, although a periodic liquid, has outstanding

---

14   "[...] *le signe linguistique est arbitraire*. Ainsi l'idée de « sœur » n'est liée par aucun rapport intérieur avec la suite des sons s – ö – r qui lui sert de signifiant" (100).

aggressive potentials, especially in languages in which it is 'rolled' or 'intermittent.' It is actually 'double-edged': on the one hand, it is periodic, on the other, it is *multiply* interrupted" (*CP* 216). As Jakobson recounts, Chastaing found that these "potentials" were indeed realized in most cases, with significantly different connotations than those produced by the other liquids: "his students felt /r/ to be 'very rough, strong, violent, heavy, pungent, hard, near-by, and bitter' in contrast to /l/, which seemed 'light-weighted [sic], debonair, clear, smooth, weak, sweet, and distant'" (Jakobson, *SS* 191). Fónagy, as well, identifies this unusual (for a non-plosive) quality in the *r*–sounds—an effect that he substantiates, not only through a variety of testing subjects, but through the statements of both poets and scholars, from Mallarmé back to the Renaissance (Ronsard, Vossius) and even the Greeks (Denys d'Halicarnasse): "Il y a un autre son – très différent des occlusives – qui est également qualifié par les grammairiens, les poètes et esthètes, comme très dur par opposition à /l/ [...]. Selon une tradition qui remonte à l'antiquité, le *r* est associé en même temps au combat" (*VV* 96). I would suggest, furthermore, that there is an additional element that adds to, or amplifies – in the most literal sense — the unique effect produced by this phoneme's "multiple interruption"—a factor in the production of speech sounds more generally that must be considered when accounting for their formation and effect. In failing to acknowledge the entire three-dimensional space in which a phoneme is produced (and additionally, in which the movements between *multiple*, successive sounds are articulated), the buccal cavity, we risk passing over (in the manner of those critics and linguists discussed above) the subtle complexities inherent in enunciated language—and poetry, in particular.

When we locate the gestures of articulation within this space, we perceive that the rough, agitated sound of the guttural French [ʀ], for instance, is produced from one of the most posterior regions possible in speech production—an attribute that produces the distinct – or rather, *in*distinct – sonority of this phoneme.[15] It should be noted here in this regard, that while we have thus far considered the *plosive* consonants as a uniform group, when we attend to the drastically different points of articulation producing them – front to back, essentially – we perceive a number of very different effects. If the bilabial (p, b) and dental (t, d) consonants of this group would initially seem to possess the most forceful, percussive quality, the posterior velars (k, g) in fact produce a

---

15 I would invite the reader at his point to begin (if he or she has not already begun) to actually produce the sounds in question—an auxiliary to the reading act that will be extremely useful, if not indispensable, to the following, more intricate readings of phonetic texture.

INTRODUCTION 13

higher level of sound—a fact that is due, logically enough, as Jakobson reminds us, to their full use of the "resonance chamber":

> for the velopalatal (or, in other terms, centrifugal) consonants the point of articulation is *behind* the sole or dominant resonance chamber, whereas for all the other consonants, i.e. for the dentals and the labials (grouped together as centripetal consonants) the point of articulation is located *in front of* this resonance chamber. The fundamental difference corresponds to the fact that the centrifugal consonants have a fuller, more perceptible sound (SM 93).

Such a distinction, which might appear insignificant out of context, becomes quite relevant when brought to bear on these articulations *in text*, as we shall see—especially in readings that are concerned, precisely, with degrees of expressive *force*, and an aesthetic of violence:

> Velar and palatal stops are more powerful than labials and dentals and display a "stronger concentration of explosion" (Fischer-Jorgensen 1959: 59), while compact vowels are more powerful than diffuse ones. Compact phonemes display a higher intra-oral air pressure according to Malécot's measurement of American English stops (Jakobson SS 104).[16]

In the poetic works we will be reading, terms that deploy such phonemes are in fact privileged in the expression of force and repulsion; an abrupt "explosion" of the voice, indeed, that is further volatilized in the following passages by the adjacent (also posterior) [R]:[17]

> Lorsque tu vis **c**racher sur ta divinité
> La **c**rapule du **c**orps de **g**arde et des **c**uisines (Baudelaire 121);[18]

> **C**rasse !
> J'ai **c**rié une chance de se re**c**ouvrer en vi**c**toire longue et
>   aplanissante (Char 107).

---

16   Fischer-Jorgensen also observes, interestingly enough, that such velar explosions are greater in duration as well as intensity (cited in in Jakobson SS, 105).
17   The following annotated citations of poetic text are taken from analyses in the following chapters, in which they will of course be contextualized, and their titles will be provided.
18   Unless otherwise noted, all citations of Baudelaire in this and following chapters are from *Les Fleurs du mal*, in the first volume of the *Œuvres complètes*.

If the effectiveness of these particular speech sounds in revolting poetry is easily perceived, however, it is only when we consider the role of the *gesture* involved in any given phonetic articulation – the physical effort and movement that produces the sound, and not merely the sound itself – that we begin to perceive the potential for complexity in such expression, beyond the more obvious categories noted thus far. As Fónagy has taken pains to verify (testing deaf children on the associations produced by the articulation of contrasting phonemes, *vv* 68–9), these gestures can in fact have an equal, if not greater role in our perception of linguistic expression. And this assertion is particularly convincing, interestingly enough, regarding the muscular tension required by the very consonants just discussed—a physical "comportment" that corresponds, as Fónagy repeatedly observes, to the most deeply rooted aggressive drives in the human mind/body: "la colère et la haine accroissent considérablement la tension musculaire. Le cadre phylogénétique proposé par Darwin nous a permis d'interpréter ce comportement vocal comme une contrefacture miniaturisée du combat" (*vv* 89). Not only does this observation further explain the expressive force of the plosive and velar consonants, noted above, but it also allows us to locate such force in other, less obvious units of speech sound. Always vigilant of the binary categories that have come to delimit inquiries into sound symbolism, we have to remember that unconsciously relying on such oppositions can prevent the perception of other expressive potentials in a given phoneme—qualities that are realized, variously, according to the semantic content in proximity to that phoneme.

Considering that the contraction of the buccal cavity, for instance (the "muscular tension," above), is required for a number of articulations, we find that the dualities inherently orienting our attempts to identify an ideal revolting poetic texture (in opposition, implicitly, to a conventionally lyrical, harmonious one)[19] – such as dark/light, hard/soft, and even consonant/vowel – do not account for the tension and associations of conflict involved in the articulation of the front *vowels*, particularly when rounded—the [y]/[œ] of "f**u**r**eu**r" in the following example from Baudelaire, for example; a poem that famously depicts, in fact, the primordial antagonism arising in human interaction ("Duellum"): "Ô f**u**r**eu**r des cœurs m**û**rs par l'amour **u**lcérés !" (36). And as this single line reveals on closer inspection, the contained tension enacted here cannot be attributed to these elements alone, but is the result of a series of contiguous phonemes—a carefully constructed texture that takes form, enunciated, in real time (the repeated [ʀ], labialized [m], and back vowels – in bold – for instance, obstinately drawing the mouth taut, further intensifying

---

19   As in Fónagy's observation, cited above (p. 12).

the enunciation): "Ô *fu*reur des c̲œurs mûrs par l'amour u̲lcérés !" Such articulations, furthermore, are often deployed for the way in which they actually force the expression of sarcastic humor (one of the predominant components of revolting poetry, as we shall see) onto the face of the reader/speaker: "[...] la *M*ort t'ad*m*ire / En tes contorsions, *r*isible Humanité" (98).[20]

This attention to gesture also allows us to perceive more subtle qualities in articulatory effects we otherwise consider self-evident. The impact of the consonantal categories discussed above, for instance, should not simply be limited to (degrees of) sonic force, but can be further differentiated, as Tsur observes, according to the contrasting sensations produced in their articulation (note: an example of a *palatal* consonant is the [ɲ] of a*gn*eau):

> the particular emotional character of palatal consonants is derived from the opposition of this articulatory gesture to its counterpart in the dental stops /n, t, d/. The opposition is between a *broad area* of contact (in palatals) and a well-defined, *clear-cut point* of contact in the dental stop. Now, the creation of such a clear-cut, well-determined point of contact (as opposed to a broad area of contact) can be interpreted (or rather perceived) as a gesture characterized by a sense of control and precision, firmness and determination, being set in purpose; whereas the creation of a broad area of contact tends to be perceived as a gesture of opposite character (*SP* 48).

Such a proposition is indeed borne out, as we shall see, in analysis of poetic text. Upon closer inspection for instance, Maldoror's beating of Mervyn, cited above, is troubling, not only due to the *sound* of force produced by the plosives, but the methodical, insistent "precision" with which they allow the poet to (re)punctuate the central gesture:

> il enleva le sac̲,\ ainsi qu'un pa̲quet de linges,\ et en fra̲p̲pa,\ à plusieurs reprises,\ le pa̲rapet du pont.\ Alors,\ le pa̲tient,\ s'étant̲ aperçu du c̲raquement d̲e\ses\os,\se\t̲ut\ (310).

It is this same control that Césaire will demonstrate, in his redemptive, visionary elaboration of poetic revolt, to enact the dawn of a new reality—a texture

---

20   Among others, see Delbouille (58) on this "grimace" produced through articulation. Grammont observes similar effects occurring with other phonemes: "les labiales *p, b,* et avec elles les labio-dentales, *f, v,* exigeant pour leur prononciation un gonflement des lèvres, sont aptes à exprimer le mépris et le dégoût, comme dans les interjections *fi, pouah*" (*PTV* 137–38).

that operates, precisely, through the type of dynamic interplay between two opposing effects described above by Tsur:

*vi*ennent *l*es **ova**i**r**es de *l*'eau où *le f*u*t*u*r* ag*i*_t_e *s*es pe_t_i_t_es _t_ê_t_es (45).[21]

This last example highlights another fact, central to the mode of analysis developed for the following studies; one more phenomenon that has too often been neglected in the existing discourse regarding sound symbolism. In their desire to confirm or negate the effect of a given phoneme – often in opposition to another category, and almost always in isolation from a continuous, coherent *sequence* of varying phonemes – linguists have generally ignored a key contributing factor in phonetic expressivity. As we have already begun to observe in the most recent citations, the role of articulatory movement in such expressivity is most evident, not in any individual instance (even in the "control and precision" of dental stops observed by Tsur, for example), but when it participates in a larger *texture*, imbricated with phonemes articulated along different points of the buccal cavity. The tendency to pass over the complexity of such sequential structures is perfectly demonstrated by the following observation by Grammont. While his sympathetic, intuitive ear allows him to identify the effect produced by these lines of Gauthier, with their predominant back vowels – "La lourdeur s'exprime par des voyelles sombres, comme la légèreté par des voyelles claires : 'La lou**r**de artillerie et les fou**r**go**n**s pes**an**ts / Ne creusent plus la **r**oute en profo**n**des ornières'" (*PTV* 132)[22] – the basic equivalence here, rear articulation = heaviness, does not account for the other phonetic components contributing to the effect in question—not only through their pitch, but through the creation of a continuous *sensation* in the articulatory movement required by this sequence. Very similar to what we observed in the lines from Baudelaire's "Duellum," analyzed above ("Ô *f*u*r*eu*r* des c̲œu*r*s mûrs pa*r* *l*'amou*r* u*l*cérés !"), the complex effect of the texture here also depends on the prominent [R] series which, along with the labialized vowels of "Ne creusent plus," and the final series of dense, monosyllabic terms, holds the buccal cavity closed and taut throughout the reading—a complexity that I would thus notate in the following manner, with these elements playing a

---

21   Unless otherwise noted, all citations of Césaire in this and following chapters are from the *Cahier*.

22   We will in fact find that this is a privileged type of texture in the revolting language of poets treated in the following studies (of Baudelaire and Césaire, in particular). As Fónagy has observed, citing Macdermott, the back, or "dark" vowels "are more frequent in lines referring to 'slow and heavy movement, or depicting hatred and struggle'" (*CP* 194).

role comparable to *all* of the "dark" rear articulations (including those ignored by Grammont, i.e.: [ã] of "en," [o], and [g]):

> La lou**r**de a**r**tille**r**ie et les fou**r**gons pesants
> Ne c**r**e**u**sent pl**U**s\la**r**oute\en\p**r**ofondes o**r**niè**r**es.

All of which forces us to acknowledge how articulation in general is an especially exploitable linguistic resource at a moment in history when poets are attempting to innovate through the marked disruption of existing conventions. As readers had grown accustomed to – and indeed *sedated* by – sonic landscapes that reproduced the continuity and harmony of phenomena valorized by the preceding lyric tradition (the mellifluous, flowing lines of Lamartine's poetry, most famously, enchanting readers through evocation of an eternal cosmos, transcending individual suffering and death), the textures utilized by the revolting poets often materialize within, and indeed *against* the intrinsic flow of the lyric, like so much debris. Just as an overabundance of rhythmic stress was considered an infraction against prosodic law, as defined by traditional French poetics,[23] particularly dense phonetic textures in poetic language – what I will refer to elsewhere as *coagulations* (a term that proves especially appropriate, given the "revolting" content to which it corresponds) – are often perceived, in being *too* perceived, as a transgression of aesthetic ideals.

While not often referenced by contemporary linguists, the experimental phonetics developed by the poet André Spire is quite relevant in this regard. A friend and collaborator of linguist Jean-Pierre Rousselot, in whose laboratory he worked, Spire developed a theory of poetic language based, not merely on the effect of linguistic sound on the reader/listener, but the physical gestures required for its production:[24]

> Balancement qui, comme tous les mouvements périodiques musculaires, est tension et détente, alternance [...] de fatigue et de repos ; et qui suscitant 'un maximum d'activité de l'organisme avec un minimum de dépense nerveuse', est générateur de plaisir quand il est modéré, de déplaisir ou de douleur quand il est excessif, anormal. Et voilà une explication infiniment plus claire de l'interdiction des rimes intérieures et de la règle de l'alternance des rimes masculines et

---

23 See Evans' excellent analysis of Baudelaire's "Les Sept vieillards," and that poem's accumulation of accentuated syllables ("the emphatically staccato hepta-accentual line," 253): "Suddenly, exact regularity provokes existential terror rather than rhythmical ecstasy, as the poet realizes the ultimate meaninglessness of nombre" (254).

24 Regarding Spire's initial work with Rousselot (to whom Ezra Pound once referred as the "Father of Experimental Phonetics") see Golston, 68–69.

féminines, que les explications d'ordre auditif. Il s'agit moins ici de déplaire à l'oreille que d'éviter la reproduction trop fréquente, donc musculairement fatigante, de mouvements laryngo-buccaux identiques ou trop voisins (143).[25]

While Spire unquestioningly posits the attainment of pleasure – or rather, a minimum of effort taxing the speaker – as the objective orienting the composition of poetic texture,[26] it is his acknowledgement of exceptional cases, where the opposite principle holds true – the poet seeking to produce an increase of "force" – that interests us: "grâce à une violation volontaire de l'*Euphonie*, il [le poète] ajoute à la force, à la valeur de suggestion de son vers" (227). For if the implicit ideal of Spire's innovative perspective on poetic aesthetics certainly holds true for most of the lyric tradition *preceding* Baudelaire, the conscious, meticulous upheaval within that tradition undertaken through *Les Fleurs du mal* will entail the frequent production of a decidedly *un*pleasant effect—the *Spleen* of existence entering poetry, not merely in the themes and imagery of the text, but *enacted*, in the tiresome articulations of the latter. Where the heavy plodding of Gauthier's sound-image, cited above, demonstrates the use of such laboriousness for momentary effect, post-Baudelairean poetry will increasingly deploy such textures on a large scale, assaulting the reader/enunciator of the poem—as, for example, in the following lines of Césaire, in the opposite phonetic "register," where the *front* area of the buccal cavity is overtaxed ("de mouvements laryngo-buccaux identiques ou trop voisins," to re-cite Spire), relentlessly communicating the "smallness" of daily oppression meted out in the history of colonization:[27]

> l'éclatante petitesse de cette mort, cette mort qui clopine de petitesses en petitesses ; ces pelletées de petites avidités sur le conquistador ; ces pelletées de petits larbins sur le grand sauvage (23).

The revolting poetic text thus quite readily becomes a nexus of aggressive, psychosomatic forces involving the writer, the object of revolt, and the reader

---

25 Spire even goes so far as to claim that, except in certain cases, in comparison to other languages, "le français répugne à l'allitération" (128).
26 He refers to the etymologically earlier, awkward phonetic configurations of certain terms, which usage has modified in the course of linguistic "evolution," as "monstres" (226). Particularly convincing, are his examples of classic verse lines, which he contrasts with reordered versions of the same lines – either by himself, or from earlier drafts of the poet's work – further supported through diagrams showing the trajectories of the respective articulatory movements (263).
27 The posterior [k] is included in the following annotation, due to its participation in the overall effect produced.

him- or herself, who is forced to "execute" the difficult articulations of the poem—a phenomenon that Vivès, once again, has insightfully identified:

> La violence phonique expose le travail pulsionnel qui agit dans le choix des consonnes les plus agressives et postule aussi une violence faite au lecteur à qui revient la dure tache d'une claire diction. Notons ainsi que, de Flaubert à Mallarmé, la lecture à haute voix devient un exercice périlleux et s'oppose à l'écoulement du lyrisme. Le texte oralisé lui-même est une violence, explosion, engagement laryngé sadique fondé sur une libération des bases pulsionnelles de la phonation (185).

We could not conclude these introductory reflections without some further discussion of these "pulsional bases" of speech production, and the linguists who first elaborated the concept: Ivan Fónagy, cited in passing above, and Julia Kristeva. While the skeptical reader may question the empirical validity of such theories, we cannot neglect to at least consider their propositions, as we attempt to understand the composition and expressive functions of revolting poetry's distinctive language, with its communication of violent emotions and acts. For as Fónagy reminds us, the so-called "speech organs" which are now responsible for the production of language evolved, long before such use, in response to the most "primary" needs and impulses of the non-signifying *body*: "[il est] indiscutable que la communication est une fonction secondaire, imprévue, greffée sur les fonctions primaires, biologiques, des organes appelés présomptueusement « organes de la parole »" (*VV* 109). From this crucial fact, generally elided by linguists in their reduction of language to signifying processes, he proceeds to explain how the articulation of certain phonemes can engage those impulses in the speaking subject that are not expressed through conventional language use. In one of his most convincing, least contestable examples, for instance, he observes that the first word acquired by most infants almost universally contains, often repeated, the phoneme [m]—the articulation of which reproduces the gesture of suckling, expressing the intense need to incorporate the maternal source of nourishment and life (Ibid. 76–77). More relevant to the present study, is Fónagy's proposition that *all* consonants, to a lesser or greater degree, involve a potential "investment" of unconscious aggressive energy, insofar as they are distinguished by an initial gesture of obstruction and retention, which precedes (and makes possible) the expulsion of the voice: "Les sons consonantiques, par opposition aux voyelles, créent et surmontent des obstacles. Ainsi, chaque son consonantique, y compris le /r/ ou le /m/, contient un élément de rétention qui permet son investissement de libido sadique-anal" (Ibid. 104).

If such propositions are generally reinforced by data, they cannot be empirically and conclusively confirmed in and of themselves, like so many claims of psychoanalytic theory, in its attempts to trace the motivation for behavior back to the amorphous terrain of the unconscious. But it becomes even more difficult to ignore them in the early work of Fónagy's protégée, Julia Kristeva—the linguist and literary theorist who brought these ideas to bear on the historical transition in aesthetics treated by the present study (indeed, making the latter possible), in her *La révolution du langage poétique*. Taking Fónagy's premise regarding the role of unconscious drives in the process of composition – a level of agency that is otherwise inherently excluded from signifying processes, and which she designates as the *semiotic* ("Nous distinguerons le sémiotique (les pulsions et leurs articulations) du domaine de la signification, qui est toujours celui d'une proposition ou d'un jugement," *RLP* 41) – she identifies the manipulation of these drives as a defining component of modern poetic expression; an activity to which she refers, significantly for us, in terms of "deformation" and "assault":

> C'est ainsi que nous pouvons penser d'ailleurs toutes les « déformations » poétiques de la chaîne signifiante et de la structure de la signification : elles cèdent sous l'assaut des « restes des premières symbolisations » (Lacan), c'est-à-dire des pulsions que la phase thétique n'a pas pu relever pour les enchaîner en signifiant/signifié (Ibid. 47).

Kristeva's fundamental insight into the function of phonetic structures in poetic language is thus double in nature. Not only does articulation allow for realization of the most powerful affective forces underlying such expression—inchoate accumulations of psychic energy in the body, otherwise inaccessible (and indeed irrelevant, at a certain point) to signification:

> Tout en conservant la fonction phonématique pour assurer la fonction symbolique – commutative – du langage, les phonèmes reprennent ce que les sons ont perdu en devenant sons d'une langue donnée : ils reprennent la topographie du corps qui s'y reproduit (Ibid. 222).

But poets' manipulation of the semiotic, much more than mere accompaniment to the dominant ideational component of language use (as the role of "formal" structures is conventionally conceived in literary analysis, in relation to "content"), comes to in fact constitute a source of liberation *from* these formal structures, as well as meaning-making itself. Concluding her detailed analysis of phonetic patterns in Mallarmé's "Prose pour Des Esseintes," she singles out the text as: "Un poème en train de se dégager des anciennes contraintes métriques et rythmiques [...] pour n'obéir qu'à un « rythme sémiotique » propre aux composantes du langage et aux articulations de la *chora* sémiotique qui les anime" (Ibid. 262).[28]

The "revolution" in poetic expression illuminated by Kristeva's seminal work is thus much more profound, in a very real sense, than the transition that is generally identified in the latter half of the 19th century. Where literary scholarship had identified this gradual historical break with poetic tradition in conceptual terms (defining Baudelaire's *mal*, for example, through its opposition to the social mores generally orienting the lyric up to that point; or understanding the Symbolists' "free" verse as the transgression of existing metrical constraints), her identification of unconscious, bodily invested forces in the creative process, lying just beneath the conscious processes of composition, allows us to perceive a more visceral, actualized form of revolt in poetic expression. And yet, the impact of Kristeva's ambitious work is significantly undermined by one glaring deficiency; and a surprising one, given the nature of her project: the hundreds of pages elaborating the dense, highly abstract theoretical discourse for this proposed method of phonetic analysis outnumber any instances – or rather, the *one instance* – of such analysis (!)—of Mallarmé's "Prose," mentioned above (*Révolution* 239–63). A theory that gains so much ground as a *critical* revolution, breaking through many of the limited constructs defining interpretation of poetic language, falls short of the *poetic* revolution it announces, in not demonstrating its propositions in any significant expanse of *text(ure)*—*un*grounded, ultimately. The following studies, highly indebted to Kristeva's brilliant work, attempt to respond to this lack, undertaking, through a relatively modest theoretical apparatus, a series of textural analyses that actually apply her theory to a number of poets' work— helping to increase the critical relevance of a perspective on modern poetic expression she revealed some forty years ago.

• • •

> Having become an entity in itself, dissonance frequently neither prepares nor anticipates anything. Dissonance is thus no more an agent of disorder than consonance is a guarantee of security (Stravinsky, cited in Friedrich 3).

---

28   It would require a number of pages to explain the singular key terms of Kristeva's discourse (such as *chora*), much less to summarize the text in greater detail. I once again leave it to the reader to familiarize him- or herself with the work in question.

In undertaking these more extensive analyses, a second issue in Kristeva's text becomes apparent, in its overt ideological orientation—not regarding the validity of her propositions in and of themselves, but the probability that the unleashed semiotic is actually capable of realizing the broader historical mission she has assigned it: was the "revolution," that is to say, in fact successful?[29] Already, in the first body of work analyzed in the following pages, Baudelaire's *Les Fleurs du mal*, where the pulsional forces bearing on composition are generally contained by the poet's continual, and indeed rigorous adherence to conventional verse forms, we begin to observe a problematic form of excess in the expressive economy of the text. The revolting discourse, we find, does not indeed "prepare or anticipate," as Stravinsky puts it, allowing the poet to lead beyond the inhibitive conventions and institutions he critiques, but in fact reproduces, paradoxically, the very qualities that are rejected. As discussed above, in the Overview, that which would break free of an apparently endless cycling of the same, is in large part constituted by repetition itself, in the very "engine" of the attack—the dynamic phonetic body of *Les Fleurs* that at once allows the enunciator of the poem to strike out against the shallow contentment of Second Empire society, and yet reconstitutes the "irreparable" the poet continues to worship:

> Nous avons, il est vrai, na*tions* **c**orrom'p**U**es,
> Aux peuples anciens des beautés inconnus :
> Des *v*isages *r*on*g*és **p**ar les *c*han**c**res d**U** `**c**œu*r* (12);
>
> L'**I**rrépara**b**le *r*on*g*e avec sa **d**ent mau**di**te
> . . . .
> L'**I**rrépara**b**le *r*on*g*e avec sa **d**ent mau**di**te (55).

The repetitive tendency of this new aesthetic becomes all the more problematic as it is increasingly accentuated in the work of those who take up and amplify the element of revolt in Baudelaire's work—Lautréamont and the Surrealists, in particular; both of whom will influence the later poets treated here.[30] If the author of *Maldoror* is ultimately an ironic, ambiguous observer of

---

29   It should be noted that Kristeva has continued to reflect on this key concept over the years – since the early days of *Tel Quel* that so infused the *Révolution* with the intellectual tenor of the time – through a series of texts (most notably, her *Sens et non-sens de la révolte*). See Sunderland for a useful summary of her evolving thought in this regard.

30   If one thinks immediately of Rimbaud as well, the same repetitions do not tend to predominate in his work, interestingly—a fact that is perhaps worthy of another study...

the no-holds-barred anarchism enacted and glorified by his protagonist (in fact condemning such extravagance in the final canto, and in the succeeding *Poésies*), this activity will be codified as an aesthetic and indeed existential principle by Breton and company; a foundational "infraction" that, as Michel Beaujour observes, justifies its endless re-enactment through the "sacred" nature attributed to it:

> La transformation, de la condition humaine est ici en jeu. [...] Promesses d'une nouvelle ère née de l'infraction d'un ordre. Peu importe l'origine de cet ordre : dogmes religieux, évolution du psychisme humain, aliénation économique, ou régimes d'oppression politique. Il suffit que la situation soit ressentie comme un interdit pour justifier un sacrilège majeur, « dans des circonstances exceptionnelles, fondamentales », qui revêtent l'acte d'une dignité sacrale : « Le surréalisme part de là ». À la suite de cette infraction initiale, le surréalisme se conçoit comme une répétition rituelle du geste libérateur, consacrant chaque fois la liberté de celui qui se livre « aveuglément » à l'automatisme (67).

Not only in the early work of Char, during the height of his involvement in the Surrealist group, do we witness these repetitive structures; but even in the carefully modulated, final ascension of Césaire's long poem, with its reiterated pronouncement of emancipation, a certain influence of this precept is detectable.

This need for repetition may derive from a more fundamental, inherent discursive structure underlying the expression of revolt—or rather, as we shall see, from the *desire* to realize such expression. For, as Laurent Jenny points out, no linguistic act can achieve the definitive resolution of an actual physical gesture. Even the most crafted blasphemy of a Lautréamont can never be assured of reaching its target; the creator/aggressor cannot avoid, however he may delude himself, being drawn into the indeterminate, volatile space of the invective:

> la parole implique le parleur toujours plus qu'il ne le croit. Les échanges d'injures enfantines le savent bien, qui s'exaspèrent sur un argument sans réplique : « Celui qui le dit y est. » Tant il est vrai qu'aucune insulte ne peut prétendre à l'énoncé pur, décoché comme un flèche, et dont le locuteur serait indemne. La destination des mots est incertaine. Avant d'atteindre qui que ce soit, ils ouvrent un espace où l'énonciateur lui-même est happé par l'effort de la représentation injurieuse. Les difficultés de la négation, qui doit poser son objet, avant de l'infirmer, sont du même ordre (120).

And indeed, we will observe the narrator of *Maldoror* continually drawn into, further elaborating his attack on – while never satisfactorily executing – the victim *at hand*—as in his recurring attacks on God, for instance: "Maniant les ironies terribles, d'une main ferme et froide, je t'avertis que mon cœur en contiendra suffisamment, pour m'attaquer à toi, jusqu'à la fin de mon existence" (140).

This particular instance of Lautréamont's invective highlights the impossibility of such a gesture actually engaging the opponent—or rather, the *object* of the attack. As Riley observes, the objectification inherent in any impassioned verbal assault ends up producing a sense of victimization in the attacker, paradoxically, as he or she is unable to exit what is essentially an endless one-way street, bearing down on a prey that can never sufficiently respond in kind:

> my very existence as the butt of his accusation is maddening to him, since under his onslaught, I'm apparently nothing for myself any longer but am turned into a mere thing-bearer of his passion. This is almost irrespective of my own passivity or my retaliation; it is because his utterance has, in its tenor, thrown me down. For the rage-speaker, I can have no life left in me, or rather none of that combative life that he needs to secure his own continuing linguistic existence for himself. Attacked, I'm rendered discursively limp, but no real relief can be afforded to my adversary by what he has produced as my rag doll quiescence. The more intense the anger, the less the sense of any agency its utterer possesses, until eventually he feels himself to be the 'true victim' in the affair (54).

That Maldoror should choose to attack an entity that is in fact *defined* by an absence of actual communication – and indeed, of substance (!): *deity* – thus highlights a problematic, if not absurd aspect of the revolting discourse more generally: by taking up a communicative gesture that is highly discursive ("calling out" the addressee, insisting on his or her presence) within a literary form of expression in which this addressee must always, irrevocably be absent, the revolting poet only aggravates the inevitable frustration that already results from the invective enunciation.

It is here, at the source of the revolting poetics – site of the initial "infraction" – that any serious inquiry into the problematic nature of such expression must eventually take place, in the perspective of the present study. While he does not proceed to an analysis of phonetic texture in literary language, Jean-Jacques Lecercle is one of the few to have identified the gestural quality of linguistic revolt, in his reflections on *lalangue*.[31] Emphasizing the play within (and outside of, in a sense) literary language (with the additional, unnecessary "la" invoking the ludic proliferation and sequencing of linguistic matter, superfluous to the process of signification), this term designates a creative principle that, according to Lecercle, is inherently disruptive of that process: "the excess of *lalangue* 'undoes' *langue* in all the senses of the word: 'lalangue défait la langue' – it overcomes, it defeats, and it deconstructs *langue*). Which means that *langue* can never be separate and abstract. It is articulated, it is in contact" (40). This useful concept for the (ultimately *non*-conceptual) source of linguistic *poïesis* is thus highly reminiscent of Kristeva's *Révolution*—not only by defining the poetic as a mode of expression that "undermines" the very system in which it takes place, but by tracing the originary impulse in such expression back to the "instinctual," non-reasoning part of the writing subject's mind/body:

> *lalangue* undermines not only discreteness, but also the arbitrary character of signs, for it opens the door to direct motivation. Proper names are ascribed meanings, phonemes are motivated by instinctual drives (39–40);[32]

> There is an inescapable materiality to language. My words emerge out of this body; other people's words penetrate it [...]. Language is not material because there is a physics of speech, but because words are always threatening to revert to screams, because they carry the violent affects of the speaker's body, can be inscribed on it, and generally mingle with it (105).

Lecercle's reflections on *lalangue* diverge significantly from Kristeva's theory of the semiotic, however, when the question of *agency* is addressed. As mentioned above, while her ideas are fundamentally aligned – like so much of the artistic and theoretical production of the time – with a *political* revolutionary agenda, claiming victories for this pulsional, disruptive force over the hegemonic discursive structures of conventional language use, Lecercle suggests that this force is not so easily appropriated or controlled. Referencing the work of Michel Schneider, he warns that this confrontation is hardly an

---

31 A term that was coined by Lacan, and then further elaborated by Jean-Claude Milner. See Pluth's article on this history of the term, referenced in my Bibliography.
32 It is thus *lalangue* that enables the writer to maintain, as Char so concisely (and yet, similarly, through *repetition*) put it, "l'amour du désir demeuré désir" (162): "[...] the textual excess that both ruins the coherence of the text and compensates for its lack. The excess of *délire* is the expression of the excess of desire" (Lecercle 5).

inevitable victory, but rather a "struggle" with the dominant group discourse, and indeed a "risky enterprise":

> Writing is always a risky enterprise, charged with emotional cathexes, because it involves a transgressive, even an incestuous relationship with the writer's mother tongue. [...] Style is the result of the separation and struggle between the writer's own language (*sa langue propre*) and the maternal tongue that he tries to appropriate (238).

The fact that this language use originates in volitional sources that are least accessible to conscious reflection, would indeed point to the unlikelihood of *any* distinct agency or telos guiding or benefitting from this activity. The totality of pulsional drives at play in such writing cannot be perceived perhaps as simply a sublimated, or otherwise temporarily obscured element of the writer's being, but should be acknowledged, at least in certain extreme cases (which many of the texts treated in the following studies certainly are), as something fundamentally *other* than the writing subject. Even the most anarchic *poète maudit*, that is to say – to return to the stakes of the present study – is perhaps incapable of controlling the forces he has engaged – if only intuitively – in the cause of revolt, truly "damned" to obey the (non-)will of a power more entrenched even than any exterior entity—"possessed":

> the linguist's failure has cast a doubt on the speaker's mastery. Emotional meaning may not be conscious; its transmission is hardly deliberate. We are closer to obsession or possession. Seen in this light, the text is the paradoxical utterance of the unutterable [...]. Language is no longer a mere instrument, it seems to have acquired a life of its own. Language speaks, it follows its own rhythm, its own partial coherence, it proliferates in apparent, and sometimes violent chaos (Lecercle 5).

Lecercle's closing formulation in fact perfectly describes the phenomenon we will observe in the following studies, where the pulsional forces driving composition are brought into relief in the phonetic textures of language. Already, in the work of Baudelaire, where these forces first begin to strain against the highly controlled structures of French poetic discourse, we find this "proliferation" of affectively charged segments of text – *intensive structures*, as I will designate them – that repeatedly rise up, as if *they*, and not the ostensible ordering principle of composition (the intended "message" of signification) justified their presence in the text; a phenomenon that, if still contained by his own adherence to formal rigor, will fully erupt into the "violent chaos" of

Lautréamont's cantos.[33] The innovation of a revolting poetics is indeed more of a "risky enterprise" than has been acknowledged, I would propose, since it infuses the already volatile, and potentially regressive activity of unrestrained linguistic play with the equally volatile and *inevitably* regressive activity in which the articulation of insulting, invective discourse engages the writer/ speaker, as discussed above.[34]

What initially appears a victory against constraining limits is itself increasingly revealed as a state of stasis, if not defeat, to the spectators of this conflict —both the "possessed" agent of the composition in progress, the writer himself, and the ultimate recipient of the text, the reader, whom the writer knows he must effectively reach. For in its reliance on the production of disruptive force, the revolting discourse is doomed to an endless repetition of its initial "infraction." This becomes apparent when, even as the object denounced appears to have no relation to any particular referent, the poetic voice must *re*-articulate the term that detonates out of its accumulation of invective force—in the passage of Char cited above, for instance, now in the context of the lines preceding it:

> L'homme a*ccr*oupi *sur ses c*end*res* in*fi*dèles a pro*gr*essé
>   par ci*catr*ices et monté la *somme* de *ses* pas à *tr*avers
>   le `*fi*ltre `*f*eint de son dépaysement
> `*Cr*asse !
> Que la *ch*amb*r*e des ma*ch*ines se *c*ou*ch*e à tes pieds
> `*Cr*asse ! (106–7).

By juxtaposing the work of the two later writers treated in the present work with that of Baudelaire and Lautréamont, I hope to demonstrate how this gamble – to somehow obtain an enduring victory over the oppressive conventions of tradition, through the most physical, untamable impulses within the poetic voice – itself calls for a sort of counter-insurgency—the return to a more *conservative* deployment of expressive force, in the most physical sense of that qualifier. Char and Césaire, that is to say, do not simply take up a more traditional aesthetic *theory* in response to the liberties of a preceding movement, merely *reactionary* (as one might identify the renewed Classicism

---

33   "[…] in [modern] verse, the autonomous dynamics of language, the need for nonmeaningful sequences of sound and curves of intensity, can go so far that the poem is no longer intelligible from its statements" (Friedrich 5).

34   For more on the regressive use of speech sound, see Jakobson, in his *Child Language, Aphasia, and Phonological Universals.*

of the Parnassians, for instance, rejecting Romanticism; or Ponge, dismissing Surrealism). Rather, as I hope the following analyses will convincingly demonstrate, these poets develop new and unique approaches to the ultimately *in*expressive gestures of the revolting poetics embraced in their youth. Not by simply smothering the energies of such writing beneath renewed formal structure, but by conserving and utilizing these forces in new ways, these inheritors of the tradition of revolt are thus able to develop voices that resonate powerfully to this day.

By patiently working the matter of language, directing – through the methodical organization of phonetic sequences – the impulsive expressive drives arising from the *chora* of the writing subject in the articulations of language, they uphold key principles of the revolting poetics, while transforming the latter, creating a new lyricism for the modern era. Such writing attains a more profound level of resonance for contemporary readers, the following studies will suggest, in being allowed to draw upon forces that are otherwise quickly dispatched only to be repeated, instead weaving them into a single, complex linguistic fabric. As the process of composition involves a higher degree of lucidity and reflection on the writing subject himself – and more importantly, on the psychosomatic "investments" of that self – the very texture of the poem becomes self-reflexive, deriving "beauty" from past "extremes":[35]

> dé*cli*nant *le refuge* des *villages* où m'a*vai*ent connu des crève-cœur ex'trêmes [...] j'avais extrait *la* signification *lo*yale d'I'rène.\ *La* beauté déferlait de sa gaine fantasque,\ donnait des roses aux fon'taines.\ (Char 134).

A metamorphosis of the creative process allows the poetic enunciation to acquire a sense of finality, thus enabling the poet to disengage from that process (with its compulsive need for repetition), "carried" onward by that which has been sufficiently expressed:

> Puis il s'éloigna,\ porté par *la* persévérance de cette houle,\ de cette 'laine (Ibid.).

While the revolting elements of existence can never be eliminated from the body of poetic language, following Baudelaire's infusion of poison, I hope to

---

35 The more complex annotation of this, and other passages cited in the Introduction, won't be entirely comprehensible until the reader has considered my elaboration of this mode of analysis, in the course of chapter 1.

INTRODUCTION   29

show that through the work of these later poets, this body in fact becomes stronger, and more vital, for having incorporated them—a body that neither languishes, melodically, before the sublime, nor gesticulates, twisted with rage, before the absurdity of human existence; a body that stands, through the force it channels... and relinquishes, "persevering":

> Et **nous sommes** d**ebout** mainte**nant**,\ **mon** pays et m*oi,*\ les *ch*e*v*eux dans le *v*ent,\ *ma m*ain pe<u>ti</u>te main<u>t</u>enant dans son p*oing* é`*nor*me et la *for*ce n'est p̲as en `<u>n</u>ous,\ mais au-dessus de `<u>n</u>ous (Césaire 57).

PART 1

Revolutions

∴

CHAPTER 1

La diction du mal: Baudelaire

> la poésie n'est plus un jeu, le plus noble des divertissements ; elle devient agression. Le lecteur ne saurait se contenter d'être le spectateur intelligent et sensible de ce que lui offre le poète [...]. Il doit être pris à son jeu.
> PICHOIS, *BET* (216).

∴

Among Baudelaire's inestimable contributions to modern poetry is his incorporation of *le mal*—not simply "evil," but a variety of previously censored, or simply devalorized aspects of human existence connoted by this rich term in French. While writers in the British Gothic tradition, as well as the *frénétique* school of French Romanticism (not to mention Poe, a well-known influence on Baudelaire) had drawn on this buried treasure in the psyche of their readers – and often with questionable artistic merit[1] – it is not until *Les Fleurs du mal* that such material becomes worthy, in and of itself, as a central subject of art —from the menagerie of humanity's sins, hidden beneath social propriety, to the rotting corpse encountered unexpectedly on a romantic stroll. And yet, it is surprising that this event has not been considered in conjunction with another of the poet's major contributions to post-Romantic poetry: the obsessive, quasi-mystical belief in the power of particular configurations of signifiers (the oft-cited "sorcellerie évocatoire") to engage readers at levels inaccessible to conventional, "prosaic" linguistic expression.[2] No extensive study has yet been undertaken, that is to say, of the ways in which *le mal* is manifested in the *body* itself of *Les Fleurs*; not simply through the introduction of new and often scandalous terms and themes, previously banished from the lyric tradition, but

---

1 It is important to note in this regard, as both Blood and Jameson have reminded readers, that there are essentially two Baudelaires: the unquestioned father of modern poetry we all know, and the poet whose first publications were widely greeted with scorn or simply indifference; not for scandalizing French society (as the infamous trial has led us to suppose) but for the perceived artificiality of his representations of evil—a "roominghouse Satan" (Brunetière, cited in Blood 30). Or, as Jameson puts it, "a second-rate post-Romantic Baudelaire, the Baudelaire of diabolism and of cheap *frisson*" (247).

2 "Manier savamment une langue, c'est pratiquer une espèce de sorcellerie évocatoire" (Baudelaire, *OC* II 118).

through the *physical* expression – in the articulated sounds imposed by the text – of precisely those "evil" sublimated drives located in the writing/speaking subject—and, by extension, in his *hypocrite lecteur* (OC I 6).

That such drives are not merely occasionally present in some form, but in fact pervade the poet's thought and work, would seem incontestable, even without the observations of his most dedicated readers—Georges Poulet, for instance: "At times sarcastic, at other times violently aggressive, Baudelaire's misanthropy is universal. It lashes out against all individuals, finding cause for resentment or contempt everywhere" (*EP* 57). Or the poet himself, for that matter, who confesses ("Il faut tout dire") to harboring the most absolute disdain for his fellow humanity—feelings and thoughts that, if they are not yet enacted, "sustain" the poet in his present state (a phenomenon, as the following pages will hopefully elucidate, that is both crucial to and highly problematic for the economy of expression in *Les Fleurs*): "Il faut tout dire, j'ai un orgueil qui me soutient, et une haine sauvage contre tous les hommes. J'espère toujours pouvoir dominer, me venger" (*Correspondance II* 96–97). The best known and most thorough exposition of this sadistic tendency in the poet's writing however, is surely, appropriately enough, Blin's *Le Sadisme de Baudelaire*. Establishing that the young poet had in fact read and appreciated the writing of the Marquis himself, Blin draws on lesser-known documents, not included in Baudelaire's published literary output, to find a number of similarities between the two writers.[3] Citing from the poet's correspondence, he observes: "Baudelaire ne se fait pas faute de cultiver « le plaisir aristocratique de déplaire ». [...] « J'ai pris une jouissance particulière à blesser, à me montrer *impertinent*, talent où j'excelle »" (36).

In a more recent study of this influence (as well as that of de Maistre and Poe) on the poet, Catani notes a number of Sadean themes in specific poems of *Les Fleurs*, including the "obsession with blood, torture, and poisoning" (996). Most revealing, in view of the present study, is his observation regarding the treatment of women in the poet's work:

> contrary to the largely positive celebration of sensuous female beauty in exotic love poems such as "La chevelure" and "Parfum exotique," there are occasions, most notably in "Une charogne," where Baudelaire dehumanizes and debases women in the manner of Sade's aristocratic libertines. The female companion

---

3 Regarding the least familiar of these documents, for example, Blin notes that a number of Baudelaire's earliest writings, unpublished and lost to posterity, went far beyond the censored poems of *Les Épaves* in the violence and depravity of their subject matter, according to secondhand accounts—including a story in which a woman is raped by an entire army (25).

evoked in this poem is objectified, denied a voice, and addressed in provocatively grotesque, humiliating terms (997).

This observation is significant, not so much for the central idea,[4] but because of a general tendency in the critical approach to Baudelaire that it highlights. While there is consensus regarding the transgressive aspect of Baudelaire's contribution to modern poetry, critics have often failed to sufficiently scrutinize this aspect of his work, continuing to orient readings according to more conventional elements of the lyric tradition, which are, admittedly, still very much present in his poetry—not only the idealized feminine other, acknowledged in the above citation as predominant ("the largely positive celebration of sensuous female beauty"), but the established aesthetic values of poetry in general; and more particularly, the formal conventions defined according to these values.[5]

Several critics have called attention to this tendency, including Evans (*Tension* 241) and Robb, both of whom trace it back to an overly facile juxtaposition of *Les Fleurs* ("[avec sa] forme conventionnelle ou quasiment classique," Robb 213) with the more experimental, avant-garde prose poems of *Spleen de Paris*.[6] Another, related cause for this misestimation of the verse poems' transgressive components lies, understandably enough, in the extreme subtlety with which they are incorporated into the poems' conventional form, as a number of critics have remarked: "Enfin, la raison sans doute la plus importante de cet oubli des innovations formelles de Baudelaire, c'est que la plupart de « licences » ou « audaces » de sa poésie en vers sont très subtiles, on pourrait même dire subreptices" (Robb 215); "Il joue sur les marges, mais ne sort pas de son cadre, et les libertés qu'il se donne ne se comprennent que par rapport à la régularité générale" (Molino/Gardes-Tamine 112–13). Through what is itself a particularly subtle figure for this phenomenon, Gendre likens Baudelaire's verse to the intentionally, only slightly imperfect spacing of the Parthenon's columns: "De même Baudelaire introduit dans ses sonnets des constructions à l'asymétrie calculée. Sans être convulsive, sa beauté naît souvent d'une série d'infractions à ce que l'on pourrait appeler le canon de l'harmonie" (175).

---

4 Which is indeed tenuous, I would think, on two counts: are the women of the "love poems" not "objectified" and "denied a voice" as well—the slumbering companion of "La Chevelure," for instance? And is the equivalence in the second half of the passage really accurate?

5 Kaddour has called into question "une tradition de lecture trop spiritualisante" in her own reading of "L'Invitation au voyage" (25).

6 "On juxtapose d'habitude les poèmes en prose [...] aux poèmes en vers, qui n'en semblent que plus conventionnels" (Robb 215); a phenomenon that is largely due, surely, to Barbara Johnson's seminal *Défigurations du langage poétique*.

Can a work truly constitute a revolution within the history of a genre, however – as most would agree is the case with *Les Fleurs du mal* – without a correspondingly dramatic, *visceral* disruption of its medium of expression— more than subtle "asymmetries"? Are the aesthetic principles of *L'Idéal* that are claimed by the poet himself, that is to say, actually maintained throughout this collection of poems to the degree we tend to assume, leaving the lines established by tradition in place?[7] Baudelaire was so successful in organizing his work according to the principles of symmetry, it would seem, that even the most perceptive readings have ended up assimilating, or simply passing over the disruptive elements they have identified.

Examining the role of evil in Baudelaire's work, Jackson suggests that the introduction of this thematic element into French poetry is inevitable at this point in the tradition, due to sociohistorical factors ("The necessary presence of evil in the poem is thus a consequence both of moral truth and of the need to address the readers in their authentic, ambivalent, constitution," *Satan* 159), and entails a significant, more than "subtle" concomitant transformation of poetic expression. Referring to Baudelaire's oft-cited definition of beauty ("Ce qui n'est pas légèrement difforme a l'air insensible ; – d'où il suit que l'irrégularité […] [est] une partie essentielle et la caractéristique de la beauté," *OC* I 656), he observes: "it is no wonder that evil becomes the mark of such 'irrégularité' and thus of modern poetics" (*Satan* 159). What is particularly noteworthy in Jackson's analysis, in my view, is the *energetic* quality he identifies in Baudelaire's valorization of irregularity. Just as the poet's assessment of (too) perfect form points to a disconnect with the physical and emotive ("a l'air insensible"), his ideal form of expression derives – in a formulation that Jackson traces back to the influence of Chateaubriand, and the latter's *Génie du christianisme* – from a form of energy arising out of the tension of opposing drives in (Christian, as opposed to Classical) humanity (Ibid. 158).[8]

---

7   A reference to one of Baudelaire's most cited poems, "La Beauté": "Je hais le mouvement qui déplace les lignes" (21).

8   It should be noted that other readers have identified this energetic principle in Baudelaire's work, if not, as Jackson has, at the formal level—Bataille being one of the earliest: "l'atmosphère de vice, de refus, de haine, répondent à cette tension de la volonté qui nie – comme l'athlète nie le poids de l'haltère – la contrainte du Bien" (*LM* 49). Catani, like Jackson, identifies the poet's interest in energy in the context of historical/ethical states of humanity. Noting Baudelaire's interest in the work of Laclos, whose willful, Machiavellian characters contrast with the bland ennui of Second Empire society, he observes, citing the poet: "This energy is, according to Baudelaire, characteristic of societies on the brink of revolution (the novel [*Les Liaisons dangereuses*] was published in 1782): 'Est-ce que la morale s'est relevée? Non, c'est que l'énergie du mal a baissé'" (Catani 3, my emphasis). Sanyal problematizes the critical trend of

Jackson comes even closer to circumscribing what I would suggest is the core of Baudelaire's new, disruptive poetics, in chapter three of his *Baudelaire sans fin*, where he elaborates more fully this energetic principle. After observing that "noise" (*le bruit*) almost always carries a negative connotation in *Les Fleurs*, he suggests that it is precisely this element, despite the privileged status accorded to musicality by Baudelaire, that distinguishes the poet's voice as distinctly modern; a phenomenon that arises in response to the urban reality of 19th-century Paris in the same way irregularity corresponds to the inner reality of modern, Christian humanity (*BSF* 64–65). Furthermore, Jackson does not simply reorient Baudelaire's poetics according to these new aesthetic principles, to the exclusion of those previously (over-)valorized by the critical tradition, but situates the latter in a newly necessary – if contradictory – mission for modern poetry: "écrire poétiquement sera poursuivre un double but contradictoire puisque l'écriture devra témoigner d'une réalité dont le bruit est l'emblème tout en visant à satisfaire l'exigence légitime d'un langage musicalisé" (Ibid. 67). More importantly, it is in fact in the *relation* between these two "exigencies" that the new aesthetic becomes, not merely a concept, but a dynamic principle. While acknowledging the traditional aesthetic that predominates in a number of Baudelaire's poems, Jackson proposes that in others, "noise" energizes traditional poetic discourse—not in and of itself, but in the *tension* it forms with the opposing drive to order and beauty: "Bien loin d'être une contradiction, la tension entre le bruit et la musique définit [...] la modalité nécessaire au chant baudelairien" (Ibid. 74).

And yet, when Jackson proceeds to analyze one of the most significant examples of this energetic phenomenon, in his reading of "Les Sept Vieillards," his demonstration is marked by a high level of abstraction—a tallying up ("quand on met en balance") of the rich and poor, the flowing and abrupt: "Quand on met en balance les éléments euphoniques et les éléments dissonants de ces quelques vers, il est facile de voir que ces derniers ne sont pas réduits à la portion congrue" (Ibid. 71). That the critic appeals to our ability to *see* (and with assured ease: "il est facile de voir") despite the auditory nature of the exercise, points to yet another tendency that continues to impede readers'

---

reading Baudelaire as a passive, traumatized barometer of modern experience: "As a mode of reading literature, such a symptomatic view short-circuits any sustained consideration of how the Baudelairean text actively engages with historical forces through irony, violence, counter-violence, and critique" (27); of the poems themselves: "their own complex deployment of violence rehearses and locates the violence of history itself in multiple sites, operations, and positionalities. This rehearsal of violence [...] is what gives the relationship between poetry and history in Baudelaire's work its ongoing critical energy" (Ibid.).

ability to fully perceive the formal innovation of Baudelaire's poetry: in accordance with a hermeneutical orientation that is particularly entrenched in the French poetic tradition, a poem's function must be understood through the highly codified set of constructs – of an often binary nature: "euphoniques"/"dissonants" – utilized and maintained by that tradition. To *hear* what distinguishes this new voice from the regulated modulations of the existing poetic canon, we must not simply count and categorize, but truly listen... to that *voice*.

There is one critic who, if he never elaborated a formal analysis of Baudelaire's work, recognized both the importance of this auditory element, and, more generally, the need to adjust the critical apparatus in order to register an aspect of linguistic expression that is far from defined, as of yet. In extensive, only recently transcribed and published notes, documenting his inquiry into the poetics of *Les Fleurs*, the linguist Benveniste proposes a different orientation for reading, or rather "reading-listening to" poetry: "le lecteur-auditeur se trouve en présence d'un langage qui échappe à la convention essentielle du discours. Il doit s'y ajuster, en recréer pour son compte les normes et le « sens »" (9). Formal analysis is not necessarily the application of mastered knowledge to a controlled object, but, first of all, the recognition of "a presence." The "matter" of poetic language physically enacts the meaning of the text—a meaning that is, Benveniste insists throughout his notes, of an affective nature: "La poésie est identification de la matière linguistique à la signification des mots. Il faut que le son suggère ou imite le sens, mais le sens pris comme suggestion émotive non comme signifié lexical" (Ibid. 546); or elsewhere, closing with a citation of Mallarmé:

> la dichotomie forme : sens a ici encore moins de sens que partout ailleurs. Le « sens » en poésie est intérieur à la « forme ». Le langage ordinaire vise une réalité, une situation qu'il dénote, qu'il décrit. Mais la langue poétique ne dénote pas, elle émeut, elle dessine dans sa forme sonore le sentiment qu'elle suggère. [...] « le rythme d'une phrase au sujet d'un acte, ou même d'un objet, n'a de sens que s'il les imite » (Ibid. 548).

To thoroughly perceive and appreciate this "moving" mode of linguistic expression – particularly in the *revolting* language introduced into poetry by Baudelaire, as I will show – requires that the reader-listener attend to the entire *body* of the text—again, that which is not simply an object, to be stratified according to existing analytical categories, but a dynamic presence, when engaged in the reading act. Several critics have approached Baudelaire's work in this manner, admittedly, though only in passing for the most part, and without sufficiently moving beyond conventional concepts of what constitutes the poetic. Vivier, for instance, who also recognizes the dynamic phenomena identified by Benveniste in Baudelaire's work, provides several wonderful examples, without however establishing recurring patterns, or distinguishing between the effects of different sounds. More importantly, even after the expressive force of a line like "*Cr*ève et *cr*ache son âme *gr*êle" (Vivier 38, his annotation) has been highlighted, all of these examples are subsumed by a single, transcendent aesthetic ideal, based on the values discussed above: "Tous ces effets de versification sont utilisés par Baudelaire principalement en vertu de l'élément de régularité qui est en eux et qui lui sert à créer l'impression de lenteur, de sérénité, d'éternité où il veut que sa poésie nous plonge" (Ibid. 46).

Vivier's tendency to either ignore or sublimate the most discordant sounds in Baudelaire's poetry into such a general "impression" points to another, more specific bias that has overdetermined readings of *Les Fleurs*—the "weight" accorded the terminal syllable, incomparably privileged in the French verse, anchoring the voice and maintaining textual symmetry at the levels of rhythm and rhyme. Perhaps because this prosodic tolling so inherently instills a sense of order in our reading of French poetry, we do not tend to perceive how Baudelaire, at the same time he rigorously maintains verse conventions, is disrupting lyric harmony in the space *before* the line ending. Given a system that mirrored the *Ancien Régime*'s conservation of authority, where dynamics that do not serve to elevate the official locus of power must be suppressed, it is logical that poetic revolt would begin in this space, straining against what has not yet been overturned. As Chesters observes: "Internal rhymes [...] subvert the anticipated regularity by their randomness and their tendency to deflect attention away from end-rhyme" (15–16); "it is argued [they] confuse the expectation of regularity and disrupt the balanced harmony of the rhyming system" (21). And in terms similar to those utilized by Jackson, above, he suggests that this disruption is not undertaken for its own sake, but in fact allows for a more authentic expression of human existence: "Versification must allow for the disturbance of its own drive towards order. In so doing, it recognizes the innate tensions of the human psyche" (105).[9]

Evans has written extensively on such disruptions at the rhythmic level of Baudelaire's verse, identifying an increase in metrical irregularity over the

---

9 It is interesting to contrast these observations with Vivier's reading of internal rhyme in *Les Fleurs*, where the critic's language "resonates" with the poet's celebrated "Correspondances": "elle étend sur le vers entier le prestige d'une résonance que le poète choisit riche et profonde. Grâce à elle, l'intérieur du vers participe à la vie sonore du poème, et non plus seulement à sa vie métrique. Le vers en devient plus vaste et plus plein. Il se prolonge dans l'espace et dans la durée" (42, my emphasis).

course of the poet's published work.[10] He notes, for instance, how Baudelaire's prosody is recurringly out of synch with the caesura, that other anchor of the alexandrine, thereby "challenging" the inherent undulations of this regal form (*Tension* 246); at times forming, in the conglomeration of multiple accents, an especially awkward, plodding *débit* (see note 23, p. 17 of the present chapter). While such metrical aberrations are a key component of Baudelaire's voice, and will be addressed in the following analyses, I will argue that it is nonetheless particularly at the phonetic or *textural* level of the poems, that Baudelaire's revolt is most keenly felt. As Chesters observes, such "phonetic patterns" do not simply serve a text's movement toward harmonic order, but, "grafted upon primary rhythmic structures […] they can emphasize or militate against the symmetry of the Classical Alexandrine" (41). And when these clusters reach a particularly high level of density and complexity, their effect is likened, in Chesters' reflections, interestingly enough, to *energy*—a phenomenon that takes place almost exclusively at the affective level of reading, independently of conceptualization: "Phonetic energy may be said to occur when there is an outburst of complex sound-patterning which, by its very richness, almost defies analysis and draws attention to itself as being a phonetic *tour de force*" (40).

Another critic who has been attentive to this "energetic" innovation in Baudelaire's writing, which he explores through a number close analyses, is Peter Broome. By engaging a wide selection of the poems, telescoping effectively between formal minutiae and the over-arching themes of the collection, he brings a refreshing approach to the language of *Les Fleurs*. After acknowledging the considerable body of scholarship dealing with the work, he calls attention to what is most dynamic, though as yet unexamined, in the poet's writing: "[…] So much is well known. What has not been so fully appreciated, however, is the extent to which Baudelaire has opened up for modern poetry, and immeasurably enlarged, the awareness of new dimensions of *active* form" (9). Unlike other critics, who have attenuated the volatile element in the poet's voice – Gendre, for instance, cited above ("Sans être convulsive, sa beauté naît souvent d'une série d'infractions") – Broome hears in *Les Fleurs*, precisely, the "convulsive" poetry demanded by Breton almost a century later, at the close of his *Nadja* (753). Baudelaire's writing cannot be reduced to the formal structures – however modified – of a detached creator, but is:

---

10   A phenomenon, interestingly, that he observes is simultaneous with, as if compensated by, an increase in verse harmony (255).

a complete and uncompromising investment of the self – its intensities, its dilemmas, its perplexities and frustrations, its irreconcilables, its 'unacceptables' – in the living act of language. Thus form is not a mould, but [...] a willed invasion, an irruption / eruption of the moment. [...] It is more that he has created a fabric, an inventive infinity of fabrics, in which self and style are consubstantial, in which the depth of the fluctuation or impulse within goes hand in hand with the visible reverberations, jolts, adjustments, contortions, unpredictabilities and palpitations of the expressive entity on the page [...][,] the battleground of spirit (10-11).

I too believe that it is to this "fabric" of Baudelaire's poetry that we must direct our attention, if we are to fully grasp the nature of the revolt attributed to it. While we will readily acknowledge such erratic "fluctuations" and "contortions" in our traversal of *Maldoror*, in the following chapter, we are not immediately conscious of these textual forces at work in a Baudelairean sonnet. Furthermore, as explained in my Introduction, I am proposing that the endeavor to illuminate such forces in the earlier poet's work is crucial, since the initial introduction of this volatile, material element into the body of French poetry also reveals a potential problem in the new (anti-)tradition it serves—a sort of linguistic virus that proliferates, as if of its own accord, overdetermining the "revolting" content and tone of the new discourse. It is interesting in this regard that Broome, who in fact selects most of his texts for close reading from the "ideal" side of *Les Fleurs*, concludes his analysis of the darker poems he does treat, by insisting on the resolution of healing and purification—recalling the optimistic readings of Vivier and others, above. In "Le Poison," for instance, an idealized essence is "cleansed" of the "verbal matter" encasing it: "Finally the word 'or' emerges, at first embedded in a thick layer of verbal matter, now cleansed of its dross" (204); a perspective that is even more evident (and more dubious) in his reading of "Une Charogne":

> The poetic experience of *Une Charogne* registers just such a conversion and becomes increasingly 'quintessential'. Gradually refining and exhausting its own inherent poisons, it takes itself 'bien loin de ces miasmes morbides' [...]. What seems first conceived under the sign of a 'muse malade' generates the health and energy of beauty (82).

The primary goal of my own analyses is not to simply contest the optimism underlying such a reading. The energetic forces identified by Broome and others are too innovative and complex to be limited to any one interpretation put forth by a given reader, in any case. The following study should be seen, rather, as taking up where Broome leaves off, in the admirable closing – or rather, *opening* – remarks of his conclusion, accepting his invitation to identify other "constellations" in the dynamic universe of Baudelaire's poetry:

> Other readers, tracing paths through the collection, could go on to create other configurations, other 'constellations', of the same. For, clearly, one poem changed, one added, one choice modified, one element of order disrupted or reversed, would give a new balance, new patterns and new distributions of poetic energy (534).

It is my hope that, through an even more extensive and focused reading of the phonetic articulations deployed throughout *Les Fleurs du mal*, the following pages will facilitate perception of the most powerful of such distributions—the intensity of which distinguishes a truly new form of poetic expression in the French language.

Decomposing Tropes

> l'air de la pourriture, avec ses charognes mélodieuses et ces cercueils qui chantent comme des boîtes à musique ...
> BONNEFIS (152).

One of the most pervasive *figurative* constellations in *Les Fleurs* involves organic processes—natural phenomena that, in distinct contrast with corresponding figures in the dissipating Romantic movement, are examples of *le mal* at the most physical level of existence. To insist here on *pervasiveness* seems appropriate, given that these allusions to disease and decay are not simply abstractions for the poet, but correspond to a very real transformation, irrevocable, in the body of poetic language. For Baudelaire, *le mal* is not in fact a phenomenon that he himself has introduced into the existing corpus of poetic expression; he is the first, rather, to diagnose a malady for which, if the symptoms have not yet reached their full "blossom" (*Les* Fleurs *du mal*), the conditions for cultivation are already in place.[11] In his ironic elegy to the passing of Romanticism,

---

11 Brunel has written extensively on this topic: "La littérature du passé n'a donc pas ignoré le Mal. L'héritage est même considérable à cet égard. C'est [...] un terreau déjà préparé sur lequel un poète moderne peut faire éclore des fleurs du Mal" (59); and, recalling Baudelaire's dedication to Gautier ("Au poète impeccable [...] Théophile Gauthier [...] je dédie ces fleurs maladives," 3): "Il convient donc de cueillir ces fleurs à la source de la *maladie*,

"Le Coucher du soleil romantique" (the poem, significantly, that introduces the collection "Épaves"—the disparate, overly "corrupt" limbs amputated by censors from the original body of *Les Fleurs*), the space of poetry becomes a dark and fetid swamp, ideal for the processes of decomposition:

> Mais je poursuis en vain le Dieu qui se retire ;
> L'irrésistible Nuit établit son empire,
> Noir, humide, funeste et pleine de frissons ;
>
> Une odeur de tombeau dans les ténèbres nage,
> Et mon pied peureux froisse, au bord du marécage,
> Des crapauds imprévus et de froids limaçons (149).

What is most significant here, however, and central to the present study, is that this is no mere diagnosis, objectively performed in the interest of aesthetic hygiene, any more than Baudelaire is actually "fearful" of what he discovers ("mon pied peureux"). The Manichean opposition at the center of *Les Fleurs* itself (*Spleen et Idéal*) is not posited as an abstraction, for the justification of *either* side, but functions as a means to reincorporate that which has been excluded from poetic expression—literary "refuse" which, like its correlate in the organic sphere, contains the most concentrated, potent source of vitality, despite (very likely *because* of, in the case of language) its banishment from visibility, below the surface of daily life. The rotting cadaver of Romanticism (and the entire lyric tradition, essentially, bloated with "ideals") opens up, in its grotesque fertility, for the appearance of a new, more vital lexicon. In a sense, it is to the underworld of poetry itself that Baudelaire escorts us, in "L'Irrémédiable"—though, in a significant twist on the first of such poetic journeys (by Orpheus), as a *final* destination; not to retrieve the ideal *from*, but to escort it *to* this hell:

> Une Idée, une Forme, un Être
> Parti de l'azur et tombé
> Dans un Styx bourbeux et plombé
> Où nul œil du Ciel ne pénètre
> . . . .
> Un damné descendant sans lampe,

---

avant de chercher leur origine dans le *Mal*. Avant toute métaphysique, devra intervenir une nosographie" (Brunel 61). See also Barbara Spackman's *Decadent Genealogies: The Rhetoric of Sickness from Baudelaire to D'Annunzio*.

> Au bord d'un gouffre dont l'odeur
> Trahit l'humide profondeur,
> D'éternels escaliers sans rampe,
> Où veillent des monstres visqueux (80).

And this journey is enacted not only at the conceptual, essentially visual level of language, as we will observe, but at its most visceral—"maggot-verses" (suggested in the "vers" of the following address, from "Le Mort joyeux") that accompany us, writhing blindly, thriving irrationally on refuse(d) matter: "Ô vers ! noirs compagnons sans oreille et sans yeux / [...] / Philosophes viveurs, fils de la pourriture" (70).

Not unexpectedly, for a poet who is still very much faithful to and working within traditional verse form, the bursts of affective intensity afforded by terms in this lexicon are often achieved, as in the preceding example, through their placement at line-endings ("[...] fils de la <u>pourriture</u>"), where the combined effects of maximum accentuation and rhyme multiply the force of the terms' emotive connotations, as in "Le Flacon":

> Je serai ton cercueil, aimable <u>pestilence</u> !
> Le témoin de ta force et de ta <u>virulence</u> (48).

The effect of such a structure is even more tangible in the following passage, from "L'Imprévu," where the "ripe" flesh of the debauched is alerted to the forces that infect and gnaw at it:

> [...] « Il est mûr,
> Le damné ! J'avertis en vain la chair in`<u>fecte</u>.
> L'homme est aveugle, sourd, fragile, comme un mur
> Qu'habite et que ronge un in`<u>secte</u> ! » (171).

The preceding citations provide a point of entry into the textual analyses that follow, in which we will observe the use of progressively complex sound structures in Baudelaire's language. The slight increase of expressive force in the above sequence of passages, in terms that are not otherwise significantly different semantically ("pestilence" => "insecte," "virulence" => "infecte") is clearly due, upon close analysis, to key differences in their phonetic structure, and the locations and components of the articulations involved. If the nasal/fricative unit of the first passage ([ã]/[s]) highlights the insidious, inconspicuous nature of the subject matter ("pesti`lence," "viru`lence"), the corresponding elements of the second passage do not merely emphasize these same qualities, but convey a distinct affective charge, traceable – implicitly – back to the writing/speaking subject. The fricatives here ([f] [s]) do not trail off at the line endings, as those used in the first example, but are employed at the *beginning* of the final, accented syllable, fluidly driving the voice into the jarring whiplash of the final consonant cluster—the articulatory movement forward ([ʃ] [s]) drawn back for the velar [k], and immediately jerked forward for the percussive dental that detonates at the line ending [t]:

in`*fe*cte / in`se*cte*
=> ↔   => ↔

The language of "pourriture" thus serves to breathe new life into the reified discourse it condemns, *physically*,[12] as the following passage from "L'Idéal" also demonstrates, surging forward in the recurring cluster of fricative [v]/palatal [ɲ]:[13]

> Ce ne seront jamais ces beautés de *vign*ettes,
> Produits a*varié*s, nés d'un siècle *vaurien*,
> ....
> Qui sauront satisfaire un cœur comme le mien (22).

In duplicitous perversity (hardly surprising for this prince of *poètes maudits*), Baudelaire *is* in fact "satisfied" by such literature, in the very act of enunciating his dissatisfaction. It is what "murmurs" in the unsavory corners of past art that captures his attention, as much as – if not more than – the beauty that is clearly visible there; voices that are "exhaled" by accumulations of filth: "Rembrandt, triste hôpital tout rempli de murmures, / [...] / Où la prière en pleurs s'exhale des ordures" ("Les Phares," 13). As we have already seen (or rather *heard*), these voices of the under-expressed are much more than a "murmur," when

---

12   Recalling the *vers* that feed on the poet's infamous "charogne," causing the latter – and the language of the poem itself – to undulate: "Tout cela descendait, montait comme une vague / [...] / On eût dit que le corps, enflé d'un souffle vague, / Vivait en se multipliant" (31).

13   Only one of the highlighted terms here of course belongs to the *champ lexical* of *pourriture*—"avarié." Far from undermining the above reading, however, this fact actually validates the present mode of analysis more generally: as suggested on pp. 7–8 of the Introduction, terms that are otherwise only partially or not at all semantically resonant can become so, due the affective "colorings" they share through phonetic texture—"*vaurien*" and even "*vign*ettes," that is to say, *become* "rotten products" in the act of reading, as they take on connotations inherent in "a*varié*s."

produced in the poet's own language, clearly and vehemently articulated. It is to these articulations, in all of their variety and complexity, that we now turn.

(Ex)Plosive Consonants

Even the least sympathetic reader of poetry must recognize the inherent expressive value in the use of those "detonators" observed above ("in`fecte" / "in`secte"). When accentuated in the texture of poetic language, through position and repetition, their explosive quality in fact becomes impossible to ignore. For the articulation of front, plosive consonants (the dentals [t] [d] and labials [p] [b]) and velar consonants ([k] [g]) involve, in the obstruction and release of breath, a palpable production of abrupt force in the mouth of the speaker. It is logical then that Baudelaire, a poet who would make his reader clearly perceive a distinct *break* with the existing lyric tradition, would utilize these phonemes to great effect in his work. Simultaneously drawing on the phonetic as well as semantic qualities of particular terms, numerous texts are thus transformed into the site of conflict depicted—as in his famous analogy between humanity and the sea, "L'Homme et la mer," where the staccato articulation of "implacable" is further amplified by the preceding accumulation of "hard" phonemes (propulsed by the liquid [l] series and open [a]), producing the *sound* of "eternal combattants":

> Tellement vous aimez le carnage et la mort,
> Ô lutteurs éternels, ô frères impla`cables ! (19).

The effect is even more apparent where such series are forced into a smaller space, seeming to not merely punctuate, but *puncture* the texture of the enunciation—perfect for distinguishing the more complex, perverse pathos of the Baudelairean subject (*victime* et *bourreau*), from the Romantic, as in "Le Vampire":

> Toi qui, comme un coup de couteau,
> Dans mon cœur plaintif es entrée (33).[14]

---

14   Broome, it should be noted, has also identified the effectiveness of this particular series, "the alliteration of which creates a serrated edge [...] aggressive and insistent" (103).

The complex subjectivity that exceeds the limitations of existing tropes available for the expression of sentiment and thought (*le vague des passions*, etc.), requiring innovation at the lexical and thematic levels, also entails a growing complexity in the gestures and sounds of the enunciated text, however. If the almost onomatopoeic function of articulation in the above "stabbing" is appropriate enough for such a passage, the majority of effects achieved through phonetic texture in *Les Fleurs* cannot be attributed to a single category of phoneme, but are the result of multiple, interactive components of the expressive act. While I will thus limit the present analysis of "hard" consonants in isolation, proceeding to introduce the function of other individual categories of phonemes in *Les Fleurs*, it will be useful at this point to acknowledge combinations of multiple phonetic components, which form more complex and dynamic effects than those observed thus far.

Often in Baudelaire's work, the envisioning or enactment of violence is all the more disturbing for the apparent disjunction between the nature of the act and the affective state of the poetic subject, expressed in the tone and texture of the enunciation.[15] We should recall, for instance, that the poem that famously announces Baudelaire's polymorphous relation to violence, "L'Héautontimorouménos" ("Je suis la plaie et le couteau ! / [...] Et la victime et le bourreau !" (79), opens by voiding affect altogether from the "beating" it promises, as the emotional intensity normally accompanying such a gesture is immediately diffused by expressions of detached agency that follow and qualify it: "Je te frapperai sans colère / Et sans haine, comme un boucher" (78). More often, however, the expression of aggressive impulses is offset by *active* contrasting emotions—a dynamic opposition that is enhanced by the texture of language. The bite of sarcasm closing the following line from "Réversibilité," for instance, is achieved as much by the seemingly adoring address that precedes it – the lulling nasals and fricative [ʒ] bobbing in the restrained *débit* ("An*g*e\ plein de bonté") – as the expression of contained "hatred," with its slight restriction of the breath and median vowel ("la '\\haine"—the effect heightened by this term's accentuation in the final position):[16]

An*g*e\ plein de bonté,\ connaissez-vous la '\\haine ? (44).

---

15   In the following chapter, we will observe that this essentially sociopathic persona adopted by the poet will appear throughout *Maldoror* as well—one of the defining attributes of Ducasse's alter egos (i.e. both Lautréamont and Maldoror).

16   Doubled back-slashes will continue to highlight the effect, however subtle, of the aspirated [h] in key terms.

By opening with an expression of (seemingly) positive, affectionate sentiment, establishing a tone (however brief) that is lilting and subdued, the poet derives an even greater force, ambushing the reader, so to speak, with the outburst that follows. In "Sonnet d'automne," before abruptly silencing his lover, both monopolizing the space of discourse, and distancing her from the interior space of feeling and thought that remains unexpressed (a gesture that is emphasized by the condensed series of occlusive [t] and [k], and that is punctuated, again, by hatred: "Je \\hais la passion"), he similarly opens with an apparently affectionate, "soft" address:

>—*Sois* c*h*arman*t*e\ et `*t*ais-`*t*oi ! Mon c*œ*ur que *t*ou*t* irri*t*e,
> ....
> Ne veut pas te montrer son secret infernal,
> [...] Je \\h**ais** la passion et l'esprit me fait mal ! (65).[17]

In one of the collection's most graphic, openly sexual acts of violence, in "À Celle qui est trop gaie," these contrasting elements are so intertwined (not merely sequential, as in the preceding examples) that they become indistinguishable—a fact that is reflected in the very texture of the poem. While the entire first two thirds of the text are utilized to establish the winsome, pleasing nature of the poem's subject, in language that is correspondingly pleasing to the ear, with its evenly spaced repetitions and flowing sound ("Ta tête, ton *g*este, ton *a*ir / *S*ont beaux comme un beau pay*s*a*g*e; / Le rire *j*oue en ton *v*isage / Comme un *v*ent *f*rais dan*s* un *ci*el clair"), the voice transitions so fluidly into the atrocity of the poem's close that our surprise is even greater, the sadistic nature of the speaker even more apparent. Without resorting to the obvious, abrupt effects at his disposal ("*c*omme un *c*oup *d*e *c*ou*t*eau"), the poet continues to utilize the fluid, resonant consonants of the preceding stanzas to do his work. The enactment of violation is all the more horrific here for the fact that it is drawn out and *not* abrupt, seemingly savored by the poet, who articulates it. The normally soothing, lyrical connotations of the fricatives, semi-vowels, and [l] correspond, strangely enough, to the speaker's complicated eroticism,

---

17   The structure of the preceding citations in fact appears several times in *Les Fleurs*—the beautiful object of desire silenced – incapable, according to the poet, of *linguistic* beauty – so that the poetic subject can dominate the space of discourse: "Et, bien que *v*otre *v*oix soit douce, *t*aisez-vous ! / *T*aisez-vous, ignoran*t*e ! âme *t*oujours ra*v*ie !" (410). Note as well, above, how the early stress created by the term in question intensifies the final, significant term of this alexandrine: "Je \\hais la passion et l'esprit me fait `*mal* !"

at the same time they enact the careful incision (with [R]) and the... *procedure* that follows:[18]

> Ainsi je voudrais, une nuit,
> ....
> Comme un lâche, ramper sans bruit,
>
> Pour c*hâ*tier ta c*hair j*oy*e*use,
> ....
> Et *f*aire à ton *f*lanc étonné
> Une b*l*essure *l*arge\ et creuse,\
>
> Et *v*ertigıneuse douc*eur* !
> À *t*ravers ces *l*èvres nou*v*el*l*es,
> Plus éc*l*a*t*an*t*es et p*l*us be*ll*es,
> T'in*f*user mon *v*enin, ma sœu*r* ! (157).

This passage not only reveals the complexity of such effects in Baudelaire's poetry, but has the additional value of further justifying the methodology of the present study, I believe. In response to those who would attempt to discredit the attribution of "sound symbolism" to poetic language, reminding us that no individual phoneme could universally and unequivocally evoke a single connotation, the above analysis demonstrates that, just as individual terms cannot definitively designate a single referent (particularly when this referent is as complicated as "desire" or "hate"), the sounds that constitute them can be utilized differently by the poet, depending on the effect he or she wishes to produce. As we look at similar, more extensive passages in *Les Fleurs*, we will see that they are constructed, not of one-to-one symbolic relationships ([t] = hard, etc.), but of complex, dynamic textures, in which these components intersect, and even change "value" in the economy of expression.

Le Mal Exposed: Front Vowels

While certain front consonants clearly provide an ideal mode of expression in this new, revolting poetics, *vowels* that are articulated from the same region of the buccal cavity are actually even more prevalent in those passages concerned

---

18   The expressive function of the recurring [R], which has been highlighted here as well for its role in this passage, will be explored in detail below.

with *le mal,* providing one of the subtler recurring effects in Baudelaire's arsenal of sound. Whereas vowels in general do not have the same degree of felt presence in linguistic expression, due to their mode of articulation (or lack thereof, essentially), they can carry strong connotations—both by their tone, and the mouth shape involved in their production. It is significant that Baudelaire often chooses to place negatively valorized terms in a final or otherwise accented position – as observed above – in which the stressed syllable contains a front, high pitched vowel. Whereas the dental [t] of "sottise" in the following passage from "Au Lecteur" clearly reinforces this term's implicit expression of judgment and condemnation, the [i], which is repeated in related terms throughout the succeeding lines, inf(l)ecting the text, also contributes significantly to the latter's tone:

> La so`tt*ise,* l'erreur, le péché, la lé`s*i*ne
> Occupent nos esprits et travaillent nos corps,
> Et nous alimentons nos aimables remords,
> Comme les mendiants nou`*rri*ssent leu*r* ver`m*i*ne (5).

The repetition of this phoneme not only connects the terms in question, emphasizing the ceaseless gnawing of sin, but involves the reader in the grimace of disgust evoked by these images, the mouth stretched taut; a gesture that is sustained, through the following "continuous" consonants, [n] [s]—at once an opening, and a closure, or rejection.[19]

To further highlight how the actual gesture (and not merely the sound) of an articulation contributes to expressivity in the Baudelairean text, we can compare a passage from the same poem, in which the deployment of other front articulations produces a similar effect, though in a different manner. While the dentals that drive the reading forward simultaneously enact relentless blows to the reader's hypocritical conscience, bringing him or her down, below the surface of *bienséance* ("Chaque jour vers l'Enfer nous descendons d'un pas"), the French [y] of "rep*U*gnant," one of the most anterior and closed vowels, contracts the buccal cavity, pursing the lips in an expression of disgust:

> Aux objets rép*U*g*n*ants nous *t*rouvons des a`*pp*as ;
> Chaque jour vers l'Enfer nous descendons d'un pas

---

[19] Compare the buccal formation of [a], [e], or even [o], to the taut, horizontal opening of [i].

LA DICTION DU MAL: BAUDELAIRE	51

Sans horreur, à travers les ténèbres qui `puent (Ibid).²⁰

Similarly, in the poet's irritated silencing of his lover, cited above, it is the piercing, excessively discrete articulations of "irrite" (arising out of the choppy series of [k] and [t]), as much as the violent "tais-toi," that expresses the poet's *humeur*, setting up the expulsion of "hate":

—Sois charmante et `tais-`toi ! Mon cœur que tout irrite,
....
Ne veut pas te montrer son secret infernal,
....
Je \\hais la passion et l'esprit me fait mal ! (65).

Compared to the consonants articulated from this area, the front vowels can be quite subtle in their effect—as in the following passage from "Une Martyre," where the progressive contraction of the buccal cavity – in the first hemistich, ending with [y] ("pointUe"), and in the second verse, with [i] and [e] ("reptile irrité") – enacts the slightly unnatural position and shape of the corpse, the jutting texture of language animated by the plosive consonants and [R]:

La \\hanche un peu pointUe et la taille frangante
Ainsi qu'un reptile irrité [...] (112).

Elsewhere, by contrast, Baudelaire reminds us through such language that even the most mundane, seemingly empty moments of the day are often keenly *felt* by wandering consciousness. In the following lines, the "prickly" experience of *spleen* (the poem's title) is given voice, not only in the imagined discourse of abandoned playing cards, with its "sinister" whispering sibilants and [R] ("Causent sinistrement"), but in the very un-lyrical sound of the lines that precede, describing the speakers themselves:

Héritage fatal d'une vieille hydro`pique,
Le beau valet de cœur et la dame de `pique
Causent sinistrement de leurs amours défunts (72).

---

20 Broome has also called attention to the awkward connotations of this articulation, in his reading of "Les Aveugles," where it reinforces the "oddity" of the subject in the terminal terms "ridicules," "singuliers," and "somnambules" (497).

As suggested in the opening remarks of the present study, it is truly the poetic *incorporation* of *le mal* – through the awkward articulations, whether vowel or consonant, front or back, that disrupt the lyric flow – that actually animates, in many instances, the otherwise conventional Baudelairean text. Where the following image from "Sépulture" is limited to a certain fixity, for instance, by the painting referenced (by Goya), frozen in time, it acquires a dynamic quality in its enunciation. The key qualifying terms surge up at the line endings, propelled by the contractions of semi-vowels ("v*iei*ll*ards") and fricative/lateral series ("sorcières *famé*l*iques"), the [ik] of the terminal syllables jutting abruptly out ("lubr**i**ques\"), suggesting the awkward, unseemly gestures of the perverse old men:

> Et des sorcières *famé*`*l*iques,\
> *L*es ébats des v*iei*ll*ards *l*u`br**i**ques\
> Et *l*es comp*l*ots des n*oirs fil*o*us\ (69).[21]

When brought into relief, the often unremarked "skeleton" of language brings the text to life, calling attention to and animating a body that would otherwise remain an abstraction ("Ce spectre"):

> Ce spe<u>c</u>tre singu*l*ier n'a pour <u>t</u>ou<u>t</u>e <u>t</u>oi*l*ette,
> <u>G</u>ro<u>t</u>esquement <u>c</u>ampé sur son *f*ront de sque*l*ette,
> <u>Q</u>u'un <u>d</u>ia<u>d</u>ème [...] (Ibid.).

An accumulation and acceleration of expressive energy that then breathes life into the figures that follow (in this instance, "le cheval"), carrying the entire image powerfully, if erratically forward:

> Sans éperons, sans *f*ouet, i*l* essou*ff*le un *ch*eva*l*,
> *F*antôme comme *l*ui, rosse <u>apocalyptique</u>,
> Qui ba*v*e des naseaux comme un <u>épileptique</u> (Ibid.).[22]

---

21 Compare a similar, *sacrilegious* use of the front vowels: "*Jé*`s**u**s, petit *Jé*`s**u**s [...] / t**u** ne serais `p*l***u**s qu'un *fœ*`t**u**s déri`soire !" 20). The back phonemes (and [a]) highlighted in the final line above ("Et les **c**o**m**pl**o**ts des n**o**irs fil**o**us"), often connote darkness and heaviness, as observed in the Introduction (p. 16); effects that will be analyzed in greater detail below. Their contribution to the suggestive "complots" here is all the more effective in contrast to the bright, angular texture of the preceding lines.

22 The final terms in these lines ("apocalyptique," "épileptique") are constituted by such dense, heterogeneous textures, "overdetermined" as such, that the attempt to parse their phonetic components seems pointless.

Mass, Weight, Density: Back Vowels

One of the things we remark when listening for phonetic textures in Baudelaire's language, is that many of them do *not* in fact contribute to a sense of movement in the reading act. If the preceding analyses have called attention to dynamics that disrupt the reification of conventional form, it should be acknowledged that movement is also one the most valued, defining qualities of the lyric genre (through the measured pulse of prosody), and conversely, that Baudelaire was, quite famously, an avid proponent of the restrictions imposed by generally concise verse forms.[23] One of the subtler ways he calls attention to that which has been sublimated by the continuous, transcendent flow of lyric discourse, is by accentuating the *substance* of the signifier itself, restricting and slowing this movement of language. Whereas series of front consonants and vowels in *Les Fleurs* often have the effect of breaking through the evenness of this discourse, accumulations of back phonemes can seem to hold the expansive surge of the lyric voice down, constricting the breath at its source.

We can begin by contrasting Baudelaire's treatment of one of the most recurring motifs in the lyric tradition, *tempus fugit* – the melancholy awareness of passing time – with that of the master of lyrical fluidity—Lamartine. In the Romantic poet's famous "Le Lac," an initial cadence pushes the lines out in a series of gentle waves, rising in all three of the front vowels ([y], [i] and [e]):

> J'ai trop vu, trop senti, trop aimé dans ma vie,
> ....
> Beaux lieux, soyez pour moi ces bords où l'on oublie (42).

The language of Baudelaire's "Le Cygne," in comparison, does not provide a soporific evasion of lived experience, but insists, precisely, on *holding* consciousness to face this past. The premature pauses and enjambments interrupt the anticipated flow of the 12 syllable line, while the back consonants and vowels of the final line, which sound out of the enclosed cavity of the mouth ([o], [u], [k], [r]), slow the voice with their apparent density:

> Paris change !\ mais rien dans ma mélancholie
> N'a bougé !\ palais neufs,\ échafaudages,\ blocs,\
> ....

---

23 Many of the *Fleurs*, for instance, are sonnets. See Poe's "The Poetic Principle," a major influence in the development of Baudelaire's aesthetic sensibility.

Et mes *chers souvenirs* sont p*lus lour*ds que des *rocs*\ (86).[24]

More often, these textures in Baudelaire's language do not explicitly subvert the expansive tendency of lyric expression through such restriction, merely calling attention to the troubled reality referenced by the poem, as in the following, similar lines from "Les Sept vieillards" and "Sépulture":

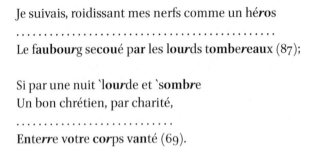

Je suivais, roidissant mes nerfs comme un hé*r*os
....
Le **fau**bou*r*g secoué par les lou*r*ds **tom**be*r*eaux (87);

Si par une nuit `lour`de et `som`b*r*e
Un **bon** chrétien, par charité,
....
Ente*rr*e votre co*r*ps vanté (69).

Instead, we observe that such articulations allow Baudelaire to *utilize* the inherent dynamism of prosody to – or rather *at* – different ends: dense phonetic textures, in seeming to obstruct the otherwise easy movement of the lyric poem, force the reading to actively strain, challenging the passive stance of the reader. In order to render the following passage from "Les Promesses d'un visage" all the more scandalous (the poem was indeed banned, only appearing in the *Épaves*), the promise in question – which involves much more than the *face* of the subject (!) – is forced into material immediacy in the text; adding, through the determined plodding of monosyllabic terms, to the sense of abrupt density produced by the back vowels, the poet embodying the "veracity" of the promise:

Tu pourras constater notre véracité
Depuis le nombril jusqu'aux fesses ;

---

24 Thus demonstrating the physical enactment of a common Baudelairean effect noted by Poulet: "A sense of heaviness is connected to time's length" ("Exploding" 70). In a similar passage, the horrific depletion of the poet's life, by the personified passing of time, is rendered more real in the heavy plodding of its expression: "[...] Maintenant dit : Je suis Autrefois, / Et j'ai **pom**pé ta vie avec ma **trom**pe i**mm**onde!" ("L'Horloge" 81). I have annotated the back consonants in this series of citations as well, despite my separate analyses of vowels and consonants. Also, while they are neither vowels nor back articulations, the labialized [m] and [b] are also annotated in bold here, and in following citations, to highlight their participation in the produced sensation of contained matter.

Tu *trou*ve*r*as au\bout\de\deux\beaux\seins\bien*l*ou*r*ds
Deux *l*a*r*ges médailles de `bron*z*e (163).

Cracher: Back Consonants

The most privileged articulations in *Les Fleurs*, however, in terms of expressive intensity, are undoubtedly the back consonants: [g] [k], and [R]. It is not insignificant that Baudelaire chooses to distance himself from the anemic poetry of his predecessors (in "Le Coucher du soleil romantique," cited above), through a figure that allows him, in its articulation, to *enact* this rejection:

Et mon pied peureux froisse, au bord du marécage,
Des crapauds imprévus [...] (149).[25]

While we have already observed the forceful, percussive effect of these phonemes in conjunction with front consonant series in *Les Fleurs* ("Toi qui, comme un coup de couteau"), we should reflect yet again on their distinctive qualities (discussed on pp. 12–13 of the Introduction)—not only at the level of sound, but in the articulatory gestures they require of the reader/speaker.

As observed earlier, where the dental and labial plosives – [d]/[t], [b]/[p] – are very clearly and succinctly articulated at the most forward point of the buccal cavity, putting the revolting enunciation literally "in your face," the corresponding back consonants have a significantly different effect.[26] Not only does their constituent friction or "detonation" involve more of the body, invested with the speaking subject's drives (with the obstruction of air taking place further back, nearer the throat). But these deeper, more visceral disruptions within the continuum of the voice also allow for a more realistic representation of force (and of the resulting penetration of matter) when

---

25 The "crapaud" will have a significant role in the bestiary of Lautréamont, in this regard— not merely for the absurdly privileged, sage-like quality assigned it, at the close of the first canto ("Pourquoi avoir ce caractère qui m'étonne ? De quel droit viens-tu sur cette terre, pour tourner en dérision ceux qui l'habitent, épave pourrie, ballotée par le scepticisme ? Si tu ne t'y plais pas, il faut retourner dans les sphères d'où tu viens" 132), but for the way in which the narrator's horrified reçognition of this figure is *expressed*, repeatedly: "Je t'abhorre autant que je le peux ; et je préfère voir un serpent, entrelacé autour de mon cou depuis le commencement des siècles, que non pas tes yeux... Comment !... c'est toi, *cr*à`paud !... *gros cr*à`paud !... infortuné *cr*à`paud !" (131).

26 As observed in the Introduction (pp. 12–13), while [R] is in fact a trill, and not a plosive, it has a comparable – if not greater – "potential" for the expression of aggression and force.

utilized in conjunction, sequentially, with those phonemes articulated further forward in the buccal cavity.[27] In a description of Baudelaire's own victimization, for instance, the "claws" of women who have (ostensibly) abused him are given a greater purchase on his heart early in the second line, in the ripping of "**gri**ffe"—the term's high [i] and fricative [f] released up and out of the preceding back consonants:

> Ce qu'elle cherche, amie, est un lieu sa*cc*agé
> Par la **gri**ffe et la dent *fé*ro*c*e de la `*f*emme (56).

In the following lines from "L'Irréparable," fricatives similarly contrast with the heavier sounds of "crushing" they follow, bringing this violence into relief and lending a weird delicacy to the horses' hooves, as they trample the body of the dying:

> Et pareil au mourant qu'é`*c*rasent les blessés,
> Que le sabot du cheval `*f*roisse (54).

That Baudelaire is undoubtedly conscious of the distinctive effect produced by the back consonants, and indeed favors them, is suggested by the fact that these phonemes are often deployed in recurring terms – particularly verbs – which thereby mimic their referent. As observed earlier (p. 52), the haunting, spectral figures that other writers would tend to overly "Romanticize," are given a presence in the text, tearing through that which separates the dead and the living—as in the following lines from "Les Phares," which utilize the back, "ripping" consonants, in conjunction with fricatives and front vowels, these articulations simulating the horrific movement of the awakened cadavers ("Déch*i*rent leur *suai*re"):

> Des *f*antômes p*ui*ssants qui dans *l*es *c*rép*u*s*cu*les
> Déch*i*rent *l*eur *suai*re en é*ti*rant *l*eurs d*oi*gts (13).

Significantly, in other instances, this recurring verb denotes an *aural*, as well as material violence—as in "Le Vin de l'assassin," when the speaker vividly hears – and indeed *feels* – his wife's yelling, in memory:

> Ses *c*ris me déch*i*raient la *f*ibre (107).

---

27   See Spire, chapter 6, on the directional nature of such movements.

By fully utilizing his innate, and heightened sensitivity to sound – not only those phenomena that can be translated into the pleasing, mellifluous tones of the conventional lyric, but those that *challenge* his ear, as well – Baudelaire forces *us* to hear/feel more acutely as well.[28] This is even more effectively demonstrated by the following lines from "Le Crépuscule du matin," in which the extended texture of enclosed articulations (which indeed suggests the "strangled sob" of the first figure) renders the physicality attributed to the final, sonic "tearing" even more palpable than in the passage just cited:

Comme un sanglot coupé par un sang écumeux
Le chant du coq au loin déchirait l'air brumeux (104).

Another recurring term in *Les Fleurs* that contains, not one, but two of these back consonants in key positions, is particularly significant. "Cracher," which gains in overall effect (due to the French guttural [R], in particular) where it loses out to the abrupt concision of the English "spit\," is an ideal term for Baudelaire, since it calls attention to the enhanced, physical orality of the poet's language, on multiple levels. For in *enacting* spitting – a gesture that is itself capable of signification, purely *as* gesture (i.e. non-linguistic) – this verb has a particular force in the development of a given image.

When the poet re-enacts the Passion of Christ, for instance, in "Le Reniement de saint Pierre," the "spitting on (His) divinity" is not only one of the most shocking images of the text, but it initiates the expression of violence and horror that follows. With each repetition, this term's propulsive cluster [kR] is further invested, finally enacting, in the signifier designating the *object* of persecution, (and not the agents, interestingly—as in Mervyn's beating, cited on

---

28 Such examples further support Jackson's reading, above (p. 37), as Baudelaire chooses to push the limits of his unusually heightened sensitivity to discordant sound by actually producing the latter in his own language. There are several passages in his *Spleen de Paris* – experiments with prose poetry which would seem to be based, in many instances, on the poet's own daily experiences as a citizen of Paris – in which such sounds "penetrate" through whatever had thus far separated a vulnerable subjectivity from a crude and malevolent world: "Un matin je m'étais levé maussade, triste, fatigué d'oisiveté […] et j'ouvris la fenêtre, hélas ! […] La première personne que j'aperçus dans la rue, ce fut un vitrier dont le cri perçant, discordant, monta jusqu'à moi à travers la lourde et sale atmosphère" ("Le Mauvais vitrier" 286); "Le temps a disparu ; c'est l'Éternité qui règne, une éternité de délices ! Mais un coup terrible, lourd, a retenti à la porte, et, comme dans les rêves infernaux, il m'a semblé que je recevais un coup de pioche dans l'estomac" ("La Chambre double" 281).

p. 10 of my Introduction) the final penetration of the martyr's "skull" ("Dans ton `crâne"):

> Lorsque tu vis cra`cher sur ta divinité
> La cra`pule du corps de garde et des cuisines,
> Et lorsque tu sentis s'enfoncer les é`pines
> Dans ton `crâne où vivait l'immense Humanité [...] (121).

In one of several instances of the poet's *own* (self-)martyrdom, "L'Amour et le crâne," the dissipation of his entire being by "Love" is enacted through such linguistic violence—an abstraction, once again, that is given a distinct immediacy through contrasting extremes, between the fragility of the "bubble," and the hard sound of its *éclatement*, "spitting out its thin soul" (further accentuated by the effective "scattering" of "Eparpille"):

> *Le globe lumineux et frêle*
> *Prend un grand essor,*
> *`Crève et `crache son âme `grêle*
> *Comme un songe d'or*
> ....
> Car ce que ta bouche cruelle
> Eparpille en l'air,
> Monstre assassin, c'est ma cervelle,
> Mon sang et ma chair ! (120).²⁹

Such articulations thus prove ideal for the revolting poetics introduced by *Les Fleurs*, allowing the voice to erupt, palpably, from its origin in the body, expelling the aggressive drives stored in the writing/speaking subject. And yet, Baudelaire develops a way to further manipulate the same textural forces, rendering them even more effective. Before proceeding to the concluding analyses of this study, in which we will observe orchestrated deployments of the various articulations analyzed thus far, I will call attention to ways in which the back consonants are used, along with other key phonemes, and in sequences similar to those observed above, to make these extended, more complex textures possible. Where the articulatory gestures observed in the preceding passages allow Baudelaire to "spit out" the resentment at the source of many of these poems,

---

29 Both Thélot ("Prière" 90) and Richter (1450) have identified correlations between the two poems just cited as well. Labarthe also identifies the effective consonant clusters above (Crève et crache) in his own analysis of "L'Amour et le crâne" (580).

the poet's ultimate goal, I would propose, is to somehow *contain* these expressive forces—not restricting entirely their volatility, but allowing them to continue straining within – and against – the confines of the text.

Contained Intensity: *ronger/se tordre*

Whatever moments of sovereignty are attained in *Les Fleurs*, allowing the poet to rise above the "miasmes morbides" of his existence (10) – whether through the bursts of invective analyzed in the present study, or the more celebrated *voyage/rêverie* poems that counterbalance them – the reality perceived by the lucid consciousness presiding over this work is always "evil," ultimately.[30] Despite the scope of his project (announced by *Spleen et Idéal*, the first and most substantial section of the work), by which it is more readily aligned with the *Divine Comedy*, or even the *Comédie humaine*, than with the preceding poetry of Romanticism, in a sense, the human existence Baudelaire sets out to depict is definitively fallen. While to the *Inferno* there corresponds a final redemption (at least potentially) in *Paradiso*, and for every Vautrin there exists a Bianchon, no inhabitants of *Les Fleurs* can hope to escape the communal curse established in the opening poem ("Hypocrite lecteur, – mon semblable, – mon frère !" 6).[31] And indeed, this curse is continually present throughout the poems in a very real sense, inevitably resurfacing in the body of language. Not only is it heard/felt, unsurprisingly, in one of the two lineages "crawling" out of Paradise:

> *R*ace de <u>C</u>aïn, dans la *fa*nge
> *R*am*p*e et *m*eurs <u>misérablement</u> ("Abel et Caïn" 122).

Even God's favored are reduced to vermin, their superior vigor evoking disdain —the salient orality of language here (in the combined front and back plosives: "<u>t</u>u <u>c</u>roîs et <u>b</u>rou<u>t</u>es") simultaneously evokes the ceaseless consumption and

---

30   It should be noted here that where *both* states of consciousness inhabit a single poem, it is generally the negative state that follows the ideal, closing the text on a note of despair ("La Chambre double" 280; "Rêve parisien" 101; "Un Voyage à Cythère" 117).

31   T.S. Eliot, an early admirer in the English-speaking world, in fact made this connection with the great Italian poet: "Baudelaire, a deformed Dante [...] aimed, with more intellect plus intensity, and without much help from his predecessors, to arrive at a point of view toward good and evil" (4).

proliferation of insects, allowing the poet to express, *physically*, his disgust for the successful bourgeois herds he must traverse daily in Second Empire Paris:

> *R*ace d'A*b*el, *tu cr*oî*s* et *b*rou*t*es
> *C*omme les p*u*nai*s*es des *b*o*is* ! (123).[32]

All of this life-force is destined, following its struggling and "contortions," to an end without transcendence—a banal passion play which serves only to amuse an "admiring" Death (note once again the grimace produced through articulation; in this instance, involving the signifier for *laughter* itself (!): "*r*i*s*i*b*le"):

> [...] la *M*ort *t*'a*d*m*i*re
> En *t*es *c*on*t*o*r*`*s*ions,\ *r*i*s*i*b*le H*u*mani*t*é (98).

Such overlap of the ontological and the aesthetic is significant: by emphatically articulating this perverse admiration for the spectacle of a continually tortured human existence, Baudelaire reveals his own participation in the production of this state. He is himself the grim reaper smiling over the world of his own creation/destruction. This is most evident in the untitled fifth poem of the collection, in which he contrasts the aesthetic values of modernity and antiquity through – significantly enough, in the perspective of the present study – the human *body*. Baudelaire the traditionalist looks back to the seemingly prelapsarian bliss of the Classical era with nostalgia, glorifying the healthy, idealized bodies of Mediterranean civilizations:

> J'aime le souvenir de ces époques nues,
> Dont Phœbus se plaisait à dorer les statues.
> Alors l'homme et la femme en leur agilité
> Jouissaient sans mensonge et sans anxiété (11).

Indeed, much in the manner of Lamartine's work, cited above, Baudelaire's language mimics the seamless confluence of nature and humanity, being and beauty, seer and seen, with its "limpid" and "flowing" prosody, in rendering homage,

---

32 Launay nonetheless sees a preference for Cain, on Baudelaire's part, reflected in his choice of tool, "l'épieu": "c'est le Mal (par Caïn) qui triomphe dans l'époque moderne et met en échec la bonne conscience endormie de la descendance passive d'Abel" (114). The present reading of the poem – particularly in light of the following analyses and concluding reflections – calls into question this "triumph."

> à l'œil limpide et clair ainsi qu'une eau courante,
> Et qui va répandant sur tout, insouciante
> Comme l'azur du ciel, les oiseaux et les fleurs,
> Ses parfums, ses chansons et ses douces chaleurs ! (12).

But it is clearly when he returns in horror to the unhealthy, deformed bodies of his own time, that the poet is most in his element—sculpting, in the dynamic medium of language, jolting the reader to attention:

> Ô mons*tr*Uos*i*t*é*s p*l*eu*r*ant *l*eu*r* vê*t*ement !
> Ô *r*idi*c*U*l*es ˋ*t*roncs\ ! ˋ*t*o*r*ses di*gn*es des mas*q*ues !
> Ô pau*v*res *c*o*r*ps *t*ord*U*s,\ maig*r*es,\ ven*tr*Us ou *fl*as*q*ues (Ibid.).

These bodies that seem to be twisted and contorted from within, by the contained articulations of the poet's language, are the *actual* "ideal" of the Baudelairean aesthetic—less a harmonious marriage of fixity and movement, concrete and amorphous,[33] than an active, dissonant confrontation of matter and force; a beauty that arises in the breaking and deformation of the object, struggling forward, beneath the material encasing it ("sous de froids tissus / Ils rampent," below)—as in "Les Petites vieilles":

> Ces *monstr*es d*i*slo*q*ués furent jadis des femmes,
> Éponine ou Laïs !\ *Monstr*es *br*isés,\ *b*oss*U*s =>
> Ou *t*ord*U*s,\ aimons-les !\ ce sont encore des âmes.
> Sous des *j*U*p*ons *tr*oués et sous de *fr*oi*d*s *t*iss*U*s
> Ils *r*am*p*ent [...] (89).

That this contained intensity is central to Baudelaire's aesthetic – enacted, if never explicitly formulated – is further substantiated by texts that, in depicting the activity of artistic creation itself, and its physical nature (*poïesis*), actually utilize the very textures observed above—as in the following brief image from "Le Jeu," where the repeated front and semi-vowels ("Qui v*i*ennent gasp*ill*er") add to the torquing effect produced by the back phonemes:

---

[33] "La modernité, c'est le transitoire, le fugitif, le contingent, la moitié de l'art, dont l'autre moitié est l'éternel et l'immuable" (from Baudelaire's *Le Peintre de la vie moderne*, OC II 695).

> [...] des fronts ténébreux de poètes i*ll*ustres
> Qui v*i*ennent gasp*ill*er *l*eurs sang*l*antes s*u*eurs (96).³⁴

Or, in a more extensive and convincing example, from one of the most cited poems in discussions of Baudelaire's conception of the poetic *métier*, "La Mort des artistes," the struggle between the poet and the ideal he would express is given a physical quality, comparable to that of the sculptor's craft, the central figure of the text:

> Nous **u**se**r**ons no**tr**e âme en de s**u**b**ti***l*s **c**omp*l*ots,
> Et nous **d**émo*l*i**r**ons main**t**e *l*our**d**e a**r**ma**tu**re,
> Avant de **c**ontemp*l*er *l*a **gr**an**d**e **Cr**éa**tu**re
> **D**ont *l*'infe**r**na*l* **d**és**ir** nous **r**emp*l*ît de san᾿**gl**ots ! (127).³⁵

The privileged function of these intensive structures in Baudelaire's craft is most strikingly apparent, however, in a text, appropriately enough, that explains (or rather, *annunciates*) his poetic mission—the second poem in the collection, "Bénédiction." This mission/texture is not articulated, in fact, by the voice we would expect – the poetic subject who speaks in most of *Les Fleurs* – but by another individual, speaking *about* him. If the poem does conclude in the voice of the more familiar subject, prophesying a Neoplatonic ascension, through his chosen status as Poet,³⁶ it is in the vituperative tirade of the poet's mother that we find the true source, in a sense, of the "evil flowers" that follow —a curse that entails a now familiar contortion of the *poet*'s voice; a *malédiction* embedded within this benediction:

> [...] [puisque] je ne puis pas rejeter dans les flammes,
> Comme un billet d'amour, ce **mon**s**tr**e **r**a**b**oug**r**i
> ....
> [...] je **t**o**rdr**ai si **b**ien ce**t** **arb**re misé**r**a**b**le,
> Qu'il ne **p**ou**rr**a **p**ouss**e**r ses **b**ou**t**ons empes᾿**t**és ! (7).

Interestingly, the language of the text becomes most dynamic at the precise moment the poet's capacity for productivity is negated. By gradually twisting,

---

34 I am not of course equating the sounds in "i*ll*ustres" and "gaspi*ll*er." The semi-vowel and liquid [l] are simply annotated in the same way in the present system of analysis.

35 The [y] and [l] have been italicized here as well – as in the preceding citation – for their participation in the "torquing" effect produced by [ʀ].

36 "Je sais que vous gardez une place au Poète / Dans les rangs bienheureux des saintes Légions" (9).

and binding back on itself the "tree" figuring the poet's being – a gesture that is remarkably palpable in the increased closure and tension of the buccal cavity, in the passage between the third and fourth lines, above – the poet produces a torsion in the voice itself, allowing an even greater sense of outward movement to follow at the line endings. Straining against what has been imposed upon it, the tree/voice grows with increased vigor, the accumulation of dynamic phonemes (fronts and sibilants: [p] [t] [e] [s]) pulsing up out of the contracted density of the rear articulations: "il ne p̲ourra p̲ousser ses b̲outons empestés !" Baudelaire is thus *already* fulfilling the prophesy announced for his poetry, if not the explicit one (i.e. the ascension, mentioned above): by carefully channeling his most violent, unexpressed drives (displaced, in the mouth of his mother) through the meticulous configuration of gestures utilized in the speech act, the poet is indeed making "flowers of evil" blossom, from the cursed buds of his true calling—an intensity that only arises, in fact, out of rejection.

L'Ensemble: The Revolting Body

If identifying the predominance of specific types of articulation in Baudelaire's language allows us to better perceive the textural dynamics animating *Les Fleurs*, proceeding in this manner has its limitations at a certain point, as suggested above. As we have already observed in the preceding citations, the recurrence of any given phoneme (or category of phonemes) only takes on a significant expressive function when imbricated with *other*, contrasting phonetic strands. The final section of the present chapter will now directly address a number of passages in which multiple strands work together, producing complex surges of intensity in the texture of Baudelaire's voice.

To fully appreciate the effect produced by such "ensembles," we can begin by focusing our attention where they are absent—for instance, in a passage from "Le Voyage," which, if it manages to significantly modify the conventional prosody of the alexandrine, does not produce the same sense of force acquired through the orchestration of contrasting articulations, instead merely disrupting the lyric flow through its irregularities. Already awkward, as a result of its frequent *coupes* (particularly in the third verse), the voice does not develop a distinct, dynamic texture, despite the recurrence of contrasting phonemes:

> La femme, esclave vile, orgueilleuse et stupide,
> Sans rire s'adorant et s'aimant sans dégoût ;
> L'homme, tyran goulu, paillard, dur et cupide,

Esclave de l'esclave et ruisseau dans l'égout (132).[37]

By contrast, in the following lines – from "Les Métamorphoses du vampire" – a fallen humanity increasingly *materializes*, dynamic, in the course of the text. The abstractions designating the two sexes in the preceding passage, joined only through the symmetrical juxtaposition of qualifiers and the clever repetition of terms ("s'adorant"/"cupide"; "esclave vile"/"Esclave de l'esclave"), are replaced with physiological terms ("os," "flancs"), placing the pair in a very real, physical relation. *This* monstrous coupling actually takes place in the text, a violent intermingling of physical bodies (down to the very "marrow") resulting in the horrific, amorphous form of the final image—a "metamorphosis" in the body of language itself, from the pursed lips sucking marrow, to the engorged, insentient carcass:

> Quand\e*ll*e\eut\de*m*es\os\sucé toute *la moell*e,
> Et que *l*angu*i*ssa*mm*ent je me tournai vers elle
> Pour lui rendre un baiser d'amour, je ne vis plus
> Qu'une\out*r*e\aux\f*l*ancs g*l*uan*t*es,\ *t*ou*t*e `p/e*i*ne de `pus ! (159).[38]

Furthermore, as if to demonstrate his mastery of this dynamic relation between image, sound and meaning, Baudelaire then continues the process of "decomposition"—first thinning out the figure *and* its texture (replacing the predominantly dense back vowels between consonants with central and front ones: "Qu'une\out*r*e\aux\f*l*ancs g*l*uan*t*es" => "des déb*r*is de squelet*t*e"), then making the "debris of (this) skeleton" indeed "tremble," in the progressive rarefication of sound we perceive in both the third and fourth lines:

> Tremblaient confusément des débris de squelet*t*e,
> Qu*i* d'eux-mêmes *r*endaient le c*r*i d'une g*i*roue*tt*e
> Ou d'une en*s*e*i*gn*e*, au bout d'une t*r*ingle de *fe*r,
> Que balance le vent pendant les nu*i*ts d'h*i*v*e*r (Ibid.).[39]

---

37 See note #23, p. 17.
38 Note as well the effect observed earlier in this chapter (pp. 47–49), in the abrupt transition from "soft" (the anticipated kiss) to "hard" (the horrific form of the lover); an effect that is heightened not only by the phonetic texture, highlighted above, but by the enjambment (which pivots, incidentally on a pursed (rounded), front vowel: "plus"): "[…] un baiser d'amour, je ne vis plus / Qu'une outre […]."
39 I have again chosen to annotate [y], not as a front vowel (as in "les *t*énèbres qui `puent," above), but according to its participation in the closure of the back series, in bold.

Through unconventional deployment of the full spectrum of articulatory dynamics, Baudelaire does not simply effect modulations in what is an otherwise continuous, evenly fluctuating voice (the goal of the traditional lyric poet), but seems to *incorporate* the very entities figured in the poem – and more importantly, the intensive, conflictual energies that pass between them – *in* that voice. In the following image/texture – again, from "Le Vin de l'assassin" – it is as if the enunciation of text reproduces the physical phenomenon depicted, as the slowly advancing wagon torques against its load (the guttural [R] held back in the throat by surrounding back vowels)—an accumulation of charged weight that renders the following contact with its victim – as it slams across the enjambment – all the more realistic and abrupt:

Le *chari*ot\aux ˋlourdes ˋ*r*oues
*Ch*a*r*gé de p̲ie*rr*es et de ˋb̲oue,
Le wag**on** en*r*agé peut bien =>

É*cr*as̲er ma t̲êt̲e c̲oup̲ab̲le\ (108).⁴⁰

A similar sound-image allows the speaker of "Femmes damnées" to convincingly contrast the tenderness of her own kisses with the brute passion of a male lover—the heavy, animal physicality of the latter effectively expressed, *felt* in her voice:

« Mes baisers sont *lég*ers comme *c*es éph*é*mères
Qui caressent *l*e soir *l*es grands *l*acs transparents,
Et *c*eux de ton amant c̲*r*euseront *l*eurs o*r*n*i*ères
C̲omme des *chari*ots ou des soc̲s déchiˋ*r*ants;\

Ils passeront sur t̲oi c̲omme un *l*ourd̲ at̲t̲eˋ*l*age » (153).

---

40   Richter, who has written an excellent lengthy analysis of the poem, nonetheless misses the full *impact* of "Écraser," following the enjambment, simply noting "une forte hésitation" in the silence between the terms in question (1275). Chesters refers to this use of phonetic patterns in the enjambment as "phonetic copula," which he identifies as mimicking gestures such as "breaking in" and "plunging into" (34–35). Murphy identifies a more subtle violence in the present poem, in the *calembour*, "tête coupable": "Baudelaire affectionnait les petites « blagues » susceptibles de provoquer l'urticaire chez le « lecteur paisible et bucolique »" (*L'Année Baudelaire* 234)

The present study of *Les Fleurs* would not be complete without turning our attention to a text in which just such a violence – at once intimate and brutal – takes place on a much grander, more elaborate scale. "À Une Madone," probably the most violent poem in the collection, is meticulously constructed to lead the unsuspecting reader to its shocking climax (the structure of the entire poem is indeed yet another example, significantly magnified, of the soft/hard dynamic identified earlier)—a climax that depends on a sustained use, over the course of an entire text, of those very phonetic strands we have observed contributing to the production, maintenance and increase of affective intensity in the space of several lines.[41]

With the opening address, we have no reason to expect any inappropriate behavior, despite several disconcerting elements—the *tutoiement* of the Virgin Mary, and the placement of her altar in "the blackest corner of [the poet's] heart," for instance:

> Je veux bâtir pour toi, Madone, ma maîtresse,
> Un autel souterrain au fond de ma détresse,
> Et creuser dans le coin le plus noir de mon cœur,
> Loin du désir mondain et du regard moqueur,
> Une nîche, d'azur et d'or tout émaillée (58).[42]

For the poet in fact proceeds to devote his craft to the consecration of embodied purity itself, situating the poem on the side of *L'Idéal* (echoing the hopeful prophesy of "Bénédiction": "ma couronne mystique / [...] / ce beau diadème éblouissant et clair," 45):

> Avec mes Vers polis, treillis d'un pur métal
> Savamment constellé de rimes de cristal
> Je ferai pour ta tête une énorme Couronne.

---

[41] I encourage the reader to consult Bonnefis' chapter on Baudelaire, in which his reading of the above poem is inflected by the poet's childhood correspondence, and very name ("Un Baudelaire, à tout prendre, n'est qu'une sorte de sabre (du bas-latin *baldarelus*)" 122) —a reading that leads him to identify a lack of closure in the poem's final lines – "Il n'est pas au pouvoir de la répétition, fût-elle incantatoire [...] d'épuiser la *choséité* de la chose" (123) – just as I will conclude, below.

[42] All other citations of the poem are from the same page, unless otherwise indicated.

Now attuned to the distinct textures of Baudelaire's voice, however, we should have already perceived a darker purpose in the opening lines—not simply in the images chosen, but in the articulation of particular terms:

> [Je veux] creuser dans le coin le plus noir de mon cœur.

And indeed, immediately following the crystalline structures figuring the poet's verses ("Vers polis, treillis d'un pur métal," "constellé de rimes de cristal"), Baudelaire re-enacts this carving gesture in a lower register, "jealously" encasing the idealized figure in a heavy material, which he "cuts out" ("tailler") in a "barbarous manner" ("Je saurai te tailler un Manteau, de façon / **Barbare** [...]"). The key qualifier here ("Barbare"), with its constitutive doubling, echoes and amplifies the propulsive bisyllabic terms of the preceding lines ("*mor*telle" "*Ma*done" "*Man*teau"), introducing an unexpected, and indeed "barbarous" tonality into the poem, as it drops abruptly over the enjambment, resonating against the premature *coupe* ("[...] de façon / => **Barbare**,\"); an awkwardness that is then drawn out, torqued by the following rear articulations and punctuation:

> Et dans ma Jalousie, ô *mor*telle *Ma*done,
> Je saurai te tailler un *Man*teau, de façon =>
> **Bar`bar**e,\ `roide et `lourd,\ et doublé de soup`çon.\

In this concurrence of the poem's two opposing motifs with its two predominant textures – which together, manifest the two, very different drives in Baudelaire's creative process, essentially: "*ri*mes de cristal" -vs- "Manteau [...] / **Bar`bar**e" – we can perceive, I would propose, how this particular text serves as an active site of conflict between opposing forces at the heart of *Les Fleurs* itself—an attempt to resolve the tension within the poet's consciousness through the matter of expression. Pursuing the present mode of analysis through to the poem's close, however, suggests that Baudelaire's poetics not only does not allow for this resolution, but in fact channels such efforts into the *reproduction* of tensions, in the particular repetitions it engenders; a problematic we will locate in a number of texts in the concluding pages of this study.

It would initially seem that the poet has achieved the lucidity necessary to avoid this pitfall of revolting discourse. As if doubting his ability to realize perfect, idealized form ("Si je ne puis [...] / [...] tailler une Lune d'argent"), he indicates that he will nonetheless vanquish – through the avatar of purity encased in this poem-altar – the force that continually "gnaws" at his better self, inciting his destructive urges: "Je mettrai le Serpent qui me mord les entrailles / Sous tes talons [...]." And yet, he immediately calls into question the authenticity of such intentions, now proposing to control his violent impulses... by enacting his violent impulses (!), deploying some of the most affectively charged figures/textures we have observed recurring throughout the present study ("**mons*t*re**," "\\haine," "**c*r*a`c*h*at**"):

> Si je ne puis, malgré tout mon art diligent,
> Pour Marchepied tailler une Lune d'argent,
> Je *me*tt*r*ai le *Ser*pent qui *me m*or*d* les en*t*r*ailles*
> Sous *t*es *t*a*l*ons,\ a*f*in que *t*u *f*ou*l*es et *f*ai*ll*es,
> *R*eine *v*ic*t*orieuse et *f*é*c*on*d*e en **r**a`*c*h*ats*,
> Ce **mons*t*re****t**ou*t***g**on*f*lé de \\haine et de **c*r*a**`*c*h*at.

As we read on, the poet would actually appear to have spit out the disruptive forces, thus restoring tranquility and order to the creative process ("Tu verras mes Pensers, rangés comme les Cierges"), all of the visceral angst introduced into the poem transmuted instantly into the ethereal substance of the Ideal:

> Et comme tout en moi te chérit et t'admire,
> Tout se fera Benjoin, Encens, Oliban, Myrrhe,
> Et sans cesse vers toi, sommet blanc et neigeux,
> En Vapeurs montera mon Esprit orageux (59).[43]

But the dark desire at the source of this creation will not be consummated through the sort of empyreal voyage undertaken in other poems. The earlier "barbarous" gestures of the text must be reintroduced, "mixed" with the poet's love, for his "black pleasure" to reach its climax ("pour mêler l'amour avec la barbarie, / Volupté noire !"). Not only do these more volatile textures resurface, transforming the poetic subject into the agent of the act to come ("**bar**bar**b**ar**ie"** => "**B**ou*rr*eau plein de *r*emor*d*s"), but the poet increasingly saturates the text with dense posterior textures, adding weight and force (particularly through nasals) to the weapon he fashions out of "sin," literally, using the linguistic material of the text ("des *sep*t Péchés **c**api*t*aux" => "je ferai *sept* **C**ou*t*eaux")— all of which he methodically controls ("comme un jongleur insensible"), through the placement of *coupes*, until the final blows surge forth, one after another:

---

[43] Note, not only the Neoplatonic motifs recalling such "ideal" poems as "Élévation," and the close of "Bénédiction," but the celebrated olfactory motif of harmony and transport found in "Correspondances."

LA DICTION DU MAL: BAUDELAIRE 69

> Enfin,\ pour compléter ton rôle de Marie,
> Et pour mêler l'amour avec la **bar**ba**r**ie,
> Volupté noire !\ des sep**t** **P**échés **c**api`taux,
> **B**ou**rr**eau **p**lein de **r**emo**r**ds, je fe**r**ai sep**t** **C**ou`teaux
> Bien a*ffi*lés,\ et,\ comme un jongleur insensi*bl*e,
> **P**renant le **p**lus **p**ro*f*ond **d**e **t**on amour pour c*i*b*l*e,
> Je les **p**lan**t**e**r**ai **t**ous **d**ans**t**on**C**œur pan**t**e`*l*ant,
> **D**ans**t**on\`**C**œur sang*l*o`tant, **d**ans**t**on\`**C**œur ru*i*sse`*l*ant ! (Ibid.)[44]

As in a number of the texts analyzed thus far, the violent element here does not merely subvert the central, idealized feminine figure of the poem. It *is* the central figure—its final enactment the true "target" of the text, the lyric figures and modes of expression utilized simply serving as a foil, helping to produce the suspense and tension required for the text's finale. The fact that this dynamic is used in the very poem in *Les Fleurs* in which the poetic subject seems most engaged in the act of force (in contrast to the insidious gesture of "A Celle qui est trop gaie," for instance), bringing a singular immediacy to this act,[45] further confirms that the intensive textures we have come to identify throughout the collection hold a privileged – if perhaps troubling – function in Baudelaire's poetry.

What is in fact problematic here, in the perspective of the present study, beyond the enactment of misogynistic violence, is the particular structure of the lines concluding the poem. If the anaphora utilized by the poet (the unrelenting series of "**d**ans**t**on**C**œu**r**") has a logical function, punctuating the climax, and effectively communicating the frenzied need to definitively consummate the twin drives at play here (erotic and violent), such repetition simultaneously points to an underlying sense of *in*effectiveness in this orchestrated series of acts: the blows that follow the initial stabbing, ostensibly helping to finalize this sacrilegious murder, suggest a possible dissatisfaction at some level with the climax and conclusion of this sequence—an unappeasable

---

[44] Other critics have commented – if in less detail – on the crucial role of the phonetic, as well as prosodic structures of the poem. See Jackson ("[the Madonna's] body becomes the aim of a near orgasmic release of sexual cruelty, noticeable in the triple repetition of the trisyllabic epithets which qualify her murdered heart," *Satan* 162); and especially, Broome's more extensive analysis of the text: "[the climax] spurts uncontrollably [...] caught as it were in the involuntary repetitions (including those of the nasal [ã] and their stream of somewhat deadening pulsations), the successive rhythmic spasms of which allow for no variations of suave and savage, fast and slow" (270).

[45] Despite the future tense—a common temporal structure for Baudelairean violence, as Catani observes: "Baudelaire imagines these acts of torture, whereas Sade's characters carry them out" (4).

desire within the agent, who must continually strive to exceed any realization of force he is able to achieve. Indeed, I would propose that, despite the production of expressive intensity witnessed in the preceding analyses of *Les Fleurs*, the primary enterprise driving these texts, if unconscious – the enactment, in language, of repressed drives within the writing subject (*la diction du mal*) – is doomed to continually repeat itself, unable to evolve beyond its conflicted source. Again, the poem we have been reading does not immediately suggest such a flaw, as the measured "beating" of this carefully wrought crescendo produces a distinct sense of finality, overriding any hints of ambiguity. But interestingly enough, when we turn our attention to other, similar texts, we find that the theme of repetitive, extended (or even endless) *duration* is often central – intimately related, it would seem – to violent phenomena in the Baudelairean universe.

In "Le Tonneau de la haine," for instance, the poet chooses to figure the most violent of emotions through the ancient myth that – along with that of Sisyphus – has come to define the notion of a fruitless, endless task: "La Haine est le tonneau des pâles Danaïdes" (71). One might suppose that this choice of figures in fact reflects a detached awareness on the part of the poet, if not a moralistic or pedagogical treatment of the subject matter. And yet, when we identify the textures employed, we find, not the cool gaze of the philosopher, but the *participation* of the poet, in a visceral re-creation of the emotions represented. The type of phonetic contrasts that are introduced in the opening line (in the opposing back and central/front vowels of "le to**nn**eau des pâles Danaïdes") not only correspond to the conflicting forces at the heart of this tragic figure (contained, controlled matter -vs- perforation and inevitable loss: "De **gra**nds `seaux pleins du `sang" => "Par où *fui*raient m**i**le ans de s**ueu**rs"), but are combined with other elements throughout the text, in order to truly incorporate these allegorical figures, and the extreme emotions that define them ("La V**e**n**g**eance éperd**U**e aux bras **r**ou**g**es et `*fo*rts"):

> La \\Hai**n**e est le to**nn**eau des pâles Danaïdes ;
> La V**e**n**g**eance éper`d**U**e aux bras **r**ou**g**es et `*fo*rts
> A beau pré**c**i**pi**ter dans ses ténèbres vides
> De **gra**nds `seaux pleins du `sang et des la**r**mes des mo**r**ts,
>
> Le Démon fait des trous secrets à ces ab**î**mes,
> Par où *fui*raient m**i**lle ans de s**ueu**rs et d'e**ff**orts,
> Quand même elle sau**r**ait ra**n**i**m**er ses victi**m**es,
> Et **p**our les **p**ress**U**rer ress**U**sc**i**ter leurs `co**r**ps (71).

Whatever "Vengeance" is capable of, the *poet* is able to "re-animate" these "victims" in the space of the text, squeezing the brute matter of language into life —a gesture, the force of which is significantly amplified by the temporality of the poem. Drawing, indirectly, on both defining events of the Prometheus myth (a favorite, of course, among poets) – the creation of human life, from inanimate matter, and an eternal cycle of (*visceral*) immolation and resuscitation – Baudelaire derives an apt poetic expression of the intoxicating passions treated in the poem.

In "Duellum," a poem that allegorizes a particular theme of violence recurring throughout *Les Fleurs* – the underlying sadism in all amorous relations[46] – it is the *endless* nature of the couple's fallen state that becomes the latter's defining, apparently ideal quality, producing the final impact of the text. But not before the poet has methodically enacted a vivid hand-to-hand combat over the course of the poem, transitioning from one mode of attack to another, as the lovers/opponents are increasingly drawn together into a single, dynamic entity of contained force (*"s'étreignant méchamment / [...] / Roulons-y sans remords"*).[47] Following the initial, civilized fencing of the first stanza (mere "games," which "click" discreetly (and dis*crete*ly) in the text: "Ces jeux, ces c*li*quet*i*s du fer"), the separation afforded by weapons is eliminated as, in conjunction with the digging in of "tooth and nail," key textures further engage the voice, introducing forces that cut both externally and internally (*"les ongles acérés*"; "*cœurs [...] par l'amour ulcérés*"):

> Les g*lai*ves sont b*ri*sés ! comme notre jeunesse
> Ma chère !\ Mais les <u>d</u>ents,\ *les* ong*les* ac*é*r*é*s,
> Ve*n*gent bientôt l'é*p*ée et la <u>d</u>ague trai*t*resse.
> Ô fu*r*eur des <u>c</u>œurs m*û*rs par *l'*amour u*l*c*é*r*é*s !

This cutting language resurfaces at the end of the following tercet, as the couple, drawn even closer together by their hateful love, find their flesh delicately lacerated by thorns; a violence that is rendered palpable, as observed in earlier examples, less by the semantic content of the key terms designating it, as by the texture surrounding those terms—the sharpness of the final "thorns" communicated as much by the qualifying "**ari<u>di</u>té**," as the final "*ronces*" that puncture:

> Nos hé*r*os,\ s'é*t*reignant mé*ch*amme*n*t,\ ont rou*l*é,
> Et *l*eur peau f*l*eu*r*ira *l'*ari<u>di</u>té des 'ro*n*ces.

---

46   Catani 997.
47   All citations of the poem are from p. 36.

The succeeding, final lines express a desire to now "eternalize" this relentless, physical violence, drawing on the multiple strands constituting it in the text ("*l'amour ulcéré*" + "*fleurira l'aridité*" = "*éterniser l'ardeur*") to build up to the final term—the aspirated "hatred" *physically* expressed, as if to guarantee its continued resonance, beyond the lovers' death:

> *Roulons*-y *s*ans *r*emo*r*ds, a*m*az*o*ne inhu*m*aine,
> Afin d'éterniser l'ardeur de notre ʽ\\haine !

Even in a poem in which the poet insists on the inevitable annihilation of *everything*, "Confession" ("<u>tout</u> craque [...] / Jusqu'à ce que l'Oubli / [le] jette dans sa hotte," my emphasis), the expression of negation becomes an opportunity to *build*, at the very moment building has been identified as futile;[48] the battered and battering language of the text stubbornly echoing, as in the above poem, into Eternity:

> « **Q**ue bâ*t*ir *s*ur les <u>c</u>œu*r*s es<u>t</u> une *c*h*o*se ʽsot<u>t</u>e ;
>   **Q**ue <u>t</u>out ʽ<u>c</u>raqu<u>e</u>,\ am*o*u*r* et beauʽ<u>t</u>é,
>   *J*usqu'à *c*e que *l*'**Oub*l*i**
>   *l*es *j*e<u>tt</u>e <u>d</u>ans sa ʽho<u>tt</u>e
>   P*o*u*r l*es *r*end*r*e à *l*'**É**<u>t</u>e*r*niʽ<u>t</u>é ! » (46).

Unable to believe, ultimately, in the possibility of an ideal state of being, Baudelaire does not abandon entirely his idolatry of poetic language. And yet, it is not simply a question of enduring his progressively bleak existential outlook by continuing to hold on to such an ideal in his work, protected from reality—as suggested by much of the critical tradition. The preceding analyses suggest, rather, that this reverence becomes truly idolatrous: no longer the belief in a spiritualized, transcendent function of language, with words leading beyond themselves, nor the purely aestheticized, *use-less* language valorized by the poet's Parnassian contemporaries, but a visceral pleasure in the brute substance of language—*craché*. For what we find is fundamentally at play in the true "flowers of evil," when reflecting on our readings of the most dynamic poems in the collection, is indeed not to be found on the conceptual plane, as I have continued to assert. It would seem that, from beneath whatever complex ideational strata critics might reveal, the *act* of composing these defining texts – the first significant example of the revolting poetics – indeed arose in

---

48   "L'œuvre de Baudelaire n'en finit pas de renaître de ses ruines… C'est aussi que la ruine est le terreau de l'œuvre. Que l'œuvre s'en nourrit, et qu'elle s'en fortifie" (Bonnefis 125).

the expression of repressed drives, stimulated in the course of reflection—that which Baudelaire did not so much strive to *represent*, as to engage and amplify on a much more immediate level of the writing process, truly *in* language. In the absence of a God who might hear – much less respond to – his lucid skepticism regarding modern existence, prayer becomes for Baudelaire, finally, an orgiastic rite; a *je m'en foutisme* that consecrates its own absurdity in the *matter* of its expression:

> [Nous avons] *Salué* l'énorme Bê`tise,
> La Bê`tise au *fr*ont de taureau\ ;
> Bai`sé la stu`pide Ma`tière
> Avec grande dévo`*tion*,
> Et de la putréfac`*tion*
> Béni la blafarde lumière (144).

And it is in this new cult of poetic language, as the concluding readings have also suggested, that the revolting poetics reveals its inherent limitations—an economy of expression that is constituted through a number of extreme, and in many ways contradictory elements. When forced to engage *le mal* pervading human existence, without the sublimation of conventional lyricism, language becomes: a medium that is recognized as inconsequential, ultimately, however much its materiality and force is still felt by the poet; an entity that, at the same moment it is acknowledged as lacking *significance*, is nonetheless utilized as a malleable *object*, serving as both weapon and target in the poet's "dual" with fallen existence; and finally, a texture that, while it allows for an experience of progressive tension and resolution in the traversal of a given text (the "intensive" structures identified in the preceding analyses), mimicking a now impossible movement toward catharsis at the semantic level, is nonetheless doomed to a certain sterility as well. The consecration of degenerate matter, however intense its expression, is always reduced in the end to the same... matter.[49] It is thus that, in the closed universe of *Les Fleurs*, the most forceful gesture must be continually repeated, as if an addiction—an articulated "fix"

---

[49] The present analysis thus arrives at a similar, and yet significantly different conclusion than that reached by Bataille, for whom – through a reading that yet again reflects an over-valorization of Baudelaire's Parnassian mastery – the blossoming of evil is reified, its authenticity paradoxically betrayed by the success of its expression: "Il est vrai que l'effort est vain, que les poèmes où ce mouvement se pétrifie (qui réduisent l'existence à l'être) ont fait du vice, de la haine et de la liberté *infinies*, les formes dociles, tranquilles, immuables que nous savons. Il est vrai la poésie, qui subsiste, est toujours un contraire de la poésie, puisque, ayant le périssable pour fin, elle le change en éternel" (*LM* 49–50).

in the mouth of the poet which, however much it rises up out of – and against – existing discourse, is doomed to gnaw on the substance it has polluted; endless contortions of the fundamentally, and in fact *willfully* "irreparable":

> [...] hélas ! pâles comme des cierges,
> **Q**ue *r*on*g*e et **q**ue **n**ou*rr*it la dé`bau*ch*e [...]
> ....
> Nous avons, il est vrai, na*t*ions **c**orrom`**p**Ues,
> Aux peuples anciens des beautés inconnus :
> Des *v*isages **r**on*g*és **p**ar les *ch*an*c*res du `**c**œu*r* (12);
>
> [...] l'obs**c**Ur Ennem**i** qui nous *r*on*g*e le `**c**œu*r*
> Du *s*ang **q**ue nous perdons `**c**roît et se *f*orti*f*ie ! (16);
>
> *L*'**I**rrépara*b*le *r*on*g*e avec sa **d**ent mau**d**i*t*e
>   No*t*re âme, **p**i*t*eux *m*onument,
> Et *s*ouvent il a*tt*aque, ainsi **q**ue le *t*er*m*i*t*e,
>   **P**ar la **b**ase le **b**â*t*i*m*ent.
> *L*'**I**rrépara*b*le *r*on*g*e avec sa **d**ent mau`**d**i*t*e ! (55).

CHAPTER 2

An Exaggerated Scale of Evil: Lautréamont

> J'ai chanté le mal comme ont fait Mickiewickz, Byron, Milton, Southey, A. de Musset, Baudelaire, etc. Naturellement, j'ai un peu exagéré le diapason pour faire du nouveau.
> LAUTRÉAMONT (378).

∴

> [...] prends garde d'augmenter, dans d'irréparables proportions, la rage qui te consume : ce n'est plus de la justice.
> LAUTRÉAMONT (256).

∴

In many ways, Lautréamont is the most direct descendent of Baudelaire—a lineage that has been somewhat neglected due to the tendency, observed in the preceding chapter, to view even the most transgressive elements of the earlier poet's work through rose-colored glasses, placing him at the head – in a somewhat forced manner – of the predominant, vaguely designated "Symbolist" poets—Mallarmé, Verlaine, Rimbaud.[1] While the extended and erratic rhetorical flights of *Maldoror* have clearly moved (or rather, *broken*) into a realm of expression entirely different than the formal tradition within which Baudelaire continued to write – however much he may have modified the latter – their creator was clearly influenced by *Les Fleurs du mal*: the fully depraved authorial persona Lautréamont creates for his text, the mission he elaborates to justify his representation of *le mal*, and the many vivid expressions of this censured subject matter originate, to a large extent, in Baudelaire's work.[2]

---

1 Pleynet has observed this tendency: "on n'attachera jamais assez d'importance à l'influence de Baudelaire, auteur des *Fleurs du mal,* sur un écrivain qui, dans *Les chants de Maldoror* et dans *Poésies*, s'attarde et met fortement en scène les divers aspects quasi sadiques du « mal » et de ses conséquences" (*Situation* 59).

2 This influence is attested to, in a more concrete manner, in the younger poet's correspondence. In a letter to Poulet-Malassis, who had published *Les Fleurs*, Ducasse requests a "supplement" to that work – from the censored *Épaves*, for the most part (Steinmetz, *Maldoror* 451, note 1) – for which he has sent money (*Correspondance, Maldoror* 381).

Such influence is not, however, the focus of the present chapter. While I will be calling attention to a number of points at which the two poets' works intersect, at levels of text where such connections would conventionally be established (*champs lexicaux*, rhetorical figures, imagery), the primary object of this chapter is to reveal that which Lautréamont takes up from Baudelaire, but which lies *beneath* the many semantic components of the text we normally perceive and analyze. I would propose that one of Baudelaire's greatest influences on *Maldoror*'s unconventional aesthetic, as yet unrecognized, is to be found in the salient *textures* we identified in the preceding study—phonetic structures that more effectively communicate, or rather *embody* the subversive drives that arise in the process of composition. In exploring how the revolting discourse evolves in the work of the later poet, we will find that the redeployment of such textures accesses yet greater expressive forces, otherwise untapped in the post-*Fleurs* tradition—an event that entails a corresponding increase of the "virus" threatening the effectiveness of these very forces: dramatically extending the range of this new poetic voice in its communication of revolting content (the "exaggerated scale" of this chapter's title), leads to a crisis in the expressive economy of *Les Chants de Maldoror* that was only faintly perceived, by comparison, in *Les Fleurs du mal*. Consequently, as we shall see, a developing awareness of this crisis forces Lautréamont to seek out, in the final canto, an equivalent to his predecessor's Parnassian adherence to formal constraint, as a way of controlling textual excess—even if this may amount to nothing more – as with so much of Lautréamont's work – than a form of subterfuge; a sleight of hand performed for the critical reader. And indeed, perhaps, for the poet himself...

...

> La statue elle-même a des muscles.
> BACHELARD (104).

One of the principal causes for neglect of the textural component of *Maldoror* can be attributed to the propensity – already observed in the preceding chapter, regarding scholarship on *Les Fleurs* – to approach the work in decidedly conceptual terms. This is particularly striking in the case of Lautréamont—a poet who was so far ahead of his time in his adamant resistance to, and subversion of the conceptual frameworks forced upon individual existence by social and linguistic conventions, and whose distinct voice has been associated with primal, *non*-linguistic expression.[3]

---

3 First citing Aragon, who was involved in the Surrealists' "discovery" of Lautréamont's work, Jean writes: "« *Maldoror* ni les *Poésies* ne pouvaient encore s'envisager comme un langage.

This is not to suggest that existing approaches to Lautréamont's revolutionary poetics are by any means dispensable in our attempt to map this uncharted territory of the text ("[des] landes inexplorées," *Maldoror* 99). As Kristeva's work has already demonstrated with such thoroughness, however much we accentuate the visceral forces at work in such a text, we cannot avoid situating them in the historico-political contexts in which they arose;[4] all acts of revolt against order and ideology, however anarchic, are also inherently and unavoidably defined through this relation. Dobelbower, for instance, has observed that the radical transgressive gesture of Lautréamont's writing cannot be attributed to its horrifying imagery and blasphemy in and of themselves, but involves a much larger, *discursive* violence committed against a system that has thus far "recuperated" all gestures of rebellion:

> Lautréamont was not interested in reproducing the reassuring and cathartic effect of conventional poetry which is never more than an opiate. It reinscribes and symbiotically requires the system it laments. His text is original and polemical. [...] It leaves no space for an ultimate recuperative gesture that would allow it to be subsumed by bourgeois culture (18).

If Baudelaire acknowledged the passing of Romanticism, in his "Coucher du soleil romantique," cited in the previous chapter (p. 43), Lautréamont even more actively assures the de-composition of that movement's central tropes and ideologies, as Winspur has noted: "By extending these landscapes to their logical extreme, Lautréamont breaks down their metaphorical purpose (the representation of an idealized inner realm of feelings, and of ethical judgments)" (84); "the battles waged by Maldoror [...] are not conflicts begun by Lautréamont but rather romanticism's own struggle played out to its final end" (87).

Another critical contribution that must be acknowledged – and which indeed constitutes a major shift in studies of Lautréamont's work, brought about, in large part, by prominent literary theorists of the sixties – lies in the *de*valorization of historical factors; a recognition of the need to replace the myth-making and conjecture of the Surrealist era with a more rigorous and fertile approach to the workings of the text itself. As Lawlor observes, in reference to the most notable of these critics (Pleynet, Kristeva and Sollers): "Malgré

Mais plus comme un cri des entrailles. » Il est bien vrai que longtemps seul le *cri* a été perceptible [...]" (in Philip 142).

4 "[L]es questions que nous nous poserons sur la pratique littéraire viseront l'horizon politique dont celle-ci est inséparable, quels que soient les efforts de l'ésotérisme esthétisant [...] pour les tenir écartés" (*Révolution* 14).

une tendance à favoriser, parfois, la méthode au dépens du texte à étudier, la critique moderne tend à ne plus faire dépendre de renseignements biographiques, historiques, etc. l'accès à un texte littéraire" (20). Nesselroth has also recognized the need to replace the biographical focus on "le cas Lautréamont" with close textual analysis, in his insightful study of the production of imagery in *Maldoror* (14).[5]

And yet, as soon as the critical gaze begins to close in on the material substance of the text – as it really must, in some manner, when it is a question of *poetic* text – we observe that *both* of these critical tendencies – historical, and purely textual – become problematic, limited by the theoretical frameworks defining them. With their jettisoning of the mystique surrounding the writer himself, in the desire to better understand the textual processes of *Maldoror*, theorists have often used the work as a platform for their *own* ideas about language, as Nesselroth suggested ("la méthode au dépens du texte à étudier"); a tendency that results in conclusions quite similar to those of the present study, in fact, but with a significant difference. If, according to such readings, Lautréamont's writing takes on a life of its own, self-propagating ("le langage engendre l'activité," below), it is in a highly "reflective" mode, in which the *visual* element overshadows the aural, language seeming to think for itself: "perçu en tant que langage, c'est un poème où les images sont plus que fantastiques et les passages sont plus qu'extraordinaires, où le langage engendre l'activité, où l'écriture écrit au sujet d'elle-même, où le texte est son propre sujet et son propre objet" (Lawlor 37).[6] Such a perspective on textual production in *Maldoror* is equally problematic, in view of the analyses that follow, when critics locate its source in the lucid consciousness of the poet himself. By treating this production – and in particular, the violence that pervades the poet's writing – from one step removed, whatever the agency, Lautréamont's language is rendered abstract, emptied of what is most volatile in it:

> There is a kind of verbal terrorism which murders sense without even disrupting legitimate verbal orders and sequences. The attack against structure in *Maldoror* is carried out in the most rigorously structured way; each sentence, each stanza,

---

5 See also Thomas' recent *Lautréamont, Subject to Interpretation*, which takes a new look at the representations and appropriations of this unknown soldier of French poetry: ("The fictional portraits of Lautréamont from 1896 to the present day [...] preserve [his] existence in spite of his absence, revealing the intolerability of an anonymous author" (25).
6 There are exceptions, admittedly. Nesselroth makes several observations regarding the sound of particular terms in the text, cited in the following pages.

each canto, and the succession of cantos are prodigies of controlled composition" (Bersani 195).[7]

As we observe, surveying existing scholarship on all of the four poets treated in the present book, the critic's own intellectual subtlety often glosses over what is truly disruptive in revolting poetry—a desire, enacted in the very matter of the poet's language, to "murder" much more than "sense"; a *coup* that destabilizes processes of "controlled composition," ultimately, establishing its own prerogative in the generation of text.

To better understand how the unique textual processes of *Maldoror* came into being and function, requires that we find a middle ground between the two positions, above. If these processes must be recognized as taking on a certain autonomy in the developing composition of the text, we nonetheless cannot avoid acknowledging their origin in an historical individual; an acknowledgement, however, that does not so much require any knowledge about that individual, beyond the fact that he existed, a living, feeling (and not merely thinking) *body*. A number of critics, for instance, have identified the overt sadism featured in *Maldoror* as a dominant force in the actual creation of the work (not simply an object of detached representation), but have focused on the possibility of a particular defining event in the psyche of the young poet (usually involving one of his boyhood friends, on whom a number of Maldoror's companion-victims would seem to be based). Bersani, for example, writes of:

> [...] [a] personal secret – not only of Maldoror, but also of Isidore Ducasse – which the literary text seeks simultaneously to hide, to reenact, and to confess. It would then have the status of a psychic origin in *Les Chants de Maldoror*; it would provide the fictional and perhaps the biographically real source for the obsession with cruelty in the work (216).

Joining an established line of *maudits*, Lautréamont is thus able to enact in writing the censorable iniquities of his past – and on a greatly "exaggerated

---

7 "L'œuvre de Lautréamont aujourd'hui nous frappe essentiellement par son aspect lucide et conscient. En d'autres termes, elle se révèle à nous comme « langage » (Jean, cited in Philip 141). There has in fact been an ongoing debate over the degree of control exercised in the composition of *Maldoror*, it should be noted, with two camps – those concurring with Blanchot, who insists that any apparent disorder in the text is conscious and part of a larger order governing the writing process ("Le lecteur [...] est environné par une vigilance supérieure, toujours prête à lui répondre," "Tête" 44), and those who call this reading into question, often basing their own reading on suppositions as to the psychological state of the writer (most famously, Soulier, in his *Lautréamont, génie ou maladie mentale ?*).

scale" – while maintaining a safe identity in society: "Lautréamont has read his Byron [and] Sade [...] all too well, since he proffers literature as a perfect way of hid[ing] oneself from persecution" (Gonsalves 30).[8] Whatever biographical sources one might hypothesize for the composition of *Maldoror* (a work that resists the validation of theories, generally), what remains clear to any attentive reader, is that the creative process of the individual writing the text – whether Ducasse, his persona, Lautréamont, or some less distinct entity in between – is highly motivated by a vivid "taste" for the sadistic, in the words of Pierre-Quint ("Ces exploits délirants de Maldoror, un mobile les domine, qui dirige sa conduite : le goût du sadisme," 72). The crucial first step, if we are to get closer to what is really happening in the language of this text (and if any text must be understood in such terms, as *event*, it is surely *Maldoror*), is to turn our attention to the traces we perceive there of the writing subject—not merely a *cogito*, but a physical, pulsional agent of composition, who is continually striving to *enact* the violence depicted.

There is one critic who has brought attention to this singular quality of the poet's writing. For Bachelard, the fundamental creative gesture in *Maldoror* is not, precisely, the product of meditated planning, but a form of spontaneous, aggressive *will*: "le *temps de l'agression* [...] toujours homogène à l'impulsion première [...] est produit par l'être qui attaque dans le plan unique où l'être veut affirmer sa violence. L'être agressif n'attend pas qu'on lui donne le temps ; il le prend, il le crée" (9). A will that is realized *physically* in the production of text, superseding the self-conscious processes of representation in which the latter is essentially *painted*, an object for viewing: "la poésie de Lautréamont est une poésie de l'excitation, de l'impulsion musculaire, et [...] n'est en rien une poésie visuelle de formes et de couleurs" (14). And yet, when Bachelard turns his attention to the aural level of the poet's language, this "impulsive" aggression is seen to coexist with, if not participate in, a "coherent" song ("la cohérence sonore," 84). While the language of *Maldoror* refuses the limits of traditional verse structure, he suggests, it binds words in harmony through a "natural force" ("Sans l'aide des rimes, sans le garde-fou d'une métrique étroite, les sons se lient comme entraînés par une force naturelle," 83). Citing Jaloux's comparison of the cantos with the meticulous prose of the master craftsman himself, Flaubert (Ibid.), Bachelard ends up sublimating the disruptive ele-

---

8   While most readers are aware of Sade's real-life exploits, not all may be aware of Byron's own run-ins with Regency society—most notably, over an incestuous relationship with his half-sister, and his probable bisexuality. On the role of sadism in *Maldoror*, see Pierre-Quint, and Durante's more recent work as well.

ment in Lautréamont's work ("une folie sans folies," below), in the same way Blanchot and others have, as mentioned above:

> Jamais une œuvre violente n'a été moins tiraillée. On peut dire que dans son aberration, elle n'aberre pas. C'est une folie sans folies, un système d'énergie violente qui brise le réel pour vivre sans scrupule et sans gêne une *réalisation* (84).

Several other critics should be acknowledged for calling attention to this material element of the text, as suggested earlier, beginning with Pleynet: "*Les Chants de Maldoror* ainsi se dérobent à toute entreprise qui ne les considère pas d'abord dans la matérialité même première-dernière, seule preuve enfin de leur existence (pour nous), leur écriture" (*Lautréamont* 109). Both Pickering and Dessons have emphasized the privileging of orality in Lautréamont's writing, the latter calling attention to the poet's use of punctuation as a means of highlighting characteristics of spoken language (90–91). In his own assessment of Lautréamont's writing process, Pierssens in fact employs the very term utilized throughout the present study, to identify this material element of the text:

> Le mélange de fluidité et de complexité de la phrase, son élan lyrique mêlé à une constante ironie, la juxtaposition des vastes envolées et des expressions crues— tout cela laisse deviner une lecture attentive, non seulement à la thématique, mais à <u>la texture même des mots</u> (80, my emphasis).

None of these critics, nevertheless, have actually developed an analytical method to investigate with any thoroughness this materiality of Lautréamont's language, through ample close readings of passages throughout the entire, evolving text.

Before presenting my own attempt at such an endeavor, one additional critical work must be acknowledged, already discussed while situating my methodology more generally, in the Introduction. Kristeva's historic *La révolution du langage poétique* is significant in this regard, not simply because she elaborates the most innovative theoretical apparatus for a "materialistic" reading of the poet's writing, but because, by undertaking this reading through a complex, conceptual discourse, even she fails to convincingly engage the texture of *Maldoror* she valorizes. Drawing on the work of linguist Ivan Fónagy, also discussed in the Introduction, she takes his reflections on the articulation of phonemes to another level: not only do the gestures involved in the production of speech sounds allow the writing subject to express drives that remain inaccessible to conventional signification ("le *dispositif signifiant* historiquement accepté," below), but they allow that subject to simultaneously transform the latter. The repeated articulations of revolt throughout *Maldoror*, arising from the deepest, most sublimated recesses of the writer/speaker's psyche, participate in an as-yet unrecognized, *semiotic* form of revolution:

> Le rejet marqué par l'abondance d'énoncés négatifs des *Chants de Maldoror* [...] est le fait d'un sujet en procès qui arrive – pour des raisons biographiques ou historiques – à remodeler le *dispositif signifiant* historiquement accepté, en proposant la représentation d'un autre rapport aux objets naturels, aux appareils sociaux et au corps propre. Un tel sujet traverse le réseau linguistique et se sert de lui pour indiquer [...] qu'il ne représente pas un réel posé d'avance et détaché à jamais du procès pulsionnel, mais qu'il expérimente ou pratique le procès objectif en s'immergeant en lui et en émergeant de lui à travers les pulsions (116).

And yet, as remarked earlier, the relatively inconsequential amount of actual *textural* analysis among the 600 plus pages of theoretical terminology treats, not the work of Lautréamont, but one poem of Mallarmé! (139–63).

My aim here is not to downplay the relevance of this, or indeed any of the scholarship mentioned thus far. In comparison to the intellectual sophistication and historical significance of Kristeva's work, in particular, the goal of the present chapter is – as already stated in the Introduction, regarding my project more generally – decidedly modest. Leaving the complex rhetorical, figural and metatextual elements to the many critics who have analyzed and will continue to analyze *Maldoror*, I would simply like to invite readers to engage with that which has too long been ignored, despite its essential role in the unique expressivity and magnetism of this work: the articulated "matter" of the text's language. For it is only then, I believe, that we can begin to fully appreciate the acknowledged *force* of Lautréamont's work—not merely in its transgression of accepted *ideas*, but as a manifestation of actual energy, as several critics have insisted: "Le beau n'est pas un simple arrangement. Il a besoin d'une puissance, d'une énergie, d'une conquête. La statue elle-même a des muscles. La cause formelle est d'ordre énergétique (Bachelard 103–04); "Ce n'est pas l'esthétique de la représentation, mais l'esthétique de l'énergie, du courant magnétique direct et foudroyant qui est illustrée" (Goraj 82).

And as I have already suggested, in tracking the shift of agency in modern poetic expression – from conscious to unconscious, mind to body – close scrutiny of these articulatory textures will tend to reveal a hidden agenda, independent of any semantic teleology the writer or critic might propose to orient reading. As Bersani has insightfully observed:

As in other modes of fantasy, the writer in the privacy and leisure of composition, may be engaged in inventing repetitions of sensual intensities. Furthermore, in the act of writing, the word itself seems to be experienced partly as an insubstantial sign referring to meanings beyond itself, and partly as a sensuous object referring to nothing but its own shape, sound and position in a design of numerous word-objects (10).

If any writer has been susceptible, in the extreme privacy of his hermetic existence, to the "sensual intensities" of spoken language, it is Lautréamont.[9] It is to the production – and *re*production – of those intensities distinguishing his unique voice, in the enactment of violence, that we now turn.

Preamble: The Menagerie

The tendency, problematized in the preceding chapter, to play down the transgressive elements of Baudelaire's work, appears less questionable when viewed in the context of *Maldoror*. Such elements appear quite tame, indeed, as the earlier poet presents the most savage, bestial impulses in the human heart – the "ménagerie infâme de nos vices" (6) of the opening "Au Lecteur" – only to cancel out the cacophony and menacing forces suggested by this allegory with the final, leveling *ennui* ("Il ferait volontiers de la terre un débris," Ibid.). Not only do these creatures fail to reappear in the succeeding poems, for the most part, instead supplanted by the refined sadism of all too human figures – the poet, his lovers, and humanity at large – but their immediate displacement in this liminal text reflects a more general tendency in the aesthetic governing the poems that follow: the *ennui* that dominates Baudelaire's "menagerie of vices," that is to say, points to the ultimate impotence of the poetic violence proposed for the work as a whole, as if predetermining the failure of its expressive economy, as suggested at the close of the preceding study. In *Maldodor*, by contrast, as anyone familiar with the text knows, the animals have clearly been let out of their cages.

---

9 The account – of questionable authenticity – provided by *Maldoror*'s third publisher, Genonceaux, has become part of the legend discussed above: "Il n'écrivait que la nuit, assis à son piano. Il déclamait, il forgeait ses phrases, plaquant ses prosopopées avec des accords" (cited in Pleynet, *Lautréamont* 15).

While the bestiary of *Maldoror* is one of the work's distinctive and most analyzed features on the figurative, *visual* plane, however,[10] its prominent *aural* presence in the work has gone largely unnoticed. The now roaming herds of predators, parasites and generally unappealing animalia – and the unrestricted drives they represent – are not only brought to life through the sounds designating them ("acting out" Baudelaire's "monstres glapissants, hurlants, grognants," 6), but this visceral mode of expression is further heightened by the accumulation of extreme articulations we will find throughout *Maldoror* more generally. Where Baudelaire expressed his disdain for the feeble post-Romantic poetry surrounding him with an abrupt croak ("Et mon pied peureux froisse, au bord du marécage, / Des crapauds imprévus [...]," 149), this same creature/exclamation sounds out multiple times in Lautréamont's text, as already observed in the preceding chapter, amplifying the shock produced by its apparition at the close of the first canto:

Comment !... c'est toi, cra`paud !... gros cra`paud !... infortuné cra`paud !... (131).

As Steinmetz observes, the names for such animals are like precious objects for the bibliophile Lautréamont, scattered throughout the cantos ("Les noms eux-mêmes valent comme des trésors, à pouvoir ainsi être déclinés," "Isidore" 153). While this naming ultimately leads, in Steinmetz's reading, to the referents in question, thus presencing anatomically these exotic creatures in the text,[11] I would propose it is the materiality of the signifier itself that becomes most present in such terms, through the extreme, awkward series of articulations constituting them. These terms stand out from, and indeed disrupt the regular progression of narrative, not only because they often exceed the vocabulary of even the most erudite reader, but because they *sound out* this incomprehensibility, at odds with the reading act on multiple levels. When Maldoror is about to witness a horrific event in IV:3, for instance (a husband being tortured by his mother and wife), his act of silent hiding, effectively communicated through the monosyllabic series of the initial clause, is disrupted by the jarring terms in the simile that follows:

---

10   Bachelard's early, seminal work on the cantos, and Le Clézio's more recent study, are two notable examples.

11   "les corps qu'il constitue comportent un coefficient de réalité surélevé. Leur présence est efficiente, étonnamment sensible et sensuelle, établie selon une relation anatomique inexistante auparavant dans les récits (excepté ceux de Sade), malgré de constants appels de la part de Balzac et autres à la phrénologie et à la pathognomonie" (Ibid. 156).

je\me\tins\tout\coi,\ comme l'acantophorus serraticornis, qui ne montre que la tête en dehors de son nid (225).[12]

When we listen more closely to such passages, and to more of the text surrounding them, we observe that these salient phonetic clusters participate – as observed in our analyses of Baudelaire's language – in larger articulatory textures. In the preceding example, for instance, the explosion of the creature itself is anticipated in the minor combustion in the first half of the passage ("je\me\tins\tout\coi,\), then redistributed to animate the final, (somewhat) clarifying image—the featureless head of the creature jutting out in the modulating series of back and front articulations:

[…] qui ne montre que\la\tête\ en dehors de\son\nid.

Such terms ("l'acantophorus serraticornis") thus function as cores of expressive energy, aural "big bangs" which are dispersed throughout the text, expanding the *Maldorean* universe. In the following, the "fascinating beauty" of the writhing "scolopendre" (*mille pattes*) evolves in the progression of text, as the creature's legs are differentiated, the undulations of initial plurisyllabic terms surging throughout the text in similar, dynamic textures, leading to the final reaction of "intense hatred":

la scolopendre ne manque pas d'ennemis ; la beauté fantastique de ses pattes innombrables, au lieu de lui attirer la sympathie des animaux, n'est, peut-être, pour eux, que le puissant stimUlant d'une jalouse irrita`tion. Et, je ne serais pas étonné d'apprendre que cet insecte est en bUtte aux \\haines les plus in`tenses (243–44).

In one of the text's celebrated "beau comme" similes, a "series" of soaring predators expands in the second half of the figure, *seizing* the reader through its jagged texture:[13]

---

12   I am expanding on Nesselroth's reading of this passage, in which he has already identified the effect of these awkward terms, without however underscoring the specific textural elements – phonetic and otherwise – contributing to this effect: "the vehicle suddenly breaks the dramatic intensity of the situation because the technical vocabulary […] renders the comparison incomprehensible and comical, the name of the bird sounding ridiculous. This is due to the Latin form whose sequence of syllables is phonetically grotesque for French ears" (*LI* 65).

13   As elsewhere, I have underlined, not simply a given creature, but other segments of text, as the notation of specific phonemes seems unnecessary for conveying the general effect

86   CHAPTER 2

> Toute une série d'oiseaux rapaces, amateurs de la viande d'autrui et défenseurs de l'utilité de la poursuite, beaux comme des <u>squelettes qui effeuillent des panoccos de l'Arkansas</u>, voltigent autour de ton front (232).[14]

It is worth noting here, in anticipation of a problematic we will increasingly observe, that these distinct sound-images often seem to function, when read in the context of surrounding passages, as a form of compensation in Lautréamont's poetics of force; an *aural* production of *enargeia*, intended to enhance an effect that has been otherwise insufficiently communicated by the principal images and events of the narrative.[15] When the narrator recounts his uncanny encounter with a strange, amphibious humanoid, for instance, his preamble overdetermines – admittedly, in a tongue-in-cheek manner – the affective charge of the event: "Hélas ! je voudrais […] [que] chacun comprenne davantage, sinon mon épouvante, du moins ma stupéfaction, quand, un soir d'été […]" (240). This is significant, in the perspective of the present study, not only because the strange event we anticipate is now presented in such a banal way – "je vis nager, sur la mer, avec de larges pattes de canard à la place des extrémités des jambes et des bras, porteur d'une nageoire dorsale, proportionnellement aussi longue et aussi éffilée que celle des dauphins, un être humain" (Ibid.) – but because it is the *following* passage that jumps out at the reader, with its torquing, baroque articulations—heard not only in key zoological terms, but in the echoes that follow: "l'anarnak groënlandais" => "de la plus grande admiration"; "le scorpène-horrible" => "les marques très-ostensibles":

> je vis nager […] un être humain que des bancs nombreux de poissons (je vis, dans ce cortège, entre autres habitants des eaux, <u>la torpille</u>, <u>l'anarnak</u>

---

      produced by such dense, complex textures. "Rapace" : "de *rapere* « saisir, ravir »" (*Robert* 1864). Most readers are familiar with these distinctive rhetorical figures, celebrated by the Surrealists: "beau comme […] la rencontre fortuite sur une table de dissection d'une machine à coudre et d'un parapluie" (*Maldoror* 289).

14 See again Nesselroth, who similarly identifies this image "implanting itself in (the reader's) mind" (23)—a phenomenon he attributes less to the sounds of the words in question, than to the obscurity of the key term "Panoccos," which cannot be located in either *Larousse* or *Littré*.

15 Zanker identifies the most thorough definition of this rhetorical term – *enargeia* – in Dionysius of Halicarnassus, which he paraphrases as: "the stylistic effect in which appeal is made to the senses of the listener and attendant circumstances are described in such a way that the listener will be turned into an eyewitness […]; he will inevitably see the events […] depict[ed] and, as it were, feel in the presence of the characters […] introduce[d]" (297).

groënlandais et le scorpène-horrible) suivaient avec les marques très-ostensibles de la plus grande admiration (Ibid.).

Displaced, what stands out most in the text – not visually, as we expect, but aurally – are the linguistic "bodies" of the underwater observers who perceive and are affected by the event, and not the event itself.

Interestingly, we increasingly observe in the rambling, surreal passages of the later cantos that such sequences are reversed, these phonetic clusters of energy instead followed by the narrator's bland, disconnected – or disconnect*ing* – observations—digressions that seem to go on forever like the boring pedants of the poet's recent youth. In the passage cited earlier, for instance, with its circling raptors, the "forehead" that closes the passage, ostensibly grounding the supporting figure in a continuing narrative, is abruptly called into question, dissipating in a paradoxically ambiguous string of objective, scientific terms: "Mais, est-ce un front ? Il n'est pas difficile de mettre beaucoup d'hésitation à le croire. Il est si bas, qu'il est impossible de vérifier les preuves, numériquement exiguës, de son existence équivoque" (232–33). Such disjunctions could be explained quite simply, at first glance, as the type of anarchic literary terrorism practiced by Lautréamont throughout the cantos—a violence that is straightforward and devoid of any conceptual goal other than *not* being meaningful. As Bersani has observed of the "beau comme" figures, mentioned above: "These comparisons have no educational, no cognitive function. What they do is simply to move us away from their supposed points of departure" (196). The prevalence or "coagulations" of linguistic sound in *Maldoror* point, however, as we will discover, to a more complicated, and in fact problematic textual process.

Setting aside these more complex forms of textual violence in the work, however, I would first like to call attention to the basic gestures in the poet's expressive arsenals, by which the latter are deployed most directly and efficiently upon their object; articulations that seem to not only strike out from the written page ("ca`nard," below), but effectively accumulate and conduct expressive energy—transforming the mocking smile of the human herd in the following example, for instance, into the reproachful invective used against it:

sachez que la poésie se trouve partout où n'est pas le sour*i*re, st*u*p*i*de-ment *raill*eur, de l'homme, à la f*i*g*U*re de ca`nard (287).[16]

---

[16] The irony, which is surely not lost on its author, if not relished, is that poetry here – Lautréamont's poetry, at least – is *precisely* where this taunting grimace is found. It is indeed constituted by it, physically, in the present instance (compare the articulation of "sourire" and "railleur" to those terms analyzed on p. 60 of chapter 1).

Like much of the infernal machinery in *Maldoror*, whatever negative consequences it may entail for the progressing composition of the cantos, Lautréamont's sounding bestiary is indeed effective in enacting *le mal* in many instances (not limited to a brief "glapissement," as in Baudelaire's "Au Lecteur"), whether it is directed against humanity ("à la figure de ca`nard") or God Himself—here, gorging on His creation:

> les supplices exercés sur la faiblesse de l'homme, dans cette mer \\hideuse de pourpre, passaient devant mon front en rugissant comme des éléphants écor`chés (156).

Creatures that reinforce, through their absurd resonance, the "autonomous" force of the writing subject, despite the "equivocal reasoning" of his discourse:

> Je veux résider seul dans mon équivoque raisonnement. L'autonomie… ou bien qu'on me change en hippopotame (260).

By introducing such creatures into his writing, many of which have never appeared – or been *heard* – in French poetry, Lautréamont takes hold of new, less refined forces of expression, rejecting the tired muse of the existing tradition:

> Je saisis la plume qui va construire le deuxième chant… instrument arraché aux ailes de quelque pygargue\`roux! (137).[17]

---

[17] It should be recalled here that Lautréamont uses such animals to denounce the poets of that tradition in his *Poésies*: "[…] les odeurs de poule mouillée, les affadissements, les grenouilles, les poulpes, les requins […] – devant ces charniers immondes, que je rougis de nommer, il est temps de réagir enfin contre ce qui nous choque et nous courbe si souverainement" (331); "Lamartine, la Cigogne-Larmoyante ; Lermontoff, le Tigre-qui-Rugit ; […] et Byron, l'Hippopotame-des-Jungles-Infernales" (340). Also noteworthy, in light of the problematic identified in the preceding pages, the confident assertion of the above citation ("Je saisis la plume […]") is immediately followed by an admission, however theatrical, of creative impotence: "[…] arraché aux ailes de quelque pygargue roux ! Mais… qu'ont-ils donc mes doigts ? Les articulations demeurent paralysées, dès que je commence mon travail. Cependant, j'ai besoin d'écrire… C'est impossible ! Et bien, je répète […]" (137). Failed expression, which is nonetheless expressive, flows out of the initial act —inarticulate, and *articulated*: "arraché […] de quelque pygargue roux" => "Les articulations […] paralysées."

Impact

> Je ne me servirai pas d'armes construites avec le bois ou le fer ; [...] la sonorité puissante et séraphique de la harpe deviendra, sous mes doigts, un talisman redoutable (*Maldoror* 219).

Lautréamont's declaration of war here is significant, for several reasons. By claiming his language will replace actual weapons, insisting on the materiality of the latter ("wood" and "iron"), he implicitly attributes a physical quality to his poetry. The force of his language is not limited to the strictly linguistic, expressive sphere – whether in the shocking imagery, or the aural disruptions identified above – he would have the reader believe, but is capable of passing into and acting upon reality. This idea is reinforced by a detail, otherwise unremarkable, in the formulation of the final image above. The fact that his fingers touch, not the strings of the harp, as one would expect, but its "sonority," reflects Lautréamont's particular relation to poetry and the act of composition: the articulation of language would actualize, not only meaning, but those aggressive drives normally channeled through the non-speaking, *acting* parts of the body. Throughout *Maldoror* we in fact observe a recurring slippage between figures for speech, and arms or hands.[18]

Maldoror's most formidable enemy, God, is attacked several times in such terms. While many of these passages in the cantos come to mind for the *image* produced (blasphemous scenes in which the deity is inebriated, or devouring men[19]—as in the passage cited earlier, for instance), the following passage conveys the impact of promised violence through the articulation of the promise itself. As in the passage just cited, the weapon of language is *handled* (emphasized through repetition: "<u>Man</u>iant les ironies terribles, d'une <u>main</u>"), the resolve and control of this statement/gesture actually setting up, in its composition, the blows that follow ("d'une main `*f*erme et `*f*roide" => "Je *f*rapperai"):

---

18   The following analysis thus resonates with (while problematizing) Bachelard's reading: "Avec la poésie <u>au poignet</u>, Maldoror aborde la réalité, il la malaxe et la pétrit, il la transforme" (109, my emphasis). Lawlor has described Lautréamont's writing in similar terms: "The written word [...] is *l'arme* of the genius poet that is capable of transforming and destroying the reader, as well as language and meaning" (*Chimères* 7).

19   III:4 and II:8, respectively.

Maniant les ironies terribles, d'une main `ferme et `froide, je t'avertis que mon cœur en contiendra suffisamment, pour m'attaquer à toi, jusqu'à la fin de mon existence. Je frapperai ta carcasse `creuse (140).

In another threatened assault on God, this wielding of language is even more conspicuous. The central act in fact stands out less ("a" life, in the abstract, ripped from the victim: "arrachant [...] une nuisible vie") than the pummeling of language that passes well beyond the fatal blow into the "contortions" of the victim's body, finally "striking" the viewer ("qui frappe sa vue et cloue [...] sa langue"):

mon bras te renversera dans la poussière, empoisonnée par ta respiration, et, arrachant de tes entrailles une nuisible vie, laissera sur le chemin ton cadavre, criblé de contorsions, pour apprendre au voyageur consterné, que cette chair palpitante, qui frappe sa vue d'étonnement, et cloue dans son palais sa langue muette, ne doit plus être comparée, si l'on garde son sang-froid, qu'au tronc pourri d'un chêne, qui tomba de vétusté ! (263).

If these passages demonstrate Lautréamont's ability to lend a visceral quality to his assaults on an abstract entity, the majority of violent scenes in *Maldoror* involve victims with distinct bodies and attributes, lending an even greater sense of actual violence to such attacks—both for the poet, who acts through his agent, Maldoror, and for the reader, who observes. In a passage from the sixth canto, already cited in my Introduction, when Maldoror throws his final victim, Mervyn, into a sack, mercilessly beating him, the compressed, percussive texture of language enacts this inescapable violence within an enclosed space, the rapid succession of blows heightened by the accentuation of monosyllabic terms ("de\ses\os,\se\tut") and punctuated pauses:

il enleva le sac,\ ainsi qu'un paquet de linges,\ et en frappa,\ à plusieurs reprises,\ le parapet du pont.\ Alors,\ le patient,\ s'étant aperçu du craquement de\ses\os,\se\tut (310).

That Lautréamont is very much aware of, and indeed relishes the sense of force produced by such compositions, is suggested by the fact that this same sound-image is reproduced several pages later, re-enacting this "rythmique pétrissage" in the very matter of the text—an effect that is amplified, in this instance, by the whirring acceleration of the "sling" preceding it, with its repeated fricatives, and [l] and [r] series:

> [...] *le jour* où *le* pont du Ca*rr*ouse*l* [...] aperçut avec ho*rr*eur *l'*ho*r*i*z*on de sa pensée s'é*l*a*r*gi*r* confusément en *cer*c*l*es *c*on*c*entriques, à *l'*appa*r*ition matina*l*e du *r*ythm**i**que p**é***tr***i**ssage **d**'un sa**c i**cosaè**d***r*e, **c**on*tr*e son pa*r*apet **c**a*l***c**aire ! (314).

Just as we observed in Baudelaire's use of such articulations (pp. 57–58), this production of perceptible impact in the texture of language need not even coincide with the representation it supports in order to be effective. There is something equally, if not more disturbing, for example, in the passage that *precedes* the explicit torture scene referenced above, on p. 84, as the strange, overwrought figure for the knocking legs of an approaching attacker is reinforced aurally—the abruptness of the sounding image heightened, as in the above citation, by the flowing fricative and [l] series that precede it:

> Les *ch*e*v*eux grisonnants de *l*a *pl*us *v*iei*ll*e *fl*ottaient au *v*ent, comme *l*es *l*ambeaux d'une *v*oi*l*e déchirée, et *l*es *ch*e*v*illes **d**e *l'*au*tr*e **c**l*aqu*aient en*tr*e e*ll*es, **c**omme *l*es **c**oups**d**e\\queue**d**'un**t**hon sur *l*a **d**une**tt**e**d**'un *v*aisseau (225).

In a work that stands out for the broad strokes of its infamously vivid and elaborate depictions of violence, however (unlike Baudelaire's encoded "infusions of venom"), it is logical that the most effective use of such aural/oral violence would be found where these textures coincide with acts committed by the central figure himself, enacted upon his many victims, and actualized in the reader's imagination—in the recurring human sling, for instance, where the density and weight connoted by back phonemes contributes to the final impact:

> son co*r*ps, *l*ancé pa*r l*a *f*o*rc*e cent*r*i*f*uge, alla **c**ogner **c**on*tr*e\\le**tr**onc**d**'un\ `*ch*ên*e*\ (246).

But before we devote further attention to this, the most sophisticated and "impactful" of Lautréamont's weapons, we should acknowledge a very different, but equally significant weapon deployed by the poet.

La douceur du poison

> Pourquoi le poète ne serait-il pas un broyeur de poisons aussi bien qu'un confiseur ?
> BAUDELAIRE (*OC* II, 237–38).

> [...] ces pages sombres et pleines de poison.
> MALDOROR (99).

As anyone familiar with *Maldodor* knows, Lautréamont's preferred modes of violence are hardly limited to the production of impact. Indeed, if I have just contrasted the direct force of his writing with the "venomous" nature of Baudelaire's imagery and tone, the latter quality is in fact distinguishable in *Maldoror* as well, and one of the most recognizable elements inherited from the earlier poet's work—not only in actual figures involving poison, which will fulfill the opening threat, cited above, but in a more general mode of expression that corresponds to mortal substances and their effects. The poison infusing the pages of Lautréamont's text is not limited to its morally degraded ideational content, as readers tend to assume, but is more intimately linked to an aesthetic of sadistic *lenteur* that is valorized throughout *Maldoror*.[20] The protagonist's most distinctive gestures are in fact those that would prolong and modulate the act of violence, in a desire to savor the domination of – and infliction of suffering upon – an objectified other, deferring any definitive consummation; an articulated "substance" that gradually and methodically kills off the implicit paradigm of lyric poetry (and the latter's equation of beauty with truth and the good), simultaneously replacing it with a new, and morbid *plaisir du texte*.[21]

This aesthetic is in fact quite clearly articulated (in the abstract sense of the term this time) in the early cantos. In the opening stanzas, which fulfill a similar function in *Maldoror* as that assigned "Au lecteur" at the opening of *Les Fleurs*, Lautréamont's own pronouncement on humanity's fundamental moral state ("les pensées hautaines et méchantes de son héros [sont] dans tous les hommes," 102), is accompanied by his proposal to "paint" the enactment – and more importantly, the enduring "delights" – of "cruelty"; an experience he would prolong to the end of human existence itself (!): "Moi, je fais servir mon

---

[20] Pickering has similarly distinguished two types of aggression in *Maldoror*, which he identifies as "sournoise" and "ouverte," both of which can be traced back to erotic impulses (40).

[21] A reference to Barthes' eponymous work.

génie à peindre les délices de la cruauté ! Délices non passagères, artificielles ; mais, qui ont commencé avec l'homme, finiront avec lui" (101). In one of the first of these crimes against humanity, in 1:6, this duration is in fact extended to eternity: "et, pendant ce temps, qui devrait durer autant que l'éternité dure, l'enfant pleure" (103). The degree to which this aestheticized, sensual perception of cruelty is privileged in Lautréamont's mind is indicated by a later passage, in which he is not even the active agent (i.e. through Maldoror) of the other's suffering. Observing from a distance the drowning victims of a shipwreck, and lingering in the passing minutes, he waxes: "Ô ciel ! comment peut-on vivre, après avoir éprouvé tant de voluptés ! [...] Minute par minute, je suivais les péripéties de leurs angoisses" (176, my emphasis).

Unremarked by most readers, however, this familiar sado-aesthetic is often enacted in the very texture of the poet's language. Its ultimate source, *prima causa* of *Maldoror* itself, *le mal*, is in fact first experienced in such a manner, as if the built-up energy of the enunciation actually reproduced a major, bodily transformation in the poetic subject—first "concentrated" through repeated punctuation, and then released in the soothing "douce," flowing out of the climactic "mal" with its trailing ellipsis:

> à cause de cette concentration qui ne lui était pas naturelle,\ chaque jour le sang lui montait à la tête ;\ jusqu'à ce que,\ ne pouvant plus supporter une pareille vie,\ il se jeta résolumment dans la carrière du 'mal... => atm*osphère* 'd*ou*ce (101).

Just as important for Lautréamont, as we will observe in greater detail below, is the effect of this *esthétique du mal* on the *reader*.[22] The introductory passage above is in fact preceded by a similar one, in 1:2, in which the narrator invests the reader with this same dark pleasure zone (immediately after expressing concern for his or her "timidity" in the face of such horrors, in the first stanza!): "Lecteur, c'est peut-être la haine que tu veux que j'invoque dans le commencement de cet ouvrage !" (100). This is significant, not only for the subtle rhetorical gesture employed here, but because the language of the text actually validates this incrimination of the reader, forcing him or her to participate in the promised savoring of evil, in articulations that mimic the undulating fluids and dilating orifices—in particular, the series of fricatives, mid and semi-vowels ("org*ueilleu*ses"), [R] and [l] ("*r*eni*fl*era"), and [m]; a "voluptuous" description that is drawn out, as in the preceding citation, through frequent pauses:

---

22 The expression is from the title of a poem by Wallace Stevens (252). See my own article – which includes the phrase in its title – on the work of Baudelaire and D'Aubigné.

Qui te dit que tu n'en reni*fl*eras pas,\ bai*g*né dans d'innombra*bl*es *v*olup-tés,\ tant que tu *v*ou*dr*as,\ avec tes narines or*g*uei*ll*euses,\ ˈ*l*ar*g*es et ˈmai*gr*es,\ [...] *l*entement et ma*g*estueusement,\ *l*es *r*ouges émanations ? (Ibid.).

And interestingly enough, when the first of *Maldoror*'s many violent acts actually take place at this point in the text – the protagonist (and his companion, the reader) no longer anticipating ("reni*fl*er<u>as</u>," "vou<u>dr</u>as"), but finally embarking on the promised "career in evil") – they are not of the "impactful" category, identified above, as we might expect. It is as if the young poet, just starting out in the "unexplored lands" of his creation (99), were slowly testing his powers there; as if, like the modern, virtual heroes of science fiction (in films such as *The Matrix* and *Avatar*), he were tentatively moving, *feeling* the limbs of his own superhuman, amoral avatar in this fantasy world—Maldoror. The first of these acts, committed against himself, in fact, reveals a secondary element in the slower category of Maldorean evil: the temporal distension observed above, with the enhanced perception it entails, often involves a more methodical, detail-oriented quality in the act's elaboration. If the "volupté" of the preceding citations is replaced in the following lines by a detached, clinical tone, a similar concentration of consciousness on the details of the event is evident—a precision that is accentuated by the distinct articulations of the text:

J'ai **p**r**i**s un **c**an**i***f* dont *l*a *l*ame avai**t** un **tr**an**ch**an**t** a**c**é**r**é, et me s**ui**s *f*en**du** les *ch*airs aux en**d**roits où se **r**é**u**n**i**ssent *l*es *l*èvres (102).

Earlier in the first canto, a similar use of language enables the narrator to more vividly imagine committing such an act – on an *other* this time – as the mellifluous sound of an initial embrace is subtly "sharpened" (s => z and **ʒ**, in bold) in the unexpected transition from paternal affection to inexplicable violence:

Qui *l*aurait dit ! *l*orsqu'i*l* embra**ss**ait un petit en*f*ant, au *v*i**s**age *r*o**s**e, i*l* aurait *v*ou*l*u *l*ui en*l*ever **s**e**s** *j*oues avec un *r*a**s**oir (101).

It is in the following stanza (1:6), however, that Lautréamont-Maldoror truly explores his capacity for extended acts of violence in the world of the text, realizing what till now has been fantasized, only potential, in relation to others ("il <u>aurait voulu</u> lui enlever ses joues [...]"). In one of the work's most disturbing scenes – largely because it is the first of its kind encountered by the reader – Maldoror carefully mutilates a child. Methodically explaining how one should go about such a procedure, it is as if describing the nuances of each gesture allowed him to actually experience its enactment, writing functioning as a sort of prosthesis. The abrupt aggressivity of the opening lines (accentuated through percussive and guttural consonants: "d'arracher brutalement de son lit") is held in check by a series of gentle, caressing gestures (again, through fricatives, the "liquid" [l], and punctuation), his fingernails finally puncturing in the accentuated nasals of "`ongles `longs":

> On doit laisser pousser ses ongles pendant `quinze `jours. Oh !\ comme il est doux d'arracher brutalement de son lit un enfant qui n'a rien encore sur la lèvre supérieure,\ et,\ avec les yeux très ouverts,\ de faire semblant de passer suavement la main sur son front,\ en inclinant en arrière les beaux cheveux ! Puis,\ tout à coup,\ au moment où il s'y attend le moins,\ d'enfoncer les `ongles `longs dans sa poitrine molle, de façon qu'il ne meure pas (103).[23]

As much as the creator of *Maldoror* would seem to produce – and experience – the highest levels of intensity in violence enacted through the "arms" of his protagonist, there are numerous passages in which he bypasses causality altogether, simply calling attention, like Baudelaire, to the blossoming putrefaction he discovers. The attribution of disease to his enemies (and to Maldoror himself) is one of the subtlest gestures in Lautréamont's arsenal of poisons because, if it does not allow for the experience of agency, its effect is in fact more immediate; indeed, *pre*-immediate—the destructive force is *already*, at the moment of attribution, *in* the objectified individual. In this sense, it is an even more formidable mode of domination since it is, implicitly, a brute fact of nature, and not a gesture that must be tested against an opposing force.

Furthermore, similar to the zoological terminology noted above, the largely Greco-Latin terms designating such maledictions, with their foreign spelling and awkward pronunciation, provide the poet with a *ready-made* linguistic weapon, disrupting the flow of familiar lexica, and jolting the reader.[24] As Hénane has observed, regarding Césaire's similar preference for such terms ("le tropisme pour le terme biomédical," CL 36):

---

23   Such analysis reinforces Bachelard's more generalized, if perceptive observation: "Lautréamont se sert de « ses griffes » en y adjoignant un mouvement raffiné. Les griffes brisent mieux par un mouvement léger et délicat de torsion" (36).

24   It should be acknowledged that a large part of such terms' effect is to be found, in many instances, on the semantic level as well, and the connotations of illicit behavior they carry. As Jacques Bosquet has observed: "Certains de ces passages sadiques sont atroces et semblent empruntés à un traité juridico-médical de pathologie sexuelle" (528).

> Ce choix si particulier est un acte délibéré qui peut faire partie d'une rhétorique de l'image. En effet, les mots de la médecine avec leurs racines gréco-latines aux sonorités glauques, leurs raucités, leur étrangeté sémantique, sont des outils lexicaux particulièrement adaptés pour participer à l'hypotypose tragique et créer un climat que l'on veut inquiétant voire mortifère (Ibid.).

One of the specific causes for this quality in many such terms, Hénane notes, lies in the recurrence of the gutteral [R]: "la fréquence des rugueuses en « r » : estropiement, prurits, urticaire, parade, risibles, etc. Sonorités rauques cohérentes avec le grattage d'une peau excoriée, prurigineuse" (AC 110). And we in fact observe precisely such effects in the deployment of similar terms in *Maldoror*, where this phoneme is often situated in a type of cluster – in which it directly follows another consonant – that not only draws on the rough quality of the guttural, but jerks the articulatory movement back, due to its extreme point of articulation ([R] being in fact among the most posterior of possible articulations), producing a *torquing* sensation in the enunciation (like that observed in chapter 1, pp. 62–63). In the following, fairly tame example, for instance, the forward movements of the [f]/[l] series – literally *blowing* to ignite the image of combustion here – are twisted back in the thudding, final terms ("ai*gr*e" "*fièvr*e"):

> la nature [...] fait *lui*re mes yeux avec la *fl*amme ai*gr*e de la *fièvr*e (171).

Leprosy is an ideal diagnosis in the world of *Maldoror*, in this regard, since the knot-like articulatory movement of this short term in French – "la lè*pr*e" – corresponds so well to the cellular disturbance it designates. In the following – Maldoror's famous metamorphosis into an immobilized, rotting entity, in IV:4 – the "flesh" of the entire passage seems to mimic the monstrous afflictions visited upon the protagonist, enacting the relentless parasites and infections that overtake his body—a complexity that is produced by a variety of elements, including the opposition of fricatives and plosives, dense back and sharp front vowels, and frequent pauses):

> Je suis sale.\ Les poux me `rongent.\ Les pourceaux,\ quand ils me regardent,\ vo`missent.\ Les croûtes et les escarres de la lèpre ont écaillé ma peau,\ couverte de pus jaunâtre (230).

As observed above, as well as in the preceding study of Baudelaire's work, such terms, with their dynamic, seemingly corporeal texture, contribute to some of the most convincing productions of destructive force in the cantos—even where they are used to designate an abstraction. In the following – another of the many assaults on God – vitiation of the divinity's omnipotence and moral clarity is figured as a *physical* deterioration; an initial (or rather, repeated: "tu retombes") fall that continues throughout the texture of the entire passage, becoming, in the coagulation of undifferentiated good and evil, a growing force in the language of the blasphemer ("comme le torrent du rocher"):

> je sais [...] que tu retombes assez souvent, toi et tes pensées, recouvertes de la lèpre noire de l'erreur, dans le lac funèbre des sombres malédic`tions.\ Je veux croire que celles-ci sont inconscientes (quoiqu'elles n'en renferment pas moins leur venin fatal) et que le mal et le bien, unis ensemble, se répandent en bonds impétueux de ta royale poitrine gangrenée, comme le torrent du rocher, par le charme secret d'une force aveugle (172).

Another consequence of the "strange sonorities" of terms for disease and physiological language more generally – and the textures they inf(l)ect – is their tendency to bring a comic element to the poet's invective. In the following threat, in which God warns humanity to cleave to the Good (immediately discredited by the narrator: "Comment les hommes voudront-ils obéir à ces lois sévères, si le législateur lui-même se refuse le premier à s'y astreindre ?" 214), it is as if Lautréamont were poking the reader, trying to incite us into adolescent laughter through the ridiculous sounding climax, the anatomically precise term ringing out – in the sudden spikes of the [i] series: "clitoris" – from the accumulation of marching, revolting language:

> sinon, malingre, et rabougris comme le parchemin des bibliothèques, ils s'avanceront à grands pas, conduits par la révolte, contre le jour de leur naissance et le clitoris de leur mère impure (Ibid.).

Indeed, such terms are often simply instances of gleeful word-play—as in the following rejection of humanity, where a description of the dense, jutting mineral formations in the initial landscape is channeled into the climactic scatology of the final absurd image:

> La nuit venue, avec son obscurité propice, ils s'élançaient des cratères, à la crête de porphyre, des courants sous-marins et laissaient, bien loin

derrière eux, le *p*ot de *ch*am*b*re *ro*c*aill*eux où se démène l'an*U*s *c*onsti*p*é des *k*a*k*a*t*oès h*U*mains (191).[25]

Through language that calls attention to *all* aspects of embodied existence, the voice of *Maldoror* derives some its most peculiar effects, dissolving the boundary between beautiful and ugly, tragic and comic, just as it confounds good and evil—as in the narrator's meeting with the mysterious toad, cited earlier:

> Qu'il est beau ! Ça me fait de la peine de le dire. [...] Mais, qu'as-tu donc *f*ait *d*e *t*es p*U*s*tU*l*e*s *v*is*q*ueu*s*es et *f*é*ti*d*e*s, pour avoir l'air si doux ? (131).

And yet, just as we will soon observe, in returning to "impactful" modes of attack in the cantos, the deployment of slower, poisoning acts of violence often reveals an underlying dissatisfaction with the actual degree of force produced —not simply in phenomena that the poet supposedly observes, such as disease, but in those acts he clearly performs (again, through Maldoror); acts that must then be repeated or somehow modified. In his attack on a strangely sentient cathedral lamp, and the spiritual purity it represents, for instance, Maldoror begins by immediately strangling his opponent (the most primal act of human violence); a gesture that is articulated, appropriately enough, through the choking gutturals:

> Et bien, le moment est venu. Avec ses *m*Us*c*les,\ il é*t*rang*l*e *l*a **g**or**g**e de *l*'an**g**e,\ qui ne peut plus respirer (168).

When this gesture, however effective in realizing its purpose, does not sufficiently satisfy the executioner's desire, he increases the degree of physical "intimacy" with his victim (a perverse embrace that recalls his first violent act, in 1:6, cited on p. 95 of the present chapter)—a corruption of the latter's purity that is enacted in the contamination of the signifier itself ("im*b*i*b*é de sa*l*ive" => "an*g*é*l*ique"):

---

25   Note the homonymy, of the highest schoolboy quality, in the choice of "kakatoès." Interestingly enough, this same term is central to a passage of Ionesco cited by Fónagy, the latter demonstrating the repeated guttural's communication of aggressivity, independent of any semantic content: "M. Smith : Kakatoes, kakatoes, kakatoes [...]. Mlle Smith: Quelle cacade, quelle cacade, quelle cacade [...]" (Fónagy *VV* 93).

il ne peut retenir son couroux. C'en est fait ; quelque chose d'horrible va rentrer dans la cage du temps ! Il se penche, et porte la langue, imbibé de salive, sur cette joue angélique (168).

Equally significant, the visual register is immediately invoked ("Oh !... voyez !... voyez donc !" below), drawing the reader in as well, as if to verify the transformative effect of this poisonous fluid—a festering that breathes ("Elle exhale") in the texture of language:

> Oh !... voyez !... voyez donc !... la joue blanche et rose est devenue noire, comme charbon ! Elle exhale des miasmes pu`trides. C'est la gan`grène (168–69).[26]

Furthermore, the narrator not only insists on showing the reader this infection taking over the entire body of the victim, but he registers his *own* reaction – through Maldoror – to the force at work:

> Le mal rongeur s'étend sur toute la figure, et là, exerce ses furies sur les parties basses ; bientôt, tout le corps n'est qu'une vaste plaie immonde. Lui-même, [il est] épouvanté (car, il ne croyait pas que sa langue contînt un poison d'une telle violence (169).

Whatever irony we might attribute to this final "touch," I would propose that it reveals a good deal about Lautréamont's evolving relation to the creative processes unleashed in the composition of *Maldoror*. With its clever inscription of superlative *linguistic* force ("sa *langue* contînt [...] une telle violence"), this passage points to the overdetermined representations of extreme violence that will be elaborated in the following cantos. Further readings will indeed suggest that similar scenes throughout *Maldoror* not only mark the points of highest intensity in the text, where the many digressive, diffusive strands of narrative content are momentarily eclipsed, but that they simultaneously reflect a sort of death drive in the textual process—an underlying desire that such passages would satisfactorily realize – through an absolute force of negation – an anticipated movement beyond the battleground of composition, with its continual "exertion of furies."

---

26   Is the resonance here with Baudelaire's famous "Élévation" coincidental?—a text in which the earlier poet invoked, interestingly, an inverse movement: "Envole-toi bien loin de ces miasmes morbides ; Va te purifier dans l'air supérieur" (10, my emphasis).

La Fronde

A number of *Maldoror*'s more elaborate productions of impact are particularly revealing, regarding the above problematic—and none moreso, perhaps, than the consecutive "sling" executions undertaken by its protagonist. If the cantos' final apotheosis of violence stands out in the memories of most readers – Maldoror launching his victim against the roof of the Panthéon – not everyone may recall that this is the third in a series of such acts, interspersed evenly throughout the work. While its final iteration will be treated extensively below, I would like to look briefly at the different ways in which the prototypes for this maneuver – clearly, the author's preferred mode of violence – are structured.[27]

Its first deployment – and the first significant act of violence in the text in general, following those early scenes in the first canto, analyzed above – takes place in II:6, as Maldoror, having noticed a girl following him during his daily walks, begins to imagine what he is capable of doing to her. It is important to keep in mind here that, as Blanchot has insisted, in traversing *Maldoror*, we are most probably retracing the real-time evolution of its composition, and not a series of passages that have been significantly reorganized during multiple revisions.[28] As Maldoror continues to adjust and modify his gestures throughout the stanza, it is as if he cannot find a mode of torture and disfigurement that is entirely satisfactory. When twisting his victim's arms proves a facile exercise, he needs the sensation of breaking them – an act that must be *heard*, in even greater resolution (the accentuated tearing of "`deux `branches `sèches") – so that by the time he forces his victim to then eat these limbs, the force employed seems superfluous:

> Dans un moment d'égarement, je pourrais te prendre les bras,\ les tordre comme un linge lavé dont on exprime l'eau, ou les casser avec fra`cas,\ comme `deux `branches `sèches,\ et te les faire ensuite manger, en employant la `force (146).

---

[27] While I am not the first to identify the importance of this figure in the work as a whole, no one else to my knowledge has considered the actual mechanics of the sling, and – most importantly – the author's "taste" for its elaboration, their observations being limited, yet again, to the conceptual: "le thème de la fronde humaine imprime à toute l'œuvre sa force à la fois sur le plan de l'imaginaire et sur celui de la cohérence structurale" (Pickering 43).

[28] "[…] il est très important, pour qui veut atteindre le « sens » d'un tel livre, de se confier à son déroulement, à son « sens » temporel. *Une œuvre se fait avec le temps*" (LS 84).

The procedure is far from over, however, as Maldoror now maintains contact with the victim in a perverse head massage. Unlike the final "ongles," in 1:6 (analyzed on p. 95 of the present chapter), which tore the flesh they had penetrated, the gesture and its object become undifferentiated here, in the fluid extraction of brains; a gentle ("doux"), unobstructed boring (the "rounded" vowels [o] [u] [õ]), pulsating evenly through frequent pauses:

> Je pourrais,\ en prenant ta tête entre mes mains,\ d'un air caressant et doux,\ enfoncer mes doigts avides dans les lobes de ton cerveau innocent,\ pour en extraire,\ le sourire aux lèvres,\ un graisse efficace qui lave mes yeux,\ endoloris par l'insomnie éternelle de la vie (Ibid.).

Only after this series of *felt* acts of violence, can the poet definitively execute his victim, rotating her body until the increasing centrifugal force slams her against a wall, punctuating, so to speak, the passage:

> Je pourrais, soulevant ton corps vierge avec un bras de fer, te saisir par les jambes, te faire rouler autour de moi, comme une fronde, concentrer mes forces en décrivant la dernière circonférence, et te lancer contre la muraille (Ibid.).

This particular passage is significant, not only because we are able to witness the poet in his development of what will become the supreme, concluding gesture of the entire work, but because it contains – in its series of intensely imagined, though ultimately unsatisfying acts, and its development of a procedure that would bring closure to this potentially endless series – a microcosm of the larger, evolving economy of *Maldoror*. While not yet fully realized in this first deployment, the sling is an ideal mechanism for Lautréamont because it helps him to override the limits of those productions of force that empowered him in his first experimentations with textual violence. As Maldoror sacrifices the immediate contact he craves in physical domination, instead distancing himself from the object of his aggression, limiting his function to that of a fixed point of anchorage – thus allowing for a regularized, contained accumulation of energy to take place – he is able to take part in a truly *physical* production of force (i.e. according to the principles of physics), which surpasses, in its apparent reality, the more fantastical gestures of the author's imagination. Furthermore, as a key instance of Lautréamont's famous use (or "misuse," in entirely plagiarized passages) of contemporary scientific work, this particular appropriation of the conceptual discourse of physics suggests that such gestures are not merely another mode of textual deviance (like his pastiches of the *roman feuilleton* that we will observe in the sixth canto, for example), as they are generally read. In many instances, they would in fact appear intended to serve, on the contrary, as an *antidote* to the excesses of expression resulting from such deviance. Reading the sling – or more accurately, the *centrifuge* – symbolically, as a figure for the process of poetic composition, we could say that the objective discourse of science imposes, like the deployment of this device itself, a necessary distance within that creative process—an affectively neutralized discursive space in which, undistracted by the self-propagating desire to "handle" the invested terms of invective and violence, in all of their sensuality and dynamic force, the writing subject obtains a degree of control over the development of text. At least, *in theory*...

That this antidote to the overly "poisonous pages" of *Maldoror* remains just that – theoretical – until the sixth canto, is reflected in the very different structure of the second centrifuge, in IV:8. It would initially seem that the poet has streamlined the procedure developed in II:6, eliminating the panoply of fantasized gestures in order to immediately undertake the preferred, definitive mode of execution. Recollecting one of several childhood friendships recounted throughout the text – in this instance, with the blond Falmer – the narrator describes how he abruptly turned on his companion one day:

> [...] un jour, parce qu'il m'avait arrêté la main, au moment où je levais mon poignard pour percer le sein d'une femme, je le saisis par les cheveux avec un bras de fer, et le fis tournoyer dans l'air avec une telle vitesse, que la chevelure me resta dans la main, et **q**ue *s*on *co*rps, *l*ancé p**a**r *l*a *f*orce cen*tr*ifuge, alla **c**ogner **c**on*tr*e\le*tr*onc*d*'un\`*ch*ên*e*\\ (246).

The economical condensation of phonetic forces that quickly accumulates at the climax of the passage corresponds perfectly to the increasingly autonomous force of the sling, its acceleration suggested by the fricative series ("lancé par la *f*orce centri*f*uge") thudding into the dense texture of the back phonemes (transferred from the body of the victim to the obstacle against which it collides: "*s*on **c**o*r*ps" => "**c**on*tr*e\le*tr*onc"), in the abrupt monosyllabic series that closes the passage.

The stanza in question is clearly not intended to reach a definitive state of closure through this violent act, however. On the contrary, the entire narrative would seem structured to reflect the continually troubled and regressive state of a mind haunted by remorse over a past action ("c'est moi-même qui, racontant une histoire de ma jeunesse, et sentant le remords pénétrer dans mon cœur... c'est moi-même, à moins que je me trompe...," 246). Within the space of several lines, the act is *re*-recounted, and – considering the role of articulated texture here, the structure of which is retained almost entirely – re-*enacted*:

AN EXAGGERATED SCALE OF EVIL: LAUTRÉAMONT 103

> Je n'ignore pas qu'un jour j'accomplis un acte infâme, tandis **que** *son* <u>c</u>o<u>r</u>ps était *lancé* p*a*r *la f*o*r*ce cen<u>t</u>r*if*uge (246–47).

Further on in the stanza, this texture/event resurfaces yet again into the narrator's rambling reflections, which are increasingly and obsessively focused less on the production of force, than its final impact, the finality of which the narrator cannot seem to verify—a change that is reflected in the progressively choppy, percussive quality of language, the contortions of a bad conscience suggested by the awkward textual body signifying it, repeatedly ("irréparablement [...] irréparablement"):

> Avec un bras de fer. Ce *ch*o<u>c</u>,\ ce *ch*o<u>c</u> l'a-<u>t</u>-il <u>t</u>*ué* ? Ses os on<u>t</u>-ils é<u>té</u> <u>b</u>r*i*sés <u>c</u>on<u>t</u>re l'a*r*<u>b</u>re... <u>irréparablement</u> ? L'a-<u>t</u>-il <u>t</u>ué, ce *ch*o<u>c</u> en*g*end*r*é par la vigueur d'un athlète ? A-t-il conservé la vie, **qu**oi**qu**e *ses os se soient* <u>irréparablement</u> <u>b</u>r*i*sés... <u>irréparablement</u> ? Ce *ch*o<u>c</u>\ l'a-<u>t</u>-il <u>t</u>*ué*? (247).

When this refrain returns, unsurprisingly, at the end of the stanza, it has been so invested with indeterminacy that it has an effect opposite to the result it initially seemed intended to produce, definitively eliminating any possibility of closure:

> M'a-t-il donc pardonné ? *Son* **c**o**r**ps alla <u>c</u>ogner <u>c</u>on<u>t</u>re\le\<u>t</u>*r*onc\<u>d</u>'un\ *ch*êne ... « Mald*o*r*o*r ! » (248).

This change in Lautréamont's "handling" of the sling further reveals the fundamental conflict in the text's violent aesthetic, observed earlier—at once a definitive, satisfactory expression of force, and a gesture that the poet feels driven to repeat, potentially without end. One could object that these scenes do not necessarily correspond to the (d)evolution of the work as whole, as I have suggested, and that such an assertion in fact forces the text to conform to the present analysis. Any one of these enactments of violence, one might argue, is simply another mutation in a fully liberated textual process that is not *intended* to have closure, until, as Blanchot suggests (cited on p. 118 below), the amorphous impulse at its source has come to term, blossoming in the final, meticulously constructed gesture. Whatever the poet's intention, however, the text itself, as an artifact in *our* hands, definitively detached from the grip (and mouth) of its creator, would suggest otherwise. For even if the regular recurrences of impact in this stanza are the result of self-possession and control of the textual process – an assertion that would be well supported by the ironic distance underlying the self-conscious pathos here ("M'a-t-il donc pardonné ?

[...] « Maldoror ! ») – as we continue our close reading of the cantos, we find that whatever degree of mastery is exerted over the forces of composition, the writer betrays a deeper uncertainty as to the ultimate success of his text in its effect upon the reader. In analyzing the increasingly dense coagulations of violent sound-images that immediately follow, in the fifth, penultimate canto, I hope to demonstrate how Lautréamont's need to prove the force of his language is itself *forced*, to a point of crisis, leading to a final attempt at closure in the concluding scene.

Advanced Symptoms

It is important to note that the next passage under scrutiny directly follows, at the opening of the fifth canto, the most recently analyzed lines, above ("*Son corps* alla *c*ogner *c*on*tr*e\le*tr*onc*d*'un*ch*êne," in the last line of the fourth canto's final stanza); and furthermore, that it deals explicitly with the question of reader reception, just evoked. The narrator in fact opens with a direct address to this reader—an expression of apparent self-deprecation that is quickly found to be facetious ("homme respectable"):

> Que le lecteur ne se fâche pas contre moi, si ma prose n'a pas le bonheur de lui plaire. Tu soutiens que mes idées sont au moins singulières. Ce que tu dis là, homme respectable, est la vérité ; mais, une vérité partiale (249).

It is harder to presume that Lautréamont is not sincerely invested on some level, however, in the analogy he now employs to defend this poetics, as he fully reveals the "truth" that has only been "partially" grasped by the critical reader. This detailed explanation of the flight pattern of a flock of starlings, lifted directly from a contemporary encyclopedia of natural history,[29] would seem ideal for justification of the poet's aesthetic, given the latter's contradictory nature. In the seemingly chaotic, inexplicable movement of the birds, which is nonetheless grounded in empirical fact, through the scientific discourse of the naturalist, the poet finds a perfect analogy for the centrifugal model of force that has come to define his ideal of textual intensity:

> [...] une espèce de tourbillon fort agité, dont la masse entière, sans suivre de direction bien certaine, paraît avoir un mouvement général d'évolution sur

---

29   Of a certain Dr. Chenu—see Steinmetz, in his footnote to this passage (*Maldoror* 411, note 1 – to p. 249).

> elle-même, [...] dans lequel le centre, tendant perpétuellement à se développer, mais sans cesse pressé, repoussé par l'effort contraire des lignes environnantes qui pèsent sur lui, est constamment plus serré qu'aucune de ces lignes [...]. Malgré cette singulière manière de tourbillonner, les étourneaux n'en fendent pas moins, avec une vitesse rare, l'air ambient, et gagnent sensiblement, à chaque seconde un terrain précieux [...]. Toi, de même, ne fais pas attention à la manière bizarre dont je chante chacune de ces strophes (249–50).

And yet, despite this assurance that his text is also succeeding in "gaining ground" through its erratic movements, the narrator's continuing oscillation between expressions of confidence and uncertainty would suggest otherwise. Soon after the above analogy, he again admits that his text may not have entirely convinced his reader, encouraging him or her to cross over ("franchir les autres degrés"); a statement that is immediately followed by an assertion that does not so much convince, as eliminate this distance altogether:

> N'est-il pas vrai, mon ami, que, jusqu'à un certain point, ta sympathie est acquise à mes chants ? Or, qui t'empêche de franchir les autres degrés ? La frontière entre ton goût et le mien est invisible ; tu ne pourras jamais la saisir : preuve que cette frontière elle-même n'existe pas (250).

What is significant at this point, is that the narrator not only proceeds to undermine *this* gesture as well, investing the reader with an active resistance to this supposedly unified aesthetic consciousness, but this hard "shell" actually takes form in the poet's language, the prosodic surges that accumulate in the phonetic texture accentuating the awkward finality of the final term:

> Il n'est pas utile pour toi que tu t'encroûtes dans la cartilagineuse carapace d'un axiome que tu crois inébranlable (250–51).

And interestingly, as this supposedly philosophical reflection becomes completely irrational, its *materiality* proves to be the most continuous, dynamic element of the discourse:

> Il y a d'autres axiomes aussi qui sont inébranlables, et qui marchent parallèlement avec le tien. Si tu as un penchant marqué pour le caramel (admirable farce de la nature), personne ne le conservra comme un crime (251).

We can now observe two developments in the text that, clearly interrelated, reflect the conflicted nature of this stanza. First of all, as similar, even more volatile textures continue to surface, they coincide with an apparent tension within the author's intent—simultaneous desires to assure the reader's seduction, as well as his or her repulsion; both of which, in a seemingly irresolvable contradiction, the narrator would effect through the increasingly shocking, and indeed repulsive language of the text. Secondly, we find that this contradictory project is articulated, on the figural plane, through the trope of poison —and more specifically, a conscious enactment of the "poisonous pages" promised in the warning of the work's opening lines.[30] And where the brief, initial appearance of this figure for the relation between reader and text was not significantly elaborated in the first stanza (its authenticity to be proven in the traversal of the following cantos), it is now *exceedingly* elaborated, calling attention to itself in a way that begins to threaten its "potency" in the reading act. For in having to insist yet again on the unusual force of his language, and in such precise, graphic detail this time – and most importantly, with such contradictory functions attributed to this force – we are led to suspect, on the contrary, that a certain crisis is transpiring in the process of composition.

Drawing once again on the detached, analytic discourse of the natural sciences, the narrator continues by assuring the reader that, like the microorganisms believed capable of surviving boiling temperatures,[31] he or she should be able to withstand imbibing the "bitter fluids" excreted by his poetry —an agitated viscosity that is indeed manifested in the language of the text (so much so, in fact, that I haven't attempted to annotate it), beginning with the (facetious) denial of provocation ("*le rôle de provoca`teur*"):

> Je parle par expérience, sans venir jouer ici le rôle de provocateur. Et, de même que les rotifères et les tardigrades peuvent être chauffés à une température voisine de l'ébullition, sans perdre nécessairement leur vitalité, il en sera de même pour toi, si tu sais t'assimiler, avec précaution, l'âcre sérosité suppurative qui se dégage avec lenteur de l'agacement que causent mes intéressantes élucubrations (251).

---

30   "Plût au ciel que le lecteur, enhardi et devenu momentanément féroce comme ce qu'il lit, trouve, sans se désorienter, son chemin abrupt et sauvage, à travers les marécages désolés de ces pages sombres et pleines de poison ; car, à moins qu'il n'apporte dans sa lecture une logique rigoureuse et une tension d'esprit égale au moins à sa défiance, les émanations mortelles de ce livre imbiberont son âme comme l'eau le sucre" (99).

31   Steinmetz observes, in his notes on this passage: "la partie antérieure du corps est garnie d'appendices ciliformes ramassés en faisceaux et produisant l'effet d'une roue quand ils entrent en mouvement" (*Maldoror* 412, note 4).

It is still apparently uncertain, however, whether or not this active substance has been successfully produced, as the narrator increases the dose—first, appending the following warning: "Mais, sois prudent. A l'heure que j'écris, de nouveaux frissons parcourent l'atmosphère intellectuelle : il ne s'agit que d'avoir le courage de les regarder en face" (251); and then, seemingly contradicting this statement, surmising that his reader has probably become *accustomed* to the shocking content of his text—a development that would correspond, he understands, to the latter's progressively purgative effect:

> puisque la répulsion instinctive, qui s'était déclarée dès les premières pages, a notablement diminué de profondeur, en raison inverse de l'application à la lecture [...] il faut espérer, quoique ta tête soit encore malade, que ta guérison ne tardera certainement pas à rentrer dans sa dernière période (251).

In order to completely "heal" the reader, the narrator proposes a remedy that would seem intended, paradoxically, to re-activate his or her "instinctive repulsion." In a significant variation of the first "sling" stanza, cited earlier ("je pourrais te prendre les bras [...] et te les faire ensuite manger"), it is now the *reader* who must consume the mutilated body: "Comme nourriture astringente et tonique, tu arracheras d'abord les bras de ta mère [...], tu les dépéceras en petits morceaux, et tu les mangeras ensuite, en un seul soir" (252). Then, in a transition that continues to echo that earlier scene, the narrator increases even further the revolting quality of the passage—though in this instance, no longer acting upon an intact body, but concocting a horrific mixture of infected organs and fluids:

> La potion la plus lénitive, que je te conseille, est un bassin, plein d'un pus blennorrhagique à noyaux, dans lequel on aura préablement dissous un kyste pileux de l'ovaire, un chancre folliculaire, un prépuce enflammé, renversé en arrière du gland par une paraphimosis, et trois limaces rouges. Si tu suis mes ordonnances, ma poésie te recevra à bras ouverts (252).[32]

In contrast to the opening stanza, in which he coyly warned the reader to become impenetrable to the poison emanating from his writing, the poet's prescription here suggests that he is not entirely confident in his ability to sustain

---

[32] Steinmetz has called attention to the choice of scientific terminology in this passage (which he likens to "les termes d'une potion de sorcières," "Isidore" 157), and throughout *Maldoror*. As in previous citations, the texture is so dense and complex here that I have refrained from annotation, relying on the reader's engagement of the text.

the transgressive force introduced in the opening cantos of his strange new work. Skipping the act of violence itself, his insistence that the reader ingest what this act has produced, suggests an anxious need to assure himself that his text is effective in its assault upon – and seduction *of* – the reader.[33]

It will be useful to return now to that privileged model for the production of force in *Maldoror*—though this time, in order to perceive, in its *absence*, how such a model becomes increasingly relevant in the final cantos. For if the centrifuge has proven to be the ideal mode of textual violence in Lautréamont's arsenals – not only in recurring enactments of the human sling itself but, as suggested earlier, in the distanced control over the writing process more generally – it could also be said to function in the same manner as its referent (when it *does* function correctly) in a much more concrete way: through a similar effect on the actual "matter" involved, counteracting the condensation of elements in an amorphous substance (the problematic "potion," just observed, for instance), the *poetic* centrifuge helps to maintain a high level of discretion (in both senses of the term) in the texture of the poet's language, even in the most expressive passages. If such an analogy seems contrived, initially, I believe the concluding analysis of this study – of the sixth, final canto – will demonstrate its pertinence. For the moment, I would like to continue focusing on what I am claiming is the *dys*function of the Maldorean textual process. In v:2, following the passages just analyzed, we can trace in even greater detail key transitions in a devolving compositional process, in which the locus of agency is progressively destabilized—a progression that leads, precisely, from the objective, empirical language of the sciences, to an even larger, more heteroclite mass of superfluous linguistic matter than that presented in the above "prescription."

The stanza begins with the mysterious introduction of several incomprehensible elements, which will be increasingly clarified – and in fact prove interrelated – over the course of the narration, however absurd, that follows. After opening, *in medias res*, with his description of an indistinct form he has chanced upon, sitting atop a pedestal ("je devinais qu'elle n'était pas d'une forme ordinaire, sans, néanmoins, préciser la proportion exacte de ses contours," 252), the narrator then observes a giant beetle ("pas de beaucoup plus grand qu'une vache !" 253), which is pushing along an amorphous ball of "matières excrémentielles" (253). If these elements begin to take on meaning once the mini-plot of this stanza is introduced (the beetle and the half-human form on the pedestal were once brothers, both betrayed by a deceased woman

---

[33] For a different perspective on this passage, see the analysis of Dobelbower, who finds in it a successfully subversive "homeopathic" use of language: "The cure for the evil produced by medical discourse is small doses of a textual homologue" (19).

whose severed body parts now constitute this ball!), the reader's attention is drawn more to what takes form, coagulating – aurally, as well as visually – at another, more visceral level of the text.

When Lautréamont proceeds to delineate the features of the first form, he borrows freely, once again, from the work of Dr. Chenu. In contrast to the previous, similar graft of the bird flock, however, with its relatively austere, abstract language ("le centre, tendant perpétuellement à se développer, mais sans cesse pressé, repoussé par l'effort contraire des lignes environnantes qui pèsent sur lui"), the following passage coagulates at the level of sound, as well. In effect, another sort of aural *ready-made*, as observed elsewhere, the linguistic elements of the original passage present their own texture (surely drawing a smile from our young lexophile, when first discovered), however unintended by the original author—series of alliterations and undulations from back to front, which Lautréamont actually mimics in the dense series he composes and places before this "citation," effectively incorporating the grafted tissue into his own text (the plagiarized section beginning with "ce bec [...]"):[34]

> Le bloc plastique que j'apercevais n'était pas une frégate. La chair cristallisée que j'observais n'était pas un cormoran. Je le voyais maintenant, *l*'homme à *l*'encéphale dépourvu de protubérance annulaire ! Je recherchais vaguement, dans les replis de ma mémoire, dans quelle contrée torride ou glacée, j'avais remarqué ce bec très-long, large, convexe, en voûte, à arête marquée, onguiculée, renflée et très crochue à son extrémité ; ces bords dentelés, droits ; cette mandibule inférieure, à branches séparées jusqu'auprès de la `pointe (253–54).

Significantly, where such use of scientific discourse in *Maldoror* would often seem intended to constitute a sort of *anti*-poetic principal, as we have observed, this passage appears to have been chosen precisely – at least in part – for the sound of the signifiers constituting it, and for its ability to thus interact with – and indeed engender – the increasingly extravagant sound-images of the poet's own creation. The language of science in such instances, that is to say, instead of defusing the proliferation of absurd, overly expressive language, in fact contributes to this tendency in the poet's creative process.

If Lautréamont appears capable of controlling this process several lines later, in his sober invocation of the scientific method – "pour la clarté de ma démonstration, j'aurais besoin qu'un de ces oiseaux fût placé sur ma table de travail, quand même il ne serait qu'empaillé" (254) – he soon returns to his

---

34   Steinmetz (*Maldoror* 413, note 4).

obsessive description of the bird-headed creature. The revolting poetics of *Maldoror* returns in full force, taking up the discourse and complex textures of the preceding passage into its famed disfigurements of that most elementary of poetic figures—the simile:

> il me paraissait beau comme *l*es deux *l*ongs *fi*laments t*enti*c*Ul*i*fo*rmes d'un inse*c*te ; ou plutôt, comme une inh*U*mat*i*on p*r*éc*i*p*i*tée ; ou encore, comme *l*a *l*oi de *l*a re*c*ons*tit*U*ti*on des **or**ganes m*Util*és ; et surtout, comme un *l*iqu*id*e ém*i*nement pU*tr*e`sc*ib*le ! (254).

Once the poet has finally disengaged himself from the multiple elaborations of this figure which have dominated the stanza up to this point, and dispensed a perfunctory narration of past events (the tragic love triangle, summarized above), he immediately returns to the production of similar textures – albeit with several important differences – in his only other extended description of the stanza's central figures. In reconstituting for us, out of discrete elements, the giant ball of excrement introduced in the opening lines, the poet performs a dismemberment and liquefaction of the body that recalls both the above citation, and the "prescription" problematized earlier. But where these earlier passages insisted, quite vehemently – through their very articulation – on maintaining the revolting quality of these "parts," which jut out of the narration, the elements constituting the following mass seem to actually cohere in the developing text. From the recurring aural inscriptions of this rolling, globular form, in the first section ("des **co***ll*iers de pe*rl*es" => "un po*l*yèdre am**o**rphe"), through the latter's relentless contact with hard, tearing objects, as it is "dragged" ("*tr*aîner, *a*vec *t*es *t*a*r*ses, à *tr*avers les *v*allées et *l*es *ch*emins, *s*u*r* les **r**on*c*es et *l*es p*ie*rres"), it is the *poet* who continuously handles the matter that coagulates, breaking down and reforming it with increasing precision and regularity ("se po*l*ir pa*r* *l*a *l*oi mécanique du *fr*ottement ro*ta*toire"), until the final geometric form is released in the smooth fricatives that have accumulated throughout the passage ("la masse d'une `*sph*ère"):

> déjà, cette femme, dont tu avais attaché, avec des **co***ll*iers *d*e p*e*rl*e*s, les jambes et les bras, de manière à réaliser un po*l*yèdre a**m**orp*h*e, a*f*in de la traîner, *a*vec *t*es *t*a*r*ses, à *tr*avers les *v*allées et *l*es *ch*emins, sur *l*es **r**on*c*es et *l*es p*ie*rres [...] a\v*U*\s*e*s\os\se *c*reuser de *bl*ess*U*res, ses **m**e**m***b*res se po*l*ir par *l*a *l*oi mécanique *d*u *fr*o*tt*ement ro*ta*toire, se *c*on*f*ondre *d*ans *l*'*U*ni*t*é de *l*a *c*oag*U*lat*i*on, et *s*on *c*orps présenter, au *l*ieu des *l*inéaments pr*i*m**o**r*d*iaux et *d*es *c*our*b*es nat*U*re*ll*es, *l*'apparence **m**onoto**n**e *d*'un seul

AN EXAGGERATED SCALE OF EVIL: LAUTRÉAMONT 111

> tout homogène qui ne ressemble que trop, par la confusion de ses divers
> éléments broyés, à la masse d'une `sphère ! (255–56).

In the end, however, whatever degree of control the poet may have demonstrated in the (de)composition of text, what is produced is not simply another in a series of bizarre figures, easily jettisoned in the continual advancement of the cantos, but a complex conglomeration of linguistic matter; the product of a meticulous orchestration of forces which, unlike the idealized separation of the centrifuge, leaves the poet (and us) with a dense, amorphous "sphere" of questionable value. Indeed, in the bird-man's wise supplication of his brother, the beetle, is the poet not perhaps addressing himself?:

> Il y a longtemps qu'elle est morte ; laisse ces dépouilles à la terre, et prends garde d'augmenter, dans d'irréparables proportions, la rage qui te consume : ce n'est plus de la justice ; car, l'égoïsme, caché dans les téguments de ton front, soulève lentement, comme un fantôme, la draperie qui le recouvre (256, my emphasis).

For if Lautréamont recognizes on some level at this point that the "rage" at the source of *his* activity could feed on itself indefinitely, expanding beyond the "justice" he would mete out for a hypocritical humanity, with its bankrupt values and discourses, he may also recognize that he has not yet managed to unburden himself—not only of the linguistic matter he has accumulated in the preceding, completed passages of his text, but more importantly, of his propensity to re-initiate the escalation of this expressive violence in what he writes next.

Conclusion

Certain reflections of *Maldoror*'s narrator, in what is essentially a prologue to the sixth and final canto, would certainly seem to confirm an awareness of the above issues, in any case. In his opening address to the reader, no longer attempting to justify the erratic, unconventional style of his text, he instead dismisses the preceding cantos, presenting the text that will follow as a clean break:

> ne croyez pas qu'il s'agisse encore de pousser, dans les strophes de quatorze ou quinze lignes, ainsi qu'un élève de quatrième, des exclamations qui passeront pour inopportunes, et des gloussements sonores de poule cochinchinoise, aussi

grotesques qu'on serait capable de l'imaginer [...]. Non : la partie la plus importante de mon travail reste à faire (283).

If this statement is immediately rendered somewhat dubious, in the perspective of the present study, by *its own* "grotesque sonority" ("des exclamations qui passeront pour inopportunes, et des gloussements sonores de poule cochinchinoise, aussi grotesque [...]"), the following explanation of how this "most important part of [his] work" will be executed seems to correspond, precisely, to the "antidote" I have proposed Lautréamont is attempting to realize on multiple levels of the text—the centrifugal production of expressive force:

> Désormais, les ficelles du roman remueront les trois personnages nommés plus haut : il leur sera ainsi communiqué une puissance abstraite. La vitalité se répandra magnifiquement dans le torrent de leur appareil circulatoire, et vous verrez comme vous serez étonné vous-même de rencontrer, là où d'abord vous n'aviez cru voir que des entités vagues appartenant au domaine de la spéculation pure, d'une part, l'organisme corporel avec ces ramifications de nerfs et ses membranes muqueuses, de l'autre, le principe spirituel qui préside aux fonctions physiologiques de la chair (283).

By maintaining a continual, *distanced* relation to the "objects" of his attention – through the controlled narrative form of the popular *roman feuilleton* that will structure the sixth canto ("the strings of the novel") – the poet will be better able to fulfill the dual charge increasingly required by his experimental poetics of force: conceiving of these characters "abstractly," he will be capable of loosening his sensual grip on them, curtailing the proliferation of self-indulgent verbiage and simultaneously investing them with a greater degree of reality ("l'organisme corporel"), assuring an engaged connection between reader and text.

As with any statement uttered by *Maldoror*'s narrator, we are hardly surprised to find that the authenticity of this project is soon discredited by the text's indomitable irony, which continually destabilizes whatever bearings we might have hoped to establish in this ambiguous moral universe. As a number of critics have observed in studies of the final canto, the *roman feuilleton* genre is not so much used here in a new manner, as it is simply grafted onto Lautréamont's text (like the passages of scientific discourse, cited above), calling attention to the latter's own superficial nature.[35] Far from leading us to identify with the feelings and thoughts of these characters, this new section

---

35 See Nathan's *Lautréamont : feuilletoniste autophage*, in particular.

of the cantos in fact has the opposite effect—as, for example, in the *rencontre*, following an extended, tension-filled period of correspondence between the youth Mervyn and his malevolent admirer, Maldoror: "c'était touchant de voir ces deux êtres, séparés par l'âge, rapprocher leurs âmes par la grandeur des sentiments. [...] ce spectacle, que plus d'un, même avec un esprit mathématique, aurait trouvé émouvant" (310). The insertion of highly abstract discourse into the narrative produces neither of the effects sought, it would seem, by the poet—distance or engagement; or, if it does so, it is in a very different, essentially "useless" manner. Like the linguistic coagulations observed earlier, though on a much smaller scale, the following nuggets of specialized terminology describing the troubled state of Mervyn enter into the text(ure), not for the sake of clarification, as one would expect, but instead calling attention to themselves *as* opaque linguistic matter, however precise:

> Ses professeurs ont observé que ce jour-là il n'a pas ressemblé à lui-même ; ses yeux se sont assombris démésurément, et le voile de la réflexion excessive s'est abaissé <u>sur la région péri-orbitaire</u> (295).

As in the above citation, such terms in the sixth canto often appear at the end of a given passage, punctuating the text with their jarring, heavy-handed specificity, producing an unmistakable rupture in the officious register of the narrative—particularly when placed in the mouth of a character (and not the narrator), as in the following exchange between Mervyn's parents, in language that is completely inappropriate for the expression of "tenderness":

> « tes yeux m'attendrissent, et tu ferais mieux de <u>refermer le conduit de tes glandes lacrymales</u> » (292).

These formulations are not suddenly introduced in the sixth canto, significantly, after the official change of course announced by the "prologue," but begin to appear just before, following the crisis of expressivity we observed at the beginning of the fifth canto (the excesses of the "potion" and "sphere"). For instance, in the narrator's request that the reader respond appropriately to the solemn event of a passing funeral procession, the logical verb choice – *s'agenouiller* – is displaced by a longer, unnecessarily explicit physiological description:

Silence ! il passe un cortège funéraire à côté de vous. Inclinez <u>la binarité de vos rotules</u> vers la terre et entonnez un chant d'outre-tombe (269).[36]

In his address to "incomprehensible pederasts," it is indeed difficult to "comprehend" the *speaker* of the enunciation, and his ultimate goal, in this violent articulation of non-violence:

> Ô pédérastes incompréhensibles, ce n'est pas moi qui lancerai des injures à votre grande dégradation ; ce n'est pas moi qui viendrai jeter le mépris sur votre <u>an**u**s in*f***u**nd*i*b**u**/*i*forme</u> (264).[37]

If the insertion of these nodes of dense, highly articulated scientific terminology into the narrative of *Maldoror* does reflect a greater degree of control over the process of composition (in contrast to excesses in the same canto, observed above), while still allowing the poet to subvert the structure of that composition, such passages hardly seem the most effective means of reaching the reader—the poet's primary concern, as I have suggested.

Regardless of its application as a generalized principle in the writing process, furthermore, Lautréamont's centrifugal poetics would face its ultimate test in the representation of violence. For, as I have proposed, it is toward a satisfactory production of extreme, physical *force* that the work fundamentally and obstinately tends, however much the sort of techniques observed above may mediate the realization of that force. It would thus seem quite logical at this point to proceed to the act of violence that closes *Maldoror*—the final, most carefully constructed apotheosis of the sling. Before doing so, however, we should conclude the present reflections with the analysis of one additional passage, in order to better appreciate precisely what that final gesture must convincingly accomplish.

There are essentially no more relevant passages left *to* analyze, in any case. After the repeated deployment of the second centrifuge, at the close of the fourth canto, and the signs of crisis that follow, in the first two stanzas of the fifth, *Maldoror* does not confront the reader with any significant scenes

---

36 Note how this formulation resonates with the preceding texture: "un co*r*tège *f*unéraire à côté *d*e *v*ous" => "la binari*t*é *d*e *v*os ro*t*ules *v*ers la *t*e*rr*e."

37 Steinmetz has also called attention to the poet's choice of terms here: "Ducasse n'a pas fini de nous surprendre, non tant dans ce cas, par la polyvalence de son imaginaire que par la pertinence des vocables employés, tout à la fois inattendus et indéniables, nous assignant à la matérialité la plus nette, cernant les bords d'un foyer réel presque insupportable" ("Isidore" 157).

of violence (with several brief exceptions), prior to the third and final sling that closes the work. It is significant, furthermore, that in the intervening stanzas – particularly in the remainder of the fifth canto – we find some of the most digressive, rambling passages of the entire work; as if the poet had been forced to remain in a sort of holding pattern, unwilling to elaborate another *act*, through Maldoror, until he could be sure to achieve the increased effect he desires. The one remarkable scene of violence in this penultimate segment of the cantos is distinguishable, interestingly, less by the quantity of force demonstrated, than by the restraint with which it is depicted—not in the manner of those savored, sadistic scenes examined earlier, but through a meticulous, unimpassioned account of conflict, anticipating – as a sort of test run, perhaps – the narrative structure of the final canto.

In yet another of those recollections of complicated boyhood friendship (with homoerotic undertones, and invariably ending in violence), the narrator recounts how his victim's body was *discovered*—significant, for *Maldoror* – along with the assertion that the victim is still alive – since the act itself has been elided from the narration:

> On constata la présence d'une blessure au flanc droit ; chacun de ces matelots expérimentés émit l'opinion qu'aucune pointe d'écueil ou fragment de rocher n'était susceptible de percer un trou si microscopique et en même temps si profond. Une arme tranchante, comme le serait un stylet des plus aigus, pouvait seule s'arroger des droits à la paternité d'une si fine blessure (277).

We should first note the insistence on extreme *finesse* here – strangely accentuated by the "profound" deadliness of the weapon – which contrasts with the often savage and exaggerated depictions of violence throughout the preceding cantos. Secondly, as observed in preceding analyses, the insertion of an objective discourse (juridical, in this instance) simultaneously establishes an affective distance, and subtly jars the reading act: replacement of the verb we would expect ("faire" or "produire") with "s'arroger des droits à la paternité d[e]," is not simply unnecessary, a weird rhetorical flourish, but seems intended to call attention to itself as such; a rupture, however "fine," in the narrative fabric of the text.

When the violence of this stanza is now (re)enacted, we do not observe the type of escalation witnessed in the earlier cantos, in any case. Not only has Maldoror mysteriously abandoned his victim after rendering this "superficial" wound, but he devotes himself to a new companion, Elsseneur, the narrator of the present stanza—not in order to make up for the ineffectiveness of the previous act, as we would expect of our miscreant hero, but to atone for his misdeed.[38] Furthermore, the high degree of subjectivity we expect from this narrator, whom we soon discover was Maldoror's next victim, is defused by his unexpectedly lucid recollection of what has taken place, his detached observations closing with a now familiar formulation:

> certains gestes dont j'avais remarqué l'irrégularité de mesure et de mouvement se présentèrent aussitôt à ma mémoire, comme les pages ouvertes d'un livre. Mes soupçons étaient confirmés. [...] Un de tes genoux sur ma poitrine, et l'autre appuyé sur l'herbe humide, tandis qu'<u>une de tes mains arrêtait la binarité de mes bras dans son étau</u> (279).

After drawing his narrative out even further, with the insertion of several dispensable background events, the speaker returns to the main storyline, bringing his account to a conclusion that is definitive indeed in its con*cision* ("Le morceau, exactement détaché, tomba par terre"), if it is less than climactic, on the affective level:

> Il n'y avait pas de temps à perdre, et c'est ce que tu compris ; craignant de ne pas parvenir à tes fins, car l'approche d'un secours inespéré avait doublé ma puissance musculaire, et t'appercevant que tu ne pouvais rendre immobile qu'un de mes bras à la fois, tu te contentas,\ par un rapide mouvement imprimé à la lame d'acier,\ de me couper le poignet droit.\ Le morceau,\ ex<u>ac</u>tement <u>dé</u>ta<u>c</u>h<u>é</u>,\ <u>t</u>om<u>b</u>a par ˋterre (279).[39]

With its focused, detailed elaboration, and the very precise result obtained, this passage clearly reflects a high degree of control – on the part of both the protagonist and the writer "moving the strings" – that is absent in many such scenes in *Maldoror*. And yet, as suggested above, if such a passage reflects an ability to master the expression of force – isolating or even eliminating the coagulations accumulating in the text, the poet demonstrating his ability to coolly "handle" the weapons at his disposal – it does not communicate such

---

38 "[...] tu résolus de racheter ta faute par le choix d'un autre ami, afin de le bénir et de l'honorer" (277); a resolution that is far from promising, as any reader of *Maldoror* who has progressed this far in the text knows.

39 Note the unnecessary precision/verbiage here, which recalls the substitutions identified above ("le conduit de tes glandes lacrymales"; "s'arroger des droits à la paternité d[e]," etc.): "[un] rapide mouvement imprimé à la lame d'acier," for "poignarder" or "un coup de couteau."

AN EXAGGERATED SCALE OF EVIL: LAUTRÉAMONT 117

force to the reader as convincingly as the more volatile passages – however problematic – that appear throughout *Maldoror*—the "incandescent, internal magma" of the text, in the words of Julien Gracq.[40]

∙ ∙ ∙

How then, does the final act of force chosen to conclude the cantos *work*? And indeed, *does* it work? Aside from its greater scale, and a certain theatricality that was absent in the above passages, it is an act that is carried out, strangely enough, in the most ordinary, matter-of-fact manner. Executed with the objective precision of an engineer, explained to the reader step-by-step, with the seemingly ingenuous enthusiasm of a middle-school science teacher, the procedure is quite simple: after quickly ascending the column of the *Plâce Vendôme*, Maldoror proceeds to rotate his victim, the adolescent Mervyn (who has been tied to the end of a long cable) in a circular manner until, having produced a satisfactory velocity, he releases the cable, allowing the "object" of this manoeuver to be projected across the Seine, making its final impact on the domed roof of the *Panthéon*.

Perhaps due to this simplicity, the significance of the final sling has not been sufficiently explored by critics, who have tended to weigh in along partisan lines, finding in it either the artificial and unconvincing resolution of an erratically constructed work,[41] or a self-evident and entirely appropriate conclusion. Most notable among the second group, as alluded to earlier, Blanchot has contested detractors' readings, suggesting that the elaboration of this final image, far from being the result of *exterior* factors (delays in publication of the cantos, for example), arose, as if organically, from within the evolving work, realizing its inherent telos (*LS* 173). After passing through the turbulent darkness of the

---

40 "Il n'est pas sans doute dans la littérature française [...] de manifestation plus exactement volcanique que cette coulée de strophes arrachées à un magma interne incandescent" (20–21). It is revealing, regarding the above citation of *Maldoror*, that in the lines that close V:2, where we identified a crisis in the expressive economy of the work, the narrator rips out a part *his own* body, at once "moved" by what he has seen – the giant ball of pulverized body parts, with its tragic origin – and yet sufficiently indifferent to refer to that tragedy as a "quadruple misfortune"; a violence within, or against the process of depicting violence: "Je m'arrachai un muscle entier dans le bras gauche [...] tant je me trouvais ému devant cette quadruple infortune. Et, moi, qui croyais que c'étaient des matières excrémentielles" (257).

41 "The text nevertheless ends – like Ducasse's own literary career – on a refusal to relinquish the solid, autonomous modern self, even at the cost of destroying a fictional alter ego or abandoning a revolutionary literary project" (Lindsay 169).

preceding cantos, he insists, the calculated, "almost too perfect" form of this image corresponds to the poet's entry into the light of a new consciousness. Identifying "le sens important et dernier d'une figure composée avec tant d'attention" (Ibid. 172), he continues: "Image monumentale, et presque trop parfaite, dont la forme calculée, en accord avec les commandements d'une raison exacte, sert pour ainsi dire de symbole à cette souveraineté nouvelle de la lumière" (Ibid.). *Maldoror* ends here, he proposes, not because any final meaning has been revealed, but because, quite simply, there is nothing more to say: "C'est l'œuvre qui lui a fait défaut, s'étant achevée dans cette lumière qu'elle avait mission d'atteindre et à partir de laquelle, achevé lui-même, il n'avait plus rien à faire et plus rien à dire qui lui importât vraiment" (Ibid.).

The final section of the present study will suggest that, neither a facile, forced resolution, nor the natural conclusion of textual processes, this scene reflects a very meticulous strategy for dealing conclusively with the production of linguistic excess in *Maldoror*, through what is not simply the most grandiose elaboration of a privileged figure, but in fact the "truest," least poetic representation of that figure's referent. Through sustained control of the writing process, drawing almost exclusively on the objective discourse of physics (i.e. not the intermittent "sound *bites*" of scientific terminology, observed above), the poet's language would attain a new degree of transparency, allowing a realistic production of force to take place in the text, as the writer and his protagonist become indistinguishable, the "arm" of poetic language definitively reaching its ultimate object—the reader.

We can find a number of reasons for Lautréamont to have chosen the *Place Vendôme* for this event. The expansive, symmetrically enclosed space, with its central, vertical site of phallic authority[42] immediately sets the stage for the dramatic enactment that will take place. In view of the poet's *physical* concerns, highlighted by the present analysis, however, this choice is significant for a more fundamental, practical reason. If the impressive height of the tower lends an epic quality to Maldoror's act here, evoking the superhuman feats of mythic heroes, it also makes the scale of this act possible in the first place, on a purely logistical level, through the spatial axes it presents. The great distance the victim will be projected, on the horizontal plane, necessitates a corresponding height, for the length of cable to sufficiently extend the protagonist's arm (the defining element in the function of an actual sling, allowing one to project an object farther than the use of one's arm alone would permit), once the object has been lifted into rotation. I would further suggest that, as much

---

42   Not only in the tower itself, but the two most powerful Frenchmen who occupied its summit, in likeness, at different periods: Louis XIV and Napoléon.

as this site makes possible the act in question, the *limitation* it places on the protagonist is of equal importance, paradoxically. In contrast to the erratic vagaries resulting from his absolute freedom in the preceding stanzas, Maldoror is now restricted to the column summit's minimal, enclosed space (within the circular balustrade), like the ascetics of antiquity who endured long periods of time atop similar structures; a restriction that will allow him, in fact, as the stable axis of rotation, to originate a more sustained and life-like production of force.

This limited sphere of agency is perhaps not only necessary for a convincing, realistic production of force to take place in the world of the text, furthermore, but the writer may sense, on some level, that it exerts a force on *him*, counteracting the spontaneous impulses of his over-active imagination. Through Zen-like focus of consciousness, verbal excursions into the fantastic and the abstract are eliminated, as full attention is devoted to each consecutive gesture:

> Après avoir amoncelé à ses pieds, sous forme d'ellipses superposés, une grande partie du câble, de manière que Mervyn reste suspendu à moitié hauteur de l'obélisque de bronze, le forçat évadé fait prendre, de la main droite, à l'adolescent, un mouvement accéléré de rotation uniforme, dans un plan parallèle à l'axe de la colonne, et ramasse, de la main gauche, les enroulements serpentins du cordage, qui gisent à ses pieds (315–16).

It is particularly significant here that, where previous acts of violence involved a slippage between the protagonist's *hand* – which "executes" physically – and the medium/organ of expression, *la langue* – which does so through the articulations imposed upon it – the hands here are entirely hands, as the right and left are observed consecutively in various interrelated gestures. No detail is omitted, as the continuum of necessary phases in this production of centrifugal force is elaborated, step-by-step:

> La fronde siffle dans l'espace ; le corps de Mervyn la suit partout, toujours éloigné du centre par la force centrifuge, toujours gardant sa position mobile et équidistante, dans une circonférence aérienne, indépendante de la matière (316).

The increasing references to physical and mathematical concepts do deviate at times from the *actual* principles that would account for these events, it must be acknowledged, whether or not Lautréamont's reader is aware. In his enthusiasm to increase the accumulation of potential energy that would project his victim, Maldoror begins to run around the balustrade of the column, after further extending the cable:

> Le sauvage civilisé lâche peu à peu, jusqu'à l'autre bout, qu'il retient avec un métacarpe ferme, ce qui ressemble à une barre d'acier. Il se met à courir autour de la balustrade, en se tenant à la rampe par une main. Cette manœuvre a pour effet de changer le plan primitif de la révolution du câble, et d'augmenter sa force de tension, déjà si considérable (Ibid.).

While the angle of the plane would indeed change, as the narrator claims here, oscillating in its rotations, this would not in fact increase the "force of tension," but would indeed have the opposite effect, diminishing this force (as I discovered, while consulting an amused colleague in the field of physics). That such a detail is erroneous is of little consequence, however, as we are caught up, as if mesmerized, by the overall development of force that continues in the text; the verisimilitude of which is guaranteed, not so much by the scientific discourse utilized, than by a more intuitive understanding we have acquired by living among, observing, and even participating in such phenomena—whether an accelerating tether-ball or a carnival ride:

> Dorénavant, il tourne majestueusement dans un plan horizontal, après avoir successivement passé, par une marche insensible, à travers plusieurs plans obliques. L'angle droit formé par la colonne et le fil végétal a ses côtés égaux ! (Ibid.).

Maldoror's arm now merged with the extended cable in a single, taut plane – "Le bras du rénégat et l'instrument meurtrier sont confondus dans l'unité linéaire" (Ibid.) – we *sense* the doubling of force taking place, as if we were participating in the movement ourselves, morphing, along with the protagonist, into this cyborg of death. Indeed, the scientific discourse inserted after the initial image of aligned "arms," supposedly allowing the poet to ground his description in empirical reality ("les théorèmes [...] me permettent de parler ainsi," below), is hardly necessary, an afterthought:

> Le bras du rénégat et l'instrument meurtrier sont confondus dans l'unité linéaire, comme les éléments atomistiques d'un rayon de lumière pénétrant dans la chambre noire. Les théorèmes de la mécanique me permettent de parler ainsi ; hélas ! on sait qu'une force, ajoutée à une autre force, engendre une résultante composée des deux forces primitives ! (Ibid.).

When Maldoror senses that his projectile has reached a sufficient velocity, he expertly executes the gestures necessary to now *use* this potential force—a manoeuver that is deceptive in its apparent simplicity. For as any sling enthusiast will confirm, it is the need to correctly time both the arresting of one's body, and release of the rotating object – relative to each other – that poses the greatest challenge, if one is to realize the maximum of accumulated velocity, and attain the greatest possible precision in determining trajectory.[43] And it is indeed, in the case of *Maldoror*, this adept ability to *stop* at the crucial moment, on *multiple* levels of the progressing text, that allows the poet's avatar to deviate from the preceding, more elaborate executions he has been assigned by his creator:

> Le corsaire aux cheveux d'or, brusquement et en même temps, arrête sa vitesse acquise, ouvre la main et lâche le câble. Le contre-coup de cette opération, si contraire aux précédentes, fait craquer la balustrade dans ses joints. Mervyn, suivi de la corde, ressemble à une comète traînant après elle sa queue flamboyante. [...] Dans le parcours de sa parabole, le condamné à mort fend l'atmosphère, jusqu'à la rive gauche, la dépasse en vertu de la force d'impulsion que je suppose infinie, et son corps va frapper le dôme du Panthéon (Ibid.).

By constructing a sort of virtual reality here, through language that is almost entirely representational, Lautréamont finally produces the centrifuge in a satisfactory manner—at once drawing the reader in to witness (and indeed participate in, on some level) the generation of force, and preserving this force from excessive digressions, over-the-top *bizarreries*, and arcane vocabulary. And yet, even if we are to accept, as Blanchot has proposed, that the cantos were composed sequentially, and that this final mastery of the text's central mechanism does appear to close the circle, so to speak, we must nonetheless wonder: what is the significance of such an act, ultimately, aside from a very convincing gymnastic? Does this final gesture, that is to say, truly resolve the chaotic excesses of the revolting poetics throughout *Maldoror*—and in particular, those coagulations that have accumulated, as the preceding analyses have demonstrated, in the *texture* of this extensive work?

There is another, more subtle mechanism at work in the sixth canto as a whole, whereby the poet would lead us to believe so—a structural device that connects this concluding event to the problematic forces manifested in the

---

43 See *Electronic Resources*, at the end of my Works Cited. A good number of these individuals actually draw on extensive physical theory and elaborate equations to explain their choices in technique and materials.

preceding cantos. While the present study has focused on the generally "normalized" writing of the final canto (the narrative structure of the *roman feuilleton*, and the spartan elaboration of the centrifuge), one cannot help remarking a curious series of absurd images and phrases that appear and reappear throughout the otherwise logical progression of events. Our attention is drawn, not to any overt strangeness in the elements themselves (which are hardly unusual for a reader who has already traversed the "abrupt and savage road" of the five preceding cantos!),[44] but to the fact, precisely, that they *reappear*, seeming to participate in the relatively coherent narrative structure of this concluding section of the text.[45] Similar in their extreme absurdity to the "beau comme" similes, these figures are nonetheless significantly different, in that they do not simply pass away as the poet continues on in the production of other, seemingly improvised and unrelated images, but re-enter the scene of action later to fulfill major – if generally arbitrary – roles in the sequence of events. Like the brief coagulations of scientific discourse we have identified, these sections of the composition are thus controlled, but within a much larger textual process; carefully, and indeed symmetrically inserted or fused into the developing narrative.

Early on, for instance, a Frankenstein-like assemblage abruptly appears within a flock of swans—an initially nonsensical apparition/articulation, the meaning of which will be made clear later in the narrative, we are assured:

> je vous dirai plus tard pourquoi il s'en trouve un de complètement noir parmi la troupe, et dont <u>le corps, supportant une enclume</u>, <u>surmontée du cadavre en putréfaction d'un crabe tourteau</u>, inspire à bon droit de la méfiance à ses autres aquatiques camarades (294).

And in fact, each of the three elements (swan, anvil, and crab), and their placement in this formation *will* be accounted for, in an extended conflict between Maldoror and an emissary of God—the two having been transformed, it is revealed, into said swan and crab, respectively. As for the anvil, even less explicable in this "aquatic" setting, it had become necessary – logically enough! – to prevent the vanquished crab/archangel from returning to life, as the swan/

---

44 Cited in note #30.
45 The following reading thus differs from that of Le Clézio, who attributes a more arbitrary, ludic source to the structure of the canto: "tout cela développe un irrationnel purement verbal, à la manière du rêve. Tout le Chant Sixième semble se construire sur quelques mots-clefs : le pont du Carrousel, l'anneau de fer, le lac des Cygnes, et l'étrange énigme : « la queue de poisson ne volera que pendant trois jours […] » (121).

Maldoror proceeded to the lake where we initially encountered him: "il se demande si la mort n'a pas été instantanée. Il a mis sur son dos une enclume et un cadavre ; il s'achemine vers une vaste pièce d'eau [...]" (309). Similarly, at another point in the sixth canto, the narrator suddenly offers us a seemingly incoherent, if highly *textured* prophesy:

> et <u>une balle cylindro-conique percera la peau de rhinocéros</u>, malgré la fille de neige et le mendiant ! <u>C'est que le fou couronné aura dit la vérité sur la fidélité des quatorze poignards</u> (299).

And indeed, just preceding the final sling, and contributing to the development of narrative tension that reaches its climax in that act, we observe Maldoror forced to prevent the attempted intervention of God Himself—an event that allows the narrator to explain these enigmatic figures, and bring to fruition the earlier prophesy:

> L'individu, qui examinait les alentours du haut de la colonne, arma son revolver, visa avec soin et pressa la détente. Le commodore qui mendiait par les rues depuis le jour où avait commencé ce qu'il croyait être la folie de son fils et la mère, qu'on avait appelée *la fille de neige*, à cause de son extrême pâleur, portèrent en avant leur poitrine pour protéger le rhinocéros. Inutile soin. La balle troua sa peau [...]. [...] Mais nous savions que, dans ce pachyderme, s'était introduite la substance du Seigneur (315).

In what is perhaps the most striking example of this *revolution* – in both senses of the term – in the sequential structure of *Maldoror*, a deceptively simple iron ring appears early in the sixth canto—a portent of terrible significance, apparently, given the physical tremor of apprehension it evokes in the narrator: "Savez-vous que, lorsque je songe à l'anneau de fer caché sous la pierre par la main d'un maniaque, un invincible frisson me passe par les cheveux" (291). Not only do we discover, as the final elements of the closing scene are falling into place, that this ring has been hidden by one of Maldoror's lackeys, to later fulfill a crucial function at the center of the final wheel of death – "Puisque, d'après vous, le moment est venu, s'écria-t-il, j'ai été reprendre l'anneau que j'avais enterré sous la pierre, et je l'ai attaché à un des bouts du câble. Voici le paquet" (313–14) – but this object ends up producing, in the final lines of the work, the last glimmer of what comes to resemble a *cosmic* force: "L'anneau de fer du nœud coulant, miroitant aux rayons du soleil, engage à compléter soi-même l'illusion" (316).

The sense of resolution produced at the close of the sixth canto thus cannot be attributed to the final sling alone, and its focused realization of force. Equally significant, is the manner in which the surreal phantasms of the poet's imagination – and more particularly, their *texture*, when expressed – are seemingly brought into the controlled movement of the narrative, coagulations of language separated out of the chaotic darkness of the preceding text (indeed, just as an actual centrifuge separates the densest matter from the most diffuse, in its acceleration), contributing to the climactic progression of events—the concluding impact of which is incidental, in a sense. Through the seemingly inconsequential insertion of an iron ring, quickly forgotten, the very core of this developing whirlwind of force, as well as the final gleam of its disappearance, are both able to take place in the text, *as if spontaneously*: "L'anneau de fer [...] compl[ète] soi-même l'illusion" – an effacement of the writer that points, obliquely, to his final assumption of control. Whether or not, when turning the final page, we forget the expanses of textual debris left by Lautréamont's revolting exploits, however, seduced by the subterfuge at the heart of this "almost too perfect" centrifuge, is another matter.

PART 2

Revolitions

∴

CHAPTER 3

Grounding Force: Césaire

> Je retrouverais le secret des grandes communications et des grandes combustions. Je dirais orage. Je dirais fleuve. Je dirais tornade. [...] Qui ne me comprendrait pas ne comprendrait pas davantage le rugissement du tigre.
>
> CÉSAIRE, *Cahier* (21).

∴

The belief that words can somehow act upon reality with the same immediacy as actual physical phenomena is hardly new when Aimé Césaire begins his literary career. Throughout human history, a select group of language users, from priests to poets, have been invested (or invested themselves) with this unique faculty. However untenable such a belief becomes in the modern era, it takes on the urgency of an imperative, for Césaire—a fact that is underscored in the above statement by an abrupt collapse of the distinction between linguistic and natural forces (underlined and italicized, respectively, below), as the initial "and" disappears, the poet *speaking storm*: "des grandes communications \et\ des grandes *combustions*" => "Je dirais *orage.*" It is this desire to access and transmit such forces, engaging the consciousness of his people and the world at large (not merely flirting with the esoteric in self-conscious parlor games, à la Hugo or the Surrealists, for instance), that has led to the unique power of the *Cahier*. A work of sustained, affectively charged expression, that has continued to captivate readers since its initial reception by thinkers as diverse – if not antithetical – as Breton and Sartre, Césaire's masterpiece demonstrates an adept merging of ethical *engagement* and anarchic revolt that few artists have attained.[1] Vividly reproducing the environment of his native Martinique – to which the reader, as well, seems to "return" – re-enacting the colonial oppression that continues to hold the spirit of his people down in the mud of the cane fields, the poet then manages to produce a sense of uprising

---

1   "Et ce cri est d'une telle beauté qu'il nous réconcilie avec la littérature engagée où l'art est trop souvent sacrifié à la cause" (Kesteloot 27). In addition to the critical work discussed in detail below, see Chambers' reflections on the ethical and aesthetic components of Césaire's poem.

in the text, liberating a new voice and a sense of purpose from the forces of entropy and silence.[2]

A number of critics have called attention to the singularly forceful, physical quality of this message of revolt and liberation. Drawing on the same imagery utilized in the above citation, Diop, for instance, identifies "a torrential flow" passing throughout Césaire's published work as a whole, surging up out of the experience of oppression into poetic language: "Forger un vocabulaire inédit, mettre à jour une syntaxe et instituer un rythme jaillissant des profondeurs de l'oppression raciale, tel est le projet éthique et esthétique que la coulée torrentueuse d'images et de vocables poursuit de poème en poème" (151). And yet, similar to what we have witnessed in the critical discourses treating Baudelaire and Lautréamont, despite his allusion to certain dynamics arising in the text, infusing signification with the visceral experience of subjugation and resentment, Diop tends to limit such observations to generalities, neglecting the actual linguistic *body* of this "torrent."

Hénane, who has written extensively on Césaire, would have a unique perspective on the salient physical qualities of the poet's voice, given his training as a physician. Beyond his thorough cataloguing of medical terminology in Césaire's work, however, he too offers few suggestions regarding the actual *articulation* of its language. Reflecting on the poet's only published analysis of a poetic text, Mallarmé's "Sonnet en *yx*," he observes: "pour Césaire comme pour Mallarmé, le mot est un signe, un hiéroglyphe, vecteur non de communication, mais de sensation, d'émotion, de saisissement" ("Lexique" 87). While Césaire's poetry is repeatedly distinguished by its "visceral" nature, ("la poésie d'Aimé Césaire est charnelle et pulsatile," AC 236; "La poésie césairienne est une création charnelle, surgie du tréfons viscéral du poète," Ibid. 19), the manner in which this poetry acts upon the reader, "awakening" him or her to the issues addressed by the poet, is left decidedly vague: "Le verbe césairien [...] infuse une énergie qui met le corps et l'esprit en éveil tendu" (Ibid. 256). However perceptive, in the few instances where the actual substance of this "carnal creation" is addressed, Hénane's analysis is generally limited to a single case of alliteration—the prevalence of words with [a], for instance (Ibid. 18), or [R], as in the passage cited in the previous chapter ("[...] la fréquence des rugueuses en « r » [...]. Sonorités rauques cohérentes avec le grattage d'une peau excoriée, prurigineuse," Ibid. 110).

---

2 The central spatial construct organizing the *Cahier* has been noted by many critics—Dash, for example: "C'est à partir de cette expérience négative et contre elle, que le poète fait appel à des forces neuves. [...] Ce dépassement se définit en termes d'un mouvement ascensionnel chez Césaire. Il parvient à ranimer ce paysage inerte, à revitaliser l'espace horizontal en faisant appel à la beauté convulsive de la montagne" ("Le cri" 103).

Ferdinand, it should be noted, has provided some valuable insights into this aspect of Césaire's voice—language that *engages* the reader... in the mouth: "les mots [du poète] épousent les lèvres et invitent à la libération de la parole étouffée, broyée, jugulée. [...] Plutôt que d'expliquer en détails le sentiment de révolte, le poète martiniquais nous fait *sentir* la révolte" (248–49). He observes how sibilants, for instance, are employed to suggest the "stifled voices" of the oppressed (243); or, in an even more convincing example, analyzes in detail a striking sound-image from *Et les chiens se taisaient* ("on a beau peindre blanc le pied de l'arbre la force de l'écorce en dessous crie," Césaire, *Chiens* 38):

> nous pouvons imaginer l'Afrique jaillir de l'arbre [...] à cause des sonorités de l'énoncé. L'allitération en [s] des mots « force », « en dessous » et « écorce », s'oppose à la sonorité en [k] du verbe crier (« crie »). Cette opposition entre une sonorité douce et le craquement dans le verbe nous prépare à une explosion (249).

If he comes closer than most critics to revealing the centrality of phonetic structures in Césaire's work, however, he too limits his remarks to several brief examples, only scratching the surface of its dense and complex textures.[3]

The distinctive voice arising in Césaire's poetry demands, perhaps more than that of any other poet, that such analysis is undertaken in depth. For however skeptically one may view the suggestion of a mystical "realizing" force in his language (a "communication-combustion," cited earlier), there is, in our reading of the *Cahier*, an undeniable sensation of forces that cannot be explained in terms of signification or through conventional formal analysis. Far from inexplicable, relegated to a realm of "sorcellerie évocatoire" (Baudelaire, *OC II* 118), these forces in fact become increasingly palpable the more we attend to the phonetic structures of the text. Such effects, we find, are not limited to individual instances of "sound symbolism" ("des rugueuses en « r »"), but are derived from complex articulatory series—textures that allow the enactment of revolt to be experienced on some level, if not literally produced, in the recitation of the text. Furthermore, where we observed recurring phonetic condensations as a problematic phenomenon in the preceding studies, we progressively discover, in accompanying Césaire on this journey, that *his* use of revolting poetics – clearly the result of significant personal evolution, both as an artist and individual – allows him to effectively control and process the matter with which he embodies and attacks a negative reality. In the final pages of the *Cahier*, the accumulated "mud" of humiliation is completely

---

3 The work of Keith Louis Walker, to which I will refer below, must be acknowledged as well.

embraced, firmly rooting the speaking subject in that reality, and *used*, for its transcendence ("boue" => "debout").

∴

> Par la seule grâce de la verbalisation, adviennent des mondes nouveaux.
> DIOP (182).

While Césaire is hardly a "nature poet," in the conventional sense of the expression, his work does reveal converging sensitivities to physical qualities of the natural world and those of language. To the attentive ear of the poet, the phonetic building blocks of language can be ordered, in conjunction with the development of a given image, to seemingly reproduce the kinetic phenomena he perceives in a world dominated by elemental forces. The wind in the following sense memory, for instance, rattling the roof of the poet's decrepit childhood home, is suggested by the interacting elements of fire and water—not merely through the figures utilized in the process of signification, but in the very material constituting them, the crackling of compressed front vowels and consonants ("un cré*pi*tement *de fri*t*U*re") subsumed by the enveloping tension of the back phonemes ("**que l'on** plonge dans l'eau"):

> et ça fait des marais de rouillure dans la pâte grise sordide empuantie de la paille, et quand le vent siffle, ces disparates font bizarre le bruit, comme un c*ré*p*i*tement *de fri*t*U*re d'abord, puis comme un *ti*son que *l'*on p*lo*nge dans *l'*eau avec *la f*U*m*ée *d*es *b*ri*ndill*es qui *s'*en'*vo*le... (18).

In an example that is even more striking, for its economy of expression, Césaire expands the entire horizon in the space of a single line. Concluding a movement that alternately contracts and expands the buccal cavity, performing the active terms ("recule et s'élargit"), the final "expansion" truly seems to open out at the line ending:

> *l'*ho*ri*zon se dé*f*ait,\ rec*U*le et s'é*l*ar`g*i*t (60).

The process of gestation and (re)birth, a central theme of the *Cahier*,[4] is similarly rendered, as the cramped front articulations of the following "small heads" break out of the diffuse "ovaries of/from water":

---

4   See Hénane, *AC* 170.

*vienn*ent *l*es o*v*ai*r*es de *l*'eau où *le f*u*t*U*r* ag*i*te *s*es *p*e*t*i*t*es *t*êtes (45).

Such textures do not arise by chance, surely, but are the product of a self-conscious process of composition, the poet confident in his ability to manipulate potential expressive force into realization. In the following line, for example, the initial indexical ("voici") calls attention to the rising fullness of voice (*voix-ci*), of which it is the source ("voici" => "virile"):

et *v*oic*i* au *b*out *d*e *c*e *p*e*t*it ma*t*in ma *pr*i*è*re *v*i`r*il*e (49).[5]

The ascending modulation of the lyric voice – or *anabasis* – that structures the preceding citations, is in fact one of the most recurring tonal patterns in the *Cahier*—hardly surprising, given that it echoes – on a smaller, microcosmic scale – the concluding movement of the text itself ("Et nous sommes debout maintenant, mon pays et moi," 57; "monte, Colombe / monte / monte / monte," 65).

If such passages demonstrate a mastery of expressive force throughout the work, they cannot of course generate in and of themselves the final, liberated voice that concludes the poem. They can however accompany (or more accurately, *embody*) the progressive evolution of this voice, as the writing subject undergoes his arduous, drawn-out struggle with the historical realities of homeland and personal identity. The momentary offering up of a "virile prayer," as above, cannot sustain the song that must "plunge" into the "mud" of reality before acquiring the ring of authenticity ("Ramper dans les boues. S'arc-bouter dans le gras / de la boue. Porter," 53). Until that moment, the text can only enact individual uprisings, unable to break free definitively from the horizontal weight of reality:

Au\bout\du *p*e*t*it ma*t*in,\ ce*tt*e ville `*p*/ate\ – éta`*l*ée...
   Elle *r*am*p*e sur les *m*ains sans *j*a*m*ais aucUne en*v*ie
de *v*ri*ll*er le *c*iel *d*'Une *s*tatUre *d*e *pr*o*t*esta`*t*io*n*\\ (17).

• • •

---

5 As in the preceding chapters, certain phonemes will be annotated according to their participation in the production of a given texture, at the expense of conformity—i.e. the labialized front [b] of "bout," above (and in "boue," throughout the text), seems to contribute to the diffuse darkness created by the back series.

Prior to its final, liberating ascension, the *Cahier* involves a recurring alternation – oriented by the spatial axes discussed above – between affirmative, expansive movements, and deflating confrontations with an oppressive reality. Both Almeida and Davis have identified this structure as a fundamental source of "oscillation" and rhythm in the work: "[…] l'oscillation constante de systoles et diastoles, […] des échecs réitérés qui accompagnent en contrepoint chaque nouveau projet d'expansion et d'affirmation" (Almeida 43); "the poem's emotional rhythm proceeds by sequences or loops, composed of elation punctured by brusque disillusionment" (Davis 196). Correspondingly, the majority of salient phonetic structures in the *Cahier* do not contribute to any sense of continuous force, instead producing abrupt bursts of expressive energy, which would counteract the forces of oppression and entropy, if only momentarily, and despite the absence of any promise of change.

For Césaire, the defining quality of a voice that can effectively rise up out of the amorphous mass of existing discourse, taking hold in the attention and memory of the auditor, is not one that we usually associate with lyric poetry, but a "guttural cacophony," carefully arranged for the "attack" of enunciation:

la cacoph*on*ie gutturale d'un *chan*tre bien d'a`tta*q*ue (15).

In addition to the alternating vowel series contributing to the jarring effect of the above texture, we find in this single line a number of Césaire's preferred weapons in the discourse of revolt—the back velars [k] [g] and guttural (!) [ʀ], and the front dentals [d] [t], the latter graphically reinforcing the effect produced (i.e., doubled: "gutturale" "attaque"). These are also key components in one of the more significant passages early in the poem—a lucid representation of the poet's homeland, and the history of oppression and violation that has shaped it. This sublimated history ("O quiètes années de Dieu") is given presence in the compressed percussion that dominates the line (heightened by the monosyllabic series "de\Dieu\sur\cette\motte"), released in the final "terra-quée !":

O quiètes années de\Dieu\sur\cette\motte terra`quée ! (60).

As observed in the preceding chapters, the dentals are particularly useful in the expression of invective, with their explosive release from a precise, complete occlusion of the buccal cavity—as in the following condemnation, further punctuated by the back nasals in accentuated positions ("tri`om*phe*," "Trahi`son"):

Ton dernier tri`omphe,\ corbeau tenace de la Trahi`son\\ (24).

The dentals are often deployed in the *Cahier* in conjunction with corresponding vowels, articulated from the same region (the front [e], and especially [i]), producing a sense of controlled, incisive force ("tri`omphe"). One of the first images we are presented of the homeland is not only seen, but *heard*, as the twin destructive forces of disease and alcoholism are enacted in the texture of language, seeming to perforate the land itself:

les Antilles grêlées de petite vérole, les Antilles dynamitées d'alcool (8).[6]

Such barrages of sound are also directed, logically enough, at the *source* of this oppression—in the forced confrontation of European aristocracy with the "savage" practices of indigenous cultures (cannibalism), for instance. If the violence in question is in fact displaced here, and not enacted in the image itself (a *past* decapitation, as in Baudelaire's morbid meditation, "Une martyre," analyzed in chapter 1, p. 51), it is nonetheless conveyed by the final "choppy" phonetic series, which seemingly beats the viewer into this "stupor":

mais est-ce qu'on tue le *Remor*ds, beau comme la *face* de stupeur d'Une dame anglaise qui trouverait dans sa soupière un crâne de \\Hottentot ?\\ (20).

And yet, throughout a great deal of the poem, Césaire would seem intent on using such textures, not to strike out at the European civilization responsible for the squalor and suffering of his people, but to reproduce that very experience. Upon the homecoming of the poem's title ("Et voici que je suis venu !" 22),[7] the poetic subject is faced with a daily life defined by the myriad "futile deaths" of the past; an impoverished, stifled existence that is continually belittled—quite literally here, in the relentless repetition of "petit":

l'éclatante petitesse de cette mort, cette mort qui clopine de petitesses en petitesses ; ces pelletées de petites avidités sur le conquistador ; ces

---

6 I am not of course attributing an [l] to "Antilles"; its semi-vowel is simply annotated in the same way in the present system of analysis as that phoneme, as acknowledged on p. 62 of chapter 1.

7 Within the world of the text at least—Césaire famously composed the poem while still living abroad (Almeida 12).

pelletées de petits larbins sur le grand sauvage, ces pelletées de petites âmes sur le Caraïbe aux trois âmes, et toutes ces morts fu`tiles (23).

In this, and similar passages, we observe that such textures involve a dual function in Césaire's poetics. The visceral quality of the enunciation not only lends a higher degree of presence to the experience of the oppressed, but allows the poet to *claim* that experience, paradoxically, in re-enacting it himself. Given that the organs utilized for articulation provide linguistic expression with its closest approximation of *physical* engagement of the real – language being otherwise limited to the abstract realm of signification – it is logical that Césaire would employ these textures in such a way, interacting with a history that would remain irrecuperable in its spectrality.

In the following violation and "consumption" of the island, for example, it is as if the poet himself were trying to obtain a greater purchase on the object in question, actually tasting it (*"lèche"*) in the transition from abrupt blows to persistent "biting" (a term that, in French, actually connotes its signified, with its repeated back guttural [R] and [d]: "mor*dre*"):

> *la mer la frappe à grands\coups\de\boxe,\ou plutôt la mer est un gros chien qui lèche et mord la plage aux jarrets, et à force de la mordre elle finira par la dévorer* (19–20).

From this embodiment of his victimized land and people, Césaire derives the predominant rhythms and timbres of his distinct voice. The taut, resistant skull of a mute student, for instance, becomes a drum in the hands of his teachers ("t[e]ndu"), the percussive consonants resonating through the dense back texture and general closure of the buccal cavity:

> *malgré leur manière si énergique à\tous\deux\de\tambouriner son crâne tondu* (11).[8]

Furthermore, it is in large part through this palpable re-enactment of victimization, re-appropriating history, that the poet will eventually develop the forces of revolt animating the final section of the poem, lifting up his people in the space of the text, as mentioned earlier. In allowing the oppressor to first

---

8 See Kubayanda on Césaire's incorporation of African idioms – actually imitating drum beats – as a way of revolting against the domination of European culture (69–71), and Dash's similar reflections on such performative language use by Caribbean writers more generally ("Introduction" xx).

GROUNDING FORCE: CÉSAIRE   135

dominate the minds and bodies of the oppressed, the poet begins to accumulate his eventual "power over destiny" in the language of the poem—allowing him to overcome the most insidious, internalized effects of colonization:

> la misère lui avait blessé poitrine et dos et on avait
> fourré dans sa pauvre cervelle qu'une fatalité pesait
> sur lui qu'on ne prend pas au collet ; qu'il n'avait pas
> puissance sur son propre destin (59).

Even when there seems to be nothing substantial or nourishing in reality to sustain it ("une faim"), the poetic voice can take hold of this lack, embodied in language—the doubled back phonemes here [g]/[ʀ] grasping what his people cannot:

> une faim qui ne sait plus grimper aux agrès de sa voix (12).

The discourse of the colonizer cannot entirely drown out the colonized, whose desire for self-expression contains forces of its own. After rising up in the growing "currents" of the fricative [f], this defiance sounds out, bursting through the "end" of an imposed – and bankrupt – "Reason" ("`fin,\" => "dé`fi =>"):

> Raison rétive tu ne m'empêcheras pas de lancer
> absurde sur les eaux au gré des courants de ma *soif*
> votre forme, îles difformes, votre `fin,\ mon dé`fi => (55).

   As suggested above, however, the destructive forces of colonization must be allowed to completely run their course in the development of the text for this cry of defiance to communicate the promise of liberation. One of most insidious of these forces appears in a figural motif that is immediately familiar, following our readings of Baudelaire and Lautréamont, reflecting a clear link with their work—decomposing (often fecal) organic matter, and its associations with other, less than desirable phenomena of existence. In the *Cahier*, such figures take on an even greater, more pressing significance, *doubled* in their force, in effect: quite real, in designating the actual day-to-day environment of contemporary Martinique (in contrast to Lautréamont's juvenile riffing on "kakatoès," for instance, analyzed on pp. 97–98 of the present work), they simultaneously point to the complex, less visible forces undermining the psychological and spiritual well-being of its people. Whereas the student in the citation above demonstrated active resistance to oppression, for instance ("*malgré* leur manière [...] de tambouriner"), the most common stance of the colonized in such situations, in Césaire's perspective, is the *absence* of any stance; a passive, silent acceptance of reality which is recurringly associated with images of rotting matter and disease.

As Hénane has already observed, devoting an entire section of one book to the language of putrefaction (*AC* 93–108), the effect rendered by such figures is due as much to the aural quality of the terms utilized, as the images themselves.[9] He observes that, with the poet's extensive knowledge of Greek and Latin, acquired during studies at *l'École Normale Supérieure*, Césaire has an ear well attuned to the "foreign," if not "disquieting" sounds of terms for disease, in particular ("leur étrangeté sémantique et leurs sonorités parfois inquiétantes," Ibid. 18). Just as *images* of physiological disorders can produce an almost visceral effect on the reader, the sounds of the terms utilized often involve a unique "emotional" charge ("ce terme sec, rugueux, lourd de sonorités étranges, est paré d'émotion," Ibid.). I would however insist that, just as we observed in the preceding chapters, such effects are not limited to the individual signifiers denoting these conditions, nor even to this particular lexicon, but are produced through complex phonetic patterns running throughout entire passages in which the terms appear. For instance, when Césaire responds to his people's silence, "unresponsive" ("qui ne répondent pas") in their quiescence and denial of truth, this pathological victimhood materializes in the poet's language, *voiced*:

et il *n'y a* que les *fien*tes accumulées de *nos* menso*n*ges – et qui *n*e ré`pon*d*ent `pas (36).

By elaborating this pervasive, amorphous state of corruption in the language of his text, the poet brings this reality to light, while simultaneously dynamizing his own discourse. To this end, such descriptions often contain some of the poem's densest textures, with highly contrasting articulations—so that "hétéro*cl*ite," for example, is expressive on two levels:

l'é*ch*ouage hétéro`*cl*ite, les p*u*anteurs exacerbées de la corr*u*p`tion, les so*d*omies monstrueuses (12).

Like its organic referent in the real, such linguistic matter coheres and condenses, only to be released in dissolution (a dynamic that is *experienced* – as

---

9 Onyeoziri also writes at length on the prevalence of such imagery, providing a catalogue of related terms (148–63). See Kouassi, as well, for a more extensive, general catalogue of the lexicon utilized in the *Cahier*.

observed in other passages, above – in the constriction and release of the buccal cavity: "qui se sou`lagent"; "crevant de pUstUles `tièdes"):

> avec ses tas d'ordUres pourri`ssant,\ ses croupes furtives qui se sou`lagent (19);

> une *vieille* misère *pourrissant sous le so*leil,\ silencieusement ;\ un *vieux* silence crevant de pUstUles `tièdes\\ (8).

The articulation of such sound-images is never deployed for shock value alone—a common proclivity toward self-gratification in the revolting poetics, as we have observed.[10] Such infection is always *engaged* in Césaire's language, reflecting an attempt to somehow reanimate the voice of the other – not merely producing a "combustion" in the poet's own acts of expression – where that voice has been silenced. Just as important as the *success* of Toussaint Louverture, in the poet's incorporation of historical events, is the *failed* revolt of American slaves, the "plugged" trumpets of their stillborn charge ("*bouchées*," in French, significantly) contributing audibly to the restricted voice of the present, *poetic* revolt:

> PUtréfactions monstrUeuses de ré`voltes
> inopé`rantes,
> marais de sang pU`trides
> trompettes absUrdement bou`chées (25).

A curious paradox becomes increasingly apparent, however, in our traversal of the *Cahier*. It would seem that the poem's evolving voice often depends for its expressive intensity on what in fact *resists* unrestrained expression. The greater the tension between that which remains *un*expressed (in the following citation: the "scandalous," "shameful," and "hatred") and the violence with which it is silenced ("suffocated," "killed"), the greater the impact of the poet's language—"immense hatred" expanding perceptibly out of the progressively contained prosody that precedes it:

> Et de petits scandales étouffés,\ de petites\`hontes\`tUes,\ de petites `\\haines i`mmenses (17).

Even the "cry" that *is* expressed takes form through failure:

---

10 "Cette poésie n'est jamais mue par le seul désir de surprendre" (Diop 184).

cette *voix* qu**i** *c*r**i**e, lente*m*ent **e**n*r*o**u**é**e**, *v*aine`m*e*nt, *v*aine`*m*ent **e**n*r*o**u**é**e** (36).

How can such a poetics serve the great ambition – successfully realized, in the view of most readers – that drives the *Cahier*? How can a voice that depends on inhibition and failure produce one of the greatest achievements of modern lyric poetry[11]—a poem that concludes in expansive affirmation, the poet claiming to have relinquished, precisely, the savor of discord ("j'accepte, j'accepte tout cela," 56)? Continuing our reading through the present mode of analysis, we find that this contradiction seemingly resolves *itself*, as the unexpressed is continually embodied in the language of the text—not merely in the dynamic discourses of violation and disease which repeatedly command our attention, however, as observed above, but through a subtler, more sustained production of intensity. Throughout the *Cahier*, and particularly in its final pages, we find a number of images in which the anticipation of liberating force is patiently maintained, the dense textures of the poem correspondingly holding the voice down in preparation for, *grounding* its final ascension.

⋯

car ce qui ouvre la route / c'est tout aussi le cri puisé au creux boueux de l'attentif gisement fidèle.
    CÉSAIRE, *Chiens* (114).

It is important to note that for Césaire, if the colonized do not yet have access to an authentic, meaningful voice ("cette foule si étrangement bavarde et muette," 9), such a voice is not in fact absent, but in close proximity ("à côté de son vrai cri," Ibid.). Interestingly, this displaced outburst, too "proud" for present circumstances, is located in "deep darkness"—an obscurity that forms in the very texture of language, enclosed:

[…] le seul qu'on eût voulu l'entendre crier parce qu'on le sent sien lui seul ; parce qu'on le sent habiter en elle dans **q**uelque *r*efuge **p**rofond **d'ombr**e et **d'orgue**il (9).

---

11 As Breton marvelled, following a chance first reading of *Tropiques*: "Je n'en crus pas mes yeux : mais ce qui était dit là, c'était ce qu'il fallait dire ! Toutes ces ombres grimaçantes se déchiraient, se dispersaient ; tous ces mensonges, toutes ces dérisions tombaient en loques : ainsi la voix de l'homme n'était pas en rien brisée, couverte, elle se redressait ici comme l'épis même de la lumière" (from the preface to the 1947 edition, *Cahier* 78).

GROUNDING FORCE: CÉSAIRE 139

We should also note in this regard, that the dark, urban underworld depicted in the poem, which introduces a crucial stage in the regenerative odyssey of the poet-hero, as a number of critics have observed, is introduced in a similar texture:[12]

> dès que t**om**bent les pre**mi**ères **om**bres su**r** le b**our**g du Gros-M**or**ne (37).

Further analysis of the poem suggests that such phonetic structures in fact quite often correspond to dual, opposingly valorized entities in the existence of the colonized. In key transformative passages of the text, as the oppression of colonialism transects with those primordial forces that continue to ground the indigenous people in their natural environment – the poet accepting his "face of mud" – the textures in which these entities are fused further intensify, propulsing the final section of the poem. Even more effectively than the stifled voices, witnessed above, these condensations in the medium of expression torque the lyric enunciation, much as we observed in the preceding chapters, deriving a source of energy from that which initially appeared an insurmountable obstacle.[13] An early description of the daily *rythme de vie* in Martinique, for example, consists of a river that entropic forces have all but immobilized

12   Almeida, for instance, has drawn attention to the "descente orphique" (61) of the poetic subject ("[...] l'espace intérieur se creusant en profondeur, comme antidote à la mort," 59–60), while Paviot has aligned this inward descent with the symbolic structures of Christian mysticism and alchemy, in particular (which Breton had already alluded to in his preface to the poem, *Cahier* 82): "Cette région du corps indiquée par Césaire, où le regard s'arrête et contemple, est appelée centre par certains, le lieu qui contient « l'essence et la vie »," Paviot 25). Most convincing, perhaps, given Césaire's extensive studies of the Classics, is Davis' identification of these motifs in a series of poetic/mythic traditions— not only in Dante and Hellenic culture (Homer), but in more ancient East Mediterranean myths. He observes that *Katabasis*, in ancient Greek, was a necessary stage preceding the hero's homecoming (*nostos*), which involved the recognition of mortality and discovery of the true self (193–95).
13   Walker and Dash read the recurring "mud" motif as an essentially negative force, which depletes energy sources: "[...] Prométhée vaincu, enchaîné et dévoré, l'homme assis, le feu éteint et « le ciel baillant d'absence noire. » Dans cet état, le soleil ne lui infuse plus ni vigueur, ni virilité verticalisantes, mais plutôt le déssèche de toute énergie et de toute volonté jusqu'à l'inertie" (Walker 57); "Chez Césaire, l'ennemi c'est la boue de ce paysage qui se colle à vous, vous paralysant" (Dash, "Le cri" 103). I am proposing that it is in fact the materialization of entropic forces ("substantialisation de l'ennui," Walker 57) that produces a sense of growing intensity. If others have already identified such a dynamic in the text at a *conceptual* level – Almeida, for instance: "l'expansion est plus large parce qu'elle prend son élan à partir des profondeurs explorées dans la deuxième partie" (45) – the

—the bright, front articulations, pushed along by fricatives and [R], struggling against back/nasal clusters and heavy punctuation:

> la *v*ie *p*ro*st*rée,\ on ne *s*ait où *d*é*p*ê*ch*er *s*es *r*êves a*v*or*t*és,\ le *fl*eu*v*e de *v*ie *d*ésespérément *t*or*p*i*d*e *d*ans *s*on li*t*,\ *s*ans *t*Urgescence ni *d*é*p*res-sion,\ ince*rt*ain de *fl*Uer,\ lamen*t*ablement *v*i*d*e,\ la lour*d*e im*p*ar*t*ialité de l'enn*ui*,\ ré*p*ar*t*issant l'ombre *s*ur *t*outes *ch*oses égales,\ l'*a*ir *st*agnant *s*ans une *t*rouée d'*o*iseau clair (17).

The most striking example of this dynamic, however, coincides with a recurring topos in the landscape of the *Cahier*—the distinctive volcanic hills, or *mornes*, of the Antilles. What seems a symbol of unrealized vitality at first appearance – "le morne oublié, oublieux de sauter" (10) – constitutes, as any reader familiar with the text knows, one of the privileged figures of the poem —less for its potential *release* of subterranean forces, than as a site where, in continuously restricting these forces, the latter are even more charged.[14] And the suggestion that this topos is intimately linked to *expression*, in particular, at its most physical level, is confirmed by the following formulation—through the latter's texture, as well as its central figure ("un sanglot"):

> l'incen*d*ie contenu\du\morne,\comme\un*s*ang*l*ot\que*l'*on a bâ*il*-*l*onné au\bor*d*\de*s*on é*cl*a*t*ement sangu*i*nai*r*e,\ en *q*uête *d*'une ignition qui *s*e dé*r*obe\\ (11).

Despite our natural tendency to identify, on the semantic level, with the awaited "éclatement" of contained fire (which is in fact produced in the texture

---

present analysis, it is hoped, will succeed in demonstrating it as an actual production of force in the physical enunciation of the text.

14   Several critics have called attention to the prevalence of contained, straining forces in the *Cahier*—though, as I have pointed out in other instances, in purely figural terms, without identifying their presence in the articulation of its language: "L'affirmation de soi et la Révolution espérées, attendues sont métaphorisées dans les images de puissances contenues ou en germe telles les ouragans enroués, les volcans enchaînés et les incendies contenus" (Walker 59); "La phrase est déferlante et ménage une tension interne, par opposition d'une lourde protase – qui s'amplifie au fur et à mesure que sont citées les servitudes, pour atteindre un point limite du « calvaire », donc de rupture – et d'une apodose où deferle, avec la sensation d'une résolution libératrice, la parole messianique du « pasteur »" (Diop 153); "[…] cette bouche-caverne, où semblent s'être accumulées la fureur et la rage après plusieurs siècles de mépris injurieux. La pression de cette fureur si longtemps contenue fait exploser le contenant, comme la lave sous pression fait exploser la montagne" (Hénane, *AC* 91).

GROUNDING FORCE: CÉSAIRE 141

here: "son éclatement sanguinaire"), the dense enclosure that withholds and "hides" this explosion resonates equally, if not moreso, in our reading. Elsewhere, these opposing forces are conjoined in a smaller textual space ("les volcans éclate`ront\\"), producing an even greater effect—the force of the explosion anticipated in the rushing fricatives and other series preceding it, and further highlighted by the contrasting "pecking" of birds that follows:

> sur cette plus fragile épaisseur de terre que dépasse de façon humiliante son grandiose avenir – les volcans éclate`ront\\ [...] et il ne restera plus qu'un bouillonnement tiède picoré d'oiseaux marins (8).

The *morne* is thus clearly one of the most privileged and consciously deployed intensive structures in the *Cahier*, reflecting an aesthetic that is deeply *felt* by the poet, communicating a life-force that is itself contained, and straining to be released. The poet's libidinal, "guttural" savoring of existence must accumulate a certain degree of tension before "tendresse" can produce "jouissance":

> ce plus essentiel pays restitué à ma gourmandise,\ non de diffuse tendresse,\ mais la tourmentée concentration sensuelle du gras téton des mornes avec l'accidentel palmier comme son germe durci,\ la jouissance saccadée des to`rrents (14).

Such intensive structures are not by necessity "grounded" in this reclaimed element of the poet's homeland, however.[15] By working and cultivating the matter of his own language ("mon labour"), in whatever form it takes, Césaire gains access to untapped expressive forces—bringing forth, in opposition to the dying civilization he leaves behind, a sturdy vessel for the liberation of a new voice, for instance:

> Au sortir de l'Europe toute révulsée de cris
> et mon labour me remémore d'une implacable
> é`trave => (35).

Indeed, it is in the poet's growing confidence in his ability to depart from his current, adopted homeland, finally arriving in the *pays natal*, that this intensity

---

15   While Dash, along with those critics cited above, identifies the *morne* as central to Césaire's project for the liberation of a new voice ("[...] de créer du volcan muet une nouvelle force subversive, de libérer la voix du volcan « bâillonné au bord de son éclatement sanguinaire »" (104), he recognizes that it is only one of the poet's figures for "intensity," among others, and part of a larger "réseau d'images de jaillissement" (104).

becomes most pronounced—a detonation that is carefully contained for the right moment ("Mon trésor de salpêtre"), preserved in its potentiality, even as it breaks through the surface of controlled expression:

> *R*aison,\ *je te* sa*c*re *v*ent du *soir*.\
> **B**ou*c*he **d**e l'or**d**re **t**on **nom** ?\
> Il m'est **c**oro**l**le du `*fou*e*t*.\
> **B**eau*t*é je *t*'appelle pé*t*ition de la **p***i*e*rr*e.\
> Mais ah ! La **rauq**ue\ **c**on*t*re**b**an**d**e
> **d**e mon *r*ire
> Ah ! **Mon *t*résor d**e sal`pê*t*re! (27).

And yet, it is as if the poet recognizes that what is most volatile at the *source* of such intensity is also that which, the more he claims and expresses it (in opposition to an *other*) becomes the most alienating of forces, ultimately, and beyond his control. A key factor contributing to the increasing dynamic quality of the *Cahier*, assuring its continual movement forward, will be found, precisely, in Césaire's ability to *abandon* the concentrated forces he has discovered within himself, at the same time he commands them, in one of the most celebrated passages of the poem:

> Mais **q**u*i* **t**ou*r*ne ma *v*oi*x* ? **q**u*i* é**c**or*c*he ma *v*oi*x* ? Me *fou*rra*n*t dans la **g**or**g**e m*i*lle **c**ro*c*s de **b**am**b**ou. M*i*lle **p***i*e*u*x **d**'our*s*in. [...] *C*'est `*t*oi `sale `\\*h*aine. *C*'est `*t*oi **p**oi**d**s de l'insul*t*e et ce*n*t ans **d**e coups **d**e `*fou*e*t*s. *C*'est `*t*oi *c*ent ans **d**e ma **p**atie*n*ce (31).

To produce, in the composition of text, this crucial transition in consciousness, the poet must find a way to jettison the material *body* of hatred in the voice. For as Diop observes, in a statement that resonates with our own findings in the first two chapters of the present work, the same emotional intensity that drives the movement toward redemption simultaneously threatens to restrict that very movement: "La colère engage le héros dans les actes les plus nobles. Mais elle peut aussi le cantonner dans les imprécations et la profération d'insanités" (178). As Césaire himself reflects, in *Et les chiens se taisaient*:

> Haïr c'est encore dépendre.
> Qu'est-ce que la haine, sinon la bonne pièce de bois attachée au cou
>   de l'esclave
>   et qui l'empêtre
> ou l'énorme aboiement du chien qui vous prend à la gorge
> et j'ai, une fois pour toutes, refusé, moi, d'être esclave (55–56).

Until he has fully acknowledged the complicated origins of this hatred, in the course of the poem, the type of expressive dynamics we have identified thus far (in the following example, from "Gon*fl*ements" to "é*cl*a*t*era-*t*-e*ll*e") can only continue to *anticipate* the dawn they announce, suspended within the continued tension of the text:

> **Gon***fl***ements** de n*ui*t aux qua*t*re *c*oi*n*s de ce pe*t*i*t* ma*t*in
> *s*oub*r*esauts de **mort** *fl*gée
> *d*es*t*in *t*ena*c*e
> **cr**i*s* *d*ebou*t* *d*e *t*erre m*u*e*tt*e
> *l*a s*pl*en*d*eu*r* *d*e *c*e *s*ang n'é*cl*a*t*era-*t*-e*ll*e `*p*oin*t*?\\ (26).

※ ※ ※

This crucial turning point, leading to the poem's final, affirmative gesture, depends on several interrelated changes in the poet's consciousness. The desire for an authentic, sustained expression of renewal will only be realized when Césaire has fully accepted his people, with all of their complicity and apathy, condemned up to this point in the text. And this change depends, in turn, on the poet's willingness to delve further into the traumatic origins of this degraded state, and his realization that he too participates in the latter's continuation, whatever pretensions to nobility he has unconsciously maintained.[16] What initially appears the fate of others ("le nègre" and "soi-même," in the following) is acknowledged as an affliction of the writing subject as well—as suggested, indirectly, by the vital force that returns to *him* following his acceptance of *their* vitiated state of being:

> et le nègre chaque jour [...] plus stérile, moins profond, plus répandu au dehors, plus séparé de soi-même [...] moins immédiat avec soi-même,
>
> j'accepte, j'accepte tout cela
> ....
> Et voici soudain que force et vie m'assaillent comme un taureau (56).

---

16   Davis, among others, has called attention to this key moment in the text: "the distance the speaker had earlier maintained between himself and his prostrate country is made to collapse abruptly, and the abject condition of the latter becomes one with the moral abjection of the former" (AC 46).

What is significant, in view of the present analysis, is that these revelations are *enacted* in the poet's writing, through the very textural forces that were deployed earlier to quite different ends. The same figures for disease that were used to embody the failings of others, for instance, are now turned back on the writing subject, who questions the excesses of his youth ("Et je ris de mes anciennes imaginations puériles", 38); a gesture that requires an ability to disengage from the discourse of aggression at the very moment it is deployed, identifying his own (linguistic) participation in the production of malignant tissue:

> *Je ref*U*se* de me donner mes **bou***rsouf*l**U***res* come d'au**t**hen**ti**ques *gloires* (38).

"Swelling" in the young poet's voice takes form in this evolving, self-reflexive discourse, so that the sharp edges of "authentic glory" can begin to pierce through, more clearly articulated. The same dynamics that were utilized to call attention to, or lash out at the corruption of others, simultaneously deriving a material force in the poetic enunciation, are now employed to evacuate what is recognized as unnecessary and self-indulgent, hindering the odyssey of the poem. The rising *anabases* of the following series, for instance, seem to transform the "passing wealth" of youth's confident knowledge into sudden, more profound "illumination":

> p̲a̲r-dessus bor**d** mes *ri*chesses p**é**r**é**gr**i**nes
> p̲a̲r-dessus bor**d** mes *faus*s̲e̲t**é***s* au**t**hen**ti**ques
> Mais quel é**t**ran*g*e orgueil **t**out sou**d**ain m'ill**Um**ine ? (44).

It is striking how the fully deployed range of articulation in fact corresponds, in a number of key passages at this point of the poem, to the liberation of forces that had previously been contained, once the speaker has accepted – actually merging his identity with – the negatively valorized elements of the text. The poet *becomes* the mud of the city he had looked down on, allowing the gesture of rejection to take on a different quality of force, in being "reclaimed"—simultaneously an invective, and a hymn of joy ("la louange [...] du / crachat"):

> Ce**tt**e *vi*l*l*e,\ ma *f*ace d̲e ˋ**b**oue.\
> *Je* ré*c̲l̲*ame **p**our ma *f*ace *la louang*e é*c̲l̲*a**t**an**t**e d̲u c̲r̲aˋ*ch*at !\\ (42).

The resilient ship's "bow" derived from the rejection of Occidental culture, cited above ("Au sortir de l'Europe [...] mon labour me remémore d'une implacable étrave"), re-emerges in the text ("proue"), the poet's language correspondingly condensing and breaking through that which continues to separate the present from the desired future ("*Fai*tes\de\ma\tête\une\tête"), allowing him to leave behind what is inauthentic and unregenerative in *himself*:

> je ne me dé*ro*be '*po*int.\\ *Fa*ites\de\ma\tête\une\tête\de\'*p*roue\\ (49).

If there remains any doubt that Césaire's experimentation with such textures is crucial to the dynamic evolution of the *Cahier* as whole, and its enactment of progressively enlightened consciousness, we have only to turn to a number of celebrated passages in the final movement of the poem, in which the poetic voice grows even more confident, its emotional intensity growing. When the poet famously reclaims his *négritude*, for instance, the rigorous articulatory gestures required by the term itself can be found throughout – indeed *constituting*, to a large degree – the tissue of the succeeding lines, binding the disparate elements of this complex passage.[17] First repelling what Negritude is *not* (any longer) – i.e. the unresponsive, entropic body of the colonized: "ma *négri*tude *n*'est *p*as une *p*ierre, sa surdité ruée [...]" – the poet then abruptly deploys this accumulating matter to reject the vertically oriented, *fabricated* civilization of Europe – "[...] *n*'est *n*i une tour *n*i une cathédrale" – all the while grounding this new identity in the elemental matter of the voice ("**d**'eau morte," etc.):

> ma *négri*tude *n*'est *p*as une *p*ierre, sa surdité ruée contre la clameur du jour
> ma *négri*tude *n*'est pas une taie d'eau morte sur l'œil mort de la terre
> ma *négri*tude *n*'est *n*i une tour *n*i une cathédrale (46–47).

Much more than a conceptual, purely figurative element of the text, this grounding *takes place* in the poem's language, through the gestures articulating it. In the continuation of the above passage, the sudden "plunge" of this new-found voice into the "flesh" of the world is accentuated, not only through the verticality of the transitional figures ("une tour," "une cathédrale"), but through repetitions that are driven into the dense matter of language itself:

> elle '*p*longe dans la chair rouge du sol
> elle '*p*longe dans la chair ardente du ciel
> elle '*t*roue l'accablement opaque de sa droite patience (47).

---

17   That Césaire is in fact conscious of such properties in this term is suggested by another poem—entitled, significantly, "Mot": "Le mot nègre / un grésillement de chairs qui brûlent" (*Cadastre* 72).

Furthermore, as suggested earlier, the controlled intensity that distinguishes the lyric voice in the final section of the *Cahier* reflects a more keenly felt experience, through rememoration, of *collective* identity. The regeneration of Negritude that will take place at the poem's close depends on the recognition and textual embodiment, not merely of the writing subject's authentic self, but the full historical reality of the people in which that self is grounded, ultimately. It is not enough that the poet's face is rendered in mud—the entire world must be similarly transformed in the language of the poem. That which would bury and stifle the voice of the colonized and enslaved yet again becomes, in the text – though even more thoroughly constructed here – that against which this voice can find itself, struggling forward ("*R*am*p*er," "*S'arc*-*bout*er"):

> *R*am*p*er *d*ans *l*es `*b*oues.\\ *S'arc*-*bout*er *d*ans *l*e *g*ras *d*e *l*a `*b*oue.\\ *P*or`ter.\\
> *Sol d*e `*b*oue.\\ Ho*r*i*z*on *d*e `*b*oue.\\ *Ciel d*e `*b*oue.\\
> Mo*r*ts *d*e `*b*oue,\\ ô noms à *r*échau*ff*er *d*ans *l*a *p*aume *d'*un sou*ffl*e *fiév*`*r*eux ! (53).

What is "the most earth of earth" is not merely recognized ("ceux sans qui la terre ne serait pas la terre / [...] / silo où se préserve et mûrit ce que la terre a de plus terre," 46), but is given a *presence* in the text, truly "grounding" the following, climactic resurrection. The Promethean transformation of this earth into an upright humanity is enacted in the ultimate realization of the poem's ascensional motif – deriving "debout" from "de boue" – through the progressively dynamic articulations that animate the textual matter established in the preceding:

> Et **nous** sommes d**e**b**o**ut main**te**nant,\ **m**on pays et m*oi*,\ les *ch*ev**e**ux dans le *v*ent,\ *m*a *m*ain *pet*ite *m*ain*t*enant dans son *p*oing é`*n*or**m**e et la *f*o*r*ce n'est *p*as **e**n `**n**ous,\ mais au-dessus de `**n**ous,\ dans une *v*oix qu**i** *vr*i*ll*e la n**u**it et l'*au*d*i*e*n*ce **c**omme la *p*é*n*é*t*rance *d*'une guêpe\apo*c*al**y**p-*t*i*qu*e.\ Et la *v*oix *p*rono*n*ce que l'Eu*r*ope nous a *p*endant des siè*c*les g**a**vés de mensonges et gon*fl*és de *p*est**i***l*en*c*es,\
> car il n'est *p*oint *v*rai que l'oeu*v*re de l'ho**mm**e est *fi*n**i**e\\ (57).

It is worth lingering here a moment, to appreciate the complexity of this passage—the continual alternation between elements of grounding (the communal "nous" which, repeated, partakes of the same dense substance as those terms designating active presence ("d**e**b**o**ut main**te**nant" "dans le *v*ent" "é`*n*or**m**e" "*f*o*r*ce"), the liberating rupture (once again, in plosives and front vowels: "la pénétrance d'une guêpe apocalyptique"), and a sense of movement that is not merely abrupt and passing, but continuous ("les cheveux dans le vent"; "une voix qui vrille la nuit").

Moreover, these sites of intensity stand out most, the voice of the poem most self-assured, at the precise moment the poet would seem to relinquish control over such forces. Effectively realizing in the progression of the poem the poetic subject's "return," promised in the title (or rather, the homeland's return *to him*: "je dirais à ce pays dont le limon entre dans la composition de ma chair [...]," 22), the voice seems to truly rise above the limitations of individual identity: "et la force n'est pas en nous, mais au-dessus de nous." It is indeed as if this force now continues on of its own accord, as the structures that had been used to contain it – not only in historical reality ("le négrier," below), but in the texture of the poem itself – begin to "crack" under the weight and tension of that which has endured the deferral of liberation:

> le négrier craque de toute part... Son ventre se convulse et ré`sonne... L'affreux ténia de sa cargaison ronge les boyaux fétides de l'étrange nourisson des mers ! (61).

In the passage that immediately follows the above sound-image, this seemingly material substance of the voice continues to produce the sense of a dynamic event taking place, with the return of the core grounding/ascensional figure, introduced earlier ("de boue" => "debout"). In these celebrated lines of the poem, with their enactment of insurrection, the anaphora that relentlessly punctuates the prosodic flow of the text communicates the repeated, emphatic dropping of feet, as one slave after another stands up ("de`bout\")—an "uprising" that takes place on multiple levels, as each site in the sequence is progressively higher: "la cale" => "les cabines" => "le pont" => "le soleil":

> la négraille assise
> inattendument de`bout\
> de`bout\ dans la cale
> de`bout\ dans les cabines
> de`bout\ sur le pont dans le vent
> de`bout\ sous le soleil (61).

As suggested above, as this force is increasingly realized in the text, a corresponding transition in the desire for possession *of* it begins to take place, in contrast to the egocentric imperative that had driven the poem at its opening (the poetic subject's wish to become the agent of just such an authentic, powerful act of expression: "Je dirais orage. Je dirais fleuve. Je dirais tornade," 21). *He would be the possessed now*, abandoning what is most elemental and vital in his thought and voice to an *other* ("je te livre ma conscience et son rythme de chair," 64), inverting one of the oldest formulas of poetic tradition by invoking his muse at the *close* of the poem. Even as he relinquishes his "abrupt speech," the language of the text writhes ("dévore et enroule-toi") in the desire to be invested with an even greater force ("d'un plus vaste frisson"); to be drawn into the wind of *real* change, joined with his risen people ("embrasse NOUS"):

> je te *livre* mes paroles abruptes\
> dévore et enroule-toi
> et t'enroulant embrasse-moi d'un plus vaste fri`sson
> embrasse-moi jusqu'au nous furieux
> em`brasse,\ embrasse `NOUS (64).

It is perhaps in the final lines of the *Cahier*, that the present mode of analysis becomes most relevant to the singular dynamics animating the text. A number of critics have called attention to the somewhat unexpected gesture that concludes the poem—the speaker's decision, at the precise moment a new level of illumination and fraternal love has been reached, to re-descend into the "great black hole" of darker forces. Davis, for instance, identifies this as the concluding iteration of a gesture that has in fact been recurring throughout the text—the same *grounding* in the real that we have observed above:

> In short, the paradise to which the poet/narrator ascends in his transfigured state is not a realm detached from mundane historical and social realities. On the contrary, it is precisely because he has been re-connected, in his visionary ascension,to his cultural umbilicus ("the very navel of the earth") that he is able to transcend the slough of oppression and racism. [...] The black hole (*trou*), then, may be read as an internal cross-reference, signifying, among other things, the spiritual space uncovered by the poet's persistent probing of the depths of a plural black identity (59–60).

In contrast to such a reading, which reduces this amorphous site to a certain level of abstraction ("his cultural umbilicus"), however much it succeeds in situating this key moment of the text in "historical social realities," the formal analyses of the present study have revealed a use of language that demonstrates – or rather, *makes felt* – the acquired mastery of those primal, volatile forces that engender the ascension of the poetic voice at the poem's close. Physically articulated, the final invocation of uprising is as much a gesture of containment, as it is an expansion. The "lasso of stars" "strangles" at the same time it is propulsed outward (through the alliteration of [t] and [l]: "m'é*t*rang*l*ant *d*e *t*on *l*asso *d*'é*t*oi*l*es," below). The repeated command that continues this tightening resonates with the earlier act of insurrection, cited above, with its vertical alignment of repeated, accentuated articulations ("*d*e`*b*out [...] / *d*e`*b*out" => "`*mont*e / `*mont*e"), the final percussive [t] detonating all the more, for being held back (by dense nasals, punctuation, and typography):

> pu*i*s,\ *m'é*t*rang*l*ant *d*e *t*on *l*asso *d*'é*t*oi*l*es
> `*mon*t*e,\ Co*l*ombe\
> `*mon*t*e\
> `*mon*t*e\
> `*mon*t*e\ (65).

Given the centrality of articulation that we have observed in Césaire's process of composition, it is not surprising that the entire poem begins to *close*, quite literally, in such a manner. Not merely through a single, accentuated phoneme but, as perceived by the reader who has attuned him- or herself to the modulations of this voice – the articulated dynamics of the entire text traversed still resonating at some level of the reading experience – through a mode of expression that is at once complex and quite simple in its immediacy.[18] Simultaneously moving toward, and out of enclosed darkness, the voice becomes more distinct and dynamic in localizing the "tongue/language of night" ("la langue [...] de la nuit")—a brief agitation that is in turn enclosed, definitively, by the back nasal punctuating the line's final syllable and the text as a whole ("*verr***ì**`*tion* !\\"):

> et le **g**ra**n**d*t*rou*noir*\où je *v*ou*l*ais me *n*oyer *l'*autre *l*une
> c'est là que je veux pêcher maintenant *l*a *l*angue ma*l*éf**i**que de *l*a *n*u*i*t en son **i**mmob**i***l*e *v*err**ì**`*tion* !\\ (65).

On the semantic level, the text would seem to produce a dead-end here; or perhaps more accurately, an escape route, whereby the poet averts the difficulty of arriving at a definitive resolution, through the mystifying contradiction of the final image—a paradoxical movement in stillness that is all the more confounding for the foreignness of the final term (a "sweeping" of the

---

18   Regarding the reference to series of individual phonemes: many detractors of efforts to put forth a theory of sound symbolism have limited the field of possibilities for such expression to one-to-one, mimetic correspondence, as observed in my Introduction, on pp. 7–8.

tongue, significantly enough (!), as we later discover, having disengaged from the text).[19] And yet, it is precisely the *opacity* of the final term, I would suggest – before we have even taken steps to locate its meaning, and discovered the paradox in which it would seem to participate – that points to the most vital element of the poem. For in suspending the consciousness of the reader here, the poet highlights, through the abrupt *experience* of the text's close – the seemingly inextinguishable movement of his song cut short in the final articulation: "son **immobi***le* **verrì**`*tion* !\\" – what is essential in the successful realization of poetic force—that which is most dynamic, rising up in the voice, when withheld.

---

19   As Igou has astutely observed (70, note 41), the term is in fact a neologism first employed, not by the poet himself, as some critics have proposed, but by the nineteenth-century *gastronome*, Brillat-Savourin, whom she cites: "[la] *verrition* (verro, lat., je balaye) […] [a lieu] quand la langue, se recourbant en dessus ou en dessous, ramasse les portions qui peuvent rester dans le canal demi-circulaire formé par les lèvres et les gencives" (Brillat-Savourin 54–55).

CHAPTER 4

The Wind's Gold: Char

> Il existe une sorte d'homme toujours en avance sur ses excréments.
> CHAR (182).

∴

> Chiure d'intérêts / Chœur / Je t'annule, je t'inhume / Je me prédis. Tais ton pas.
> CHAR, cited in Mathieu (71).

∴

For many readers of French poetry, the work of René Char, increasingly one of the most respected, and securely canonized figures of the twentieth century, might seem out of place among the examples of revolting poetics gathered here. If the theme of revolt is certainly present in his most famous writing (the poems collected in *Les Matinaux*, and especially, in *Fureur et mystère*—much of which was composed during the second world war), the aesthetic of this work is oriented by very different principles than those observed in the preceding studies. Indeed, his often hermetic, laconic voice would appear intentionally opposed to the revolting poetics (particularly in the work of Lautréamont), pervaded as it is by a distinct sense of *conscience*—the dual faculties, conveyed by this single term in French, of awareness and moral imperative.[1] An unwavering lucidity in the creative process seems to check the tendency of poetic expression to intoxicate, allowing him to bypass, precisely, the repeated invectives and verbal inflation we have identified as problematic in the work of others: "Ce qui importe le plus dans certaines situations c'est de maîtriser à temps l'euphorie" (194); "Vers ta frontière, ô vie humiliée, je marche maintenant au pas des certitudes [...]. Folle sœur de ma phrase, ma maîtresse scellée, je te sauve d'un hôtel de décombres" (147).

And yet, in lesser-known publications preceding *Fureur*, a quite different mode of expression predominates—often vehement, exclamatory language

---

[1] Interestingly, Maldoror in fact hunts down and executes an anthropomorphized "conscience" in II:15. See my article analyzing this stanza ("Unexorcised Conscience").

© KONINKLIJKE BRILL NV, LEIDEN, 2016 | DOI 10.1163/9789004324572_006

that, if it is also oriented by moral purpose in many instances (similar to the discourse of the *Cahier*), recalls the revolting poetics observed in the first section of the present work. In contrast to the reserved concision that will be necessary to the *maquisard* ("L'intelligence avec l'ange, notre primordial souci. (Ange, ce qui à l'intérieur de l'homme, tient à l'écart [...] la parole du plus haut silence)," 179), the poetic voice erupts in condemnation, *repeatedly*. The collection *Placard pour un chemin des écoliers*, for instance, dedicated to children killed in the Spanish Civil War, opens with the imprecation: "Incomparables bouchers! Honte! Honte! Honte!" (89). In the publication that follows *Placard*, *Dehors la nuit est gouvernée*, such enunciations recur even more frequently, and in a very specific discourse, familiar to us at this point. While Char's language is at once more esoteric and politically engaged than the assaults undertaken by Baudelaire and Lautréamont, his own attack – on humanity's attachment to and accumulation of things and ideas – also relies on figures from the least savory areas of physical existence, in order to vivify denunciation: "La vieillesse caresse les cartels de ce monde d'aubaines / En souille les paniers" (106); "tu berçais lumière égoïstement ta crasse" (110); "l'aventure du repos n'est plus martelée de sueurs des / irrésistibles gourmandises d'ordures" (104); "Collecteur de la retentissante pourriture cyclique / Ses ressources le dégradent" (116). While largely ignored, in comparison to the masterpieces of those poets treated in the first three chapters of the present study, *Dehors* clearly participates in the same "tradition," and indeed expands the latter's range, as this single *champ lexical* allows the poet to wage war on multiple fronts: political, ethical, artistic, and even "intro-muros" (176)—i.e., within his own mind and creative process.

These elements in *Dehors* have received some critical attention, it should be acknowledged. Voellmy, for instance, has noted the prevalence of exclamations in the work, and their origin in the "double menace" of impending war and serious illness confronting the poet: "exténué par la maladie, il doit lutter à la double menace en l'exprimant avec les sons comme avec les images, et en s'en remettant aux propriétés stimulantes du verbe. Les exhortations à soi-même, les invectives et les défis scandent ces versets fiévreux" (356). And Mathieu has identified Char's use of excess matter in the work as a motif that allows the poet to figure – and transform, in the material of the poem's language – the inequities of society (discussed below). Upon further analysis, however, we find that the repeated elaboration of this motif, particularly *as* exclamation ("Crasse ! / J'ai crié une chance de se recouvrer en victoire," Char 107), has unwanted consequences for the poet's project, unexplored in any depth by critics until now, if immediately familiar to readers of the preceding studies—a production of excess within the writing process itself, whereby *lin-*

guistic matter reproduces itself for the sake of expressive intensity, despite the poet's ostensible control of this process.

As in the first three chapters, this study thus responds to a prevailing critical perspective – in this instance, a tendency to lionize Char as an historical figure – that often glosses over certain "inefficient" structural details of the work in question (recent publications by Bellec and the Bibliothèque nationale, for instance, have focused on biographical circumstances, interspersing passages of text – including reproductions of original manuscripts – with numerous photographs).[2] The present study is not simply intended to call into question a production of myth that has diverted attention from close reading, however, in order to identify inconsistencies within the writing of an often overlooked work (for critical perspectives on such issues, see the iconoclastic statements of Crouzet and Prigent, and the more recent, nuanced analyses of Née and Van Rogger Andreucci). Rather, by situating key texts from *Dehors* in relation to work that follows – several of the first, most lyrical poems appearing in *Seuls demeurent*, published in *Fureur et mystère*, the collection for which Char is first recognized as a major poet – we learn a great deal about how the earlier work evolves into the mature voice of the post-war period.

While the sequence of these works marks a clear, and indeed dramatic transition in Char's writing for the majority of readers,[3] no one has sufficiently analyzed this stage in the development of the poet's distinct voice, down to its very *texture*, as a self-reflexive evolution within the textual process. Through attentive analysis of poems in both phases, we find that the poet, after undergoing a transformative internal experience, has gained a degree of distance in the later period—not only from a previous state of subject-hood, but from a particular relation to language inherent in that state. The "irrésistibles gourmandises d'ordures" of which he himself had become guilty, in savoring his invectives against the forces of oppression and illness, are brought under control within the process of composition.[4] If *matter* is still a central concern in

---

2 Michel has also identified this tendency: "Jusqu'à la fin de sa vie, et au-delà, sa place dans la cité restera marquée par une singulière valorisation de son nom dans l'imaginaire social et politique. [...] (ce qui) tend parfois à recouvrir la lecture de l'œuvre" (9). There are of course exceptions—Schulz's detailed semiotic readings of just three poems, for example, and Mathieu's monumental study of the poet's evolving work.

3 Mathieu, most notably, has traced Char's odyssey through the "night" of historical and internal demons, identifying the catalyst for the poet's release in a powerful romantic encounter (14).

4 This study thus implicitly calls into question readings of *Dehors*, not only by Mathieu (discussed in the following pages), but by the poet Jacques Dupin, and Gourio, the latter having written an excellent analysis of the role of Char's "traversal of night" in Dupin's own work ("La violence, ainsi, sera *exorcisée* par l'écriture, une qui se montre tout à la fois le véhicule de cette

the later work, it is considered from a new level of consciousness—a perspective that allows the poet to finally disengage from his own accumulations of language, leaving behind the "retentissante pourriture cyclique" of earlier writing. In the context of those works problematized in the first section of my book then (*Les Fleurs* and *Maldoror*), this final study is intended to demonstrate – pinpointing in even greater detail the types of metamorphoses we witnessed in the writing process of Césaire – how the revolting poetics comes to transcend its own limitations—dominating no *other* more than itself.

Dehors la nuit est gouvernée: The Economy of *Crasse*

The motif of excess matter, with its various associations, is most clearly and succinctly elaborated in *Dehors* in the short poem "Passerelle." In the first stanza, accumulation and retention ("cartels [...] d'aubaines") are critiqued through the basic oppositions of age and youth, past and future ("vieillesse"/"frai"):

> La vieillesse caresse les cartels de ce monde d'aubaines
> En souille les paniers.
> La troupe chasse les gardiennes du frai
> La babel de langueur se referme toujours indemne (106).[5]

In addition to the political ideology suggested here – the Marxist critique of capitalist society, embraced by the Surrealists during this period – these lines demonstrate the complexity of the *crasse* motif in Char's writing, as this very topical, political discourse intersects with another, distinctly Charian critique.[6] The current, imperfect state of human existence is not simply the result of actual "cartels," and the proletariat's failure to confront them, but is maintained through a continual recycling of existing language, with its pre-formed structures and unvarying meanings. The "babel de langueur" is the fate of any unreflective use of words that fails to move beyond this state of closure ("se referme"); a state that must be disrupted, as the following lines suggest, through

---

 monstruosité et l'épreuve de son assomption. Char n'aurait donc bâti une « *prison* » poétique que pour briser les murs qui le maintiennent sous le joug des puissances de mort," Gourio 151).
5 All further citations of a given poem in the following readings are from the same page, unless otherwise noted.
6 It is important to note that, while Char was influenced early on by the revolutionary politics of the Surrealist group, closely following and identifying with the workers' movement in France (as discussed in the following pages), he would refuse to officially support the Communist party (Leclair 87).

an antidote that "burns" as it liberates, waking us to reality—the *revolting* language of poetry: "Traverse-nous brûlant / Aquilin breuvage de liberté."

There is another element in the elaboration of this motif that reveals a great deal about the function of *crasse* in Char's poetics at this point in his career. As in other texts addressed by the present study, such language becomes most significant for the manner in which it is *invested*—not simply with meaning, but the emotive charge of particular terms when amplified by the structure of the text. Rereading the opening lines of "Passerelle," for instance, we perceive a subtle insistence in the alliteration of the first words—a pattern that not only enacts the "caressing" condemned here – the languorous, delicate gesture effected through the lilting prosody, semi-vowels, and fricatives – but that sets up the accentuated key term in this critique, rendering apparent wealth "filthy":

> La *vieilless*e ca*ress*e les cartels de *c*e monde d'aubaines
> En *souille* les pan*ie*rs.

What is condemned is not merely material excess, but the manner in which it is "handled." As we will observe throughout *Dehors*, such excess is most offensive when fondled and savored—the degree of the poet's disgust corresponding to the amount of pleasure – usually connoted with effeminate, decadent behavior – derived by an *other*. Secondly, these moments of intensity in the poetic voice are heightened by the prosodic and phonetic structures of the language used. While the second of these observations, in and of itself, might seem commonplace in a work of poetic analysis, we will find that the deployment of such effects becomes problematic in these particular texts, actually working against the poet's intentions: the very excess that is condemned is reproduced in the poet's own language. Dense, highly charged passages of the invective discourse reveal an obsession that in fact impedes the poet's desire to leave behind the "night" that oppresses him (*"la nuit* [...] *gouvernée"*).

This symptom of Char's early writing becomes particularly apparent in the longer poem, "Tous Compagnons de lit," a paean to the recent successes of the newly formed workers' movement, *Le Front populaire* (Mathieu 60). An initial reading of the poem would suggest that the more numerous and elaborate articulations of the *crasse* motif here are used productively, in order to be rejected in the space of poem, leading to the statement of conviction in the final lines – "Nous ne nous avouons pas vaincu" – as Mathieu has concluded in his close reading of the poem:

> L'aliénation, alchimie inversée, enlise le « pourvoyeur d'or » dans l'attrait excrémentiel d'une vie plombée [...]." [...] l'insistance des signifiants [...] acccomplit dans le langage le renversement des valeurs, le redressement des allongés : l'or, d'abord engagé dans un contexte sonore où il s'allie à l'aliénation, s'en dégage pour se lier au « repos » « populaire » (61).

And yet, despite the poem's implicit claim to re-enact and help protect this moment of liberation, a closer look at the language of the text, and the way this "matter" is phonetically and emotively invested by the poet, suggests an attachment to the past that inhibits this process.

The opening lines celebrate an emancipated present, in which both the working class and the poet – who has been similarly oppressed, during a recent convalescence – can "flourish" in the recuperative rest that has been won.[7] This positive, forward movement into a new future is accentuated through the overt presence of breath, in repeated fricatives:

> Tous compagnons de lit *fl*orissant dans le *s*ommeil
>   d'au*j*ourd'hui *fr*aternel.
> *S*ur quoi reposent et *v*eillent leurs outils in*fr*anc*h*issables
>   conquis *s*ur la pares*s*e et l'e*x*ploit de tra*v*ail (104).

The same articulations that are deployed to help definitively distance an oppressive past, preserving the victory of this new present, however, are soon used in a return to, and condemnation of the earlier state. The unsavory past is "vomited" up ("temps vomis") in the choking of the back articulations that accompany the resuscitated capitalist "entourage" [ã] [ur], into the halting staccato of the poet's accusation. The material of his "indomitable tools" ("outils in*fr*anc*h*issables") returns in even greater density, as the percussive dentals and labials [t] [d] [p] and compressed, front vowels [i], now also accentuated, allow him to spit out his invective:

> <u>T</u>emps *v*om<u>i</u>s ils roulaient dociles aux avant-postes du
> néant re<u>d</u>ou<u>t</u>ant le *s*or<u>di</u>de en<u>t</u>ou*r*age
> <u>P</u>our*v*oyeurs <u>d</u>'or mais à <u>p</u>eine moins c*h*é<u>ti</u>*f*s q'une
> mo<u>tt</u>e <u>d</u>e c*h*ien<u>d</u>ent\<u>d</u>ans un he<u>ct</u>a*r*e en `*fr*<u>i</u>c*h*e.

---

7 In 1935, Char suffered from a belatedly diagnosed case of blood poisoning, necessitating a month-long hospitalization and a period of convalescence that would last over a year (Leclair 89). Both Leclair and Mathieu (13–14) have provided detailed accounts of this physically painful and psychologically trying experience, and its effect on the poet's creative process.

In the same manner, when the "false dawn" offered by the Church (accomplice in the domination of the working class) is ostensibly left behind, these lines instead move *back* in time, in order to enact the reification of authentic "love" and "hope" effected by organized religion. The end of the passage is punctuated, not by an affirmation of the present (as the opening "aujourd'hui fraternel"), but by a condensation of the past, the dense and heavy qualities of key terms reinforced by the back phonemes ("b**ou**e"/"fa*r*deau"):

> Il ne croisent plus sur la pente affûtée la fausse aurore
> dallée de fossiles célestes et de bissacs de larmes
> Où fatalement l'a*m*our se t*r*ans*m*uait en boue et l'esp**o**ir
> en far`deau.

Whatever the intended movement and effect of the poem, such "regressive" passages stand out as the most dynamic—most markedly, in the reappearance of the extreme, torquing textures we witnessed in the preceding lines (re-cited below, in parentheses), the poetic voice once again leaving the present "adventure of rest" to re-enact perversions of the past:

> L'aventu*r*e d**u** *r*epos n'est pl**u**s ma*r*telée d̲e s**u**eu*r*s d̲es i*r*résis̲t̲ibles
> gou*r*mand̲ises d̲'o*r*du*r*es
> (P̲ou*r*voyeu*r*s d̲'o*r* mais à p̲eine moins chétifs qu̲'une
> mot̲te d̲e chien d̲ent\dans un hectare en f*r*iche).

While such passages do not actually re-enact historical events, of course, the expressive intensity brought into relief leads one to suspect that the poet himself is indeed savoring (and inviting us to savor) this "irresistible gluttony." The fundamental, if un-avowed motivation for the act of composition here, paradoxically, may not be his desire to transcend a corrupt, unjust past, but rather, a need to *articulate* that past state—an opportunity to condemn (and to relish condemning) the oppressor. By the time we arrive at the poem's close, these passages still resonating, it is hard not to question the claimed intransigence of the final lines: "Nous ne tolérons pas d'être interrompus par la laideur comédienne d'une voix / Nous ne nous avouons pas vaincu [...]" (105). The poet has not only "tolerated," but has actively participated in the "ugly interruptions" of his own voice.

A reading of "Confins" proves significant at this point, for the way this poem both aligns with, and deviates from the content and structure of the text just analyzed. Recounting Char's extended illness and convalescence, noted above, it grounds the declaration of solidarity with the oppressed in personal experience. And as in "Tous compagnons," the poet envisions a new state of well-being, unencumbered by oppressive forces (in this case, both physical and psychological). It differs from the earlier poem, however, in situating the instant of the enunciation *in medias res*—a brief "pause" in the state of oppression, assigned the task of actually "composing" the movement into a liberated present:

> Clarté frugale un bien limpide à la pause
> Chemise prête au vœu de vêtir une larme
> Pour composer la plus inoccupée des routes (106).

If a negative past is revisited here, it would seem to serve, not merely as an object of condemnation, but as something to be definitively transcended. While, in the following lines, the reward for lucidity initially appears limited to the knowledge that one's life has been irreparably broken ("tout bénéfice au conservateur du phare / le calendrier mis en pièces"), such awareness will perhaps also allow one to move beyond the burdensome remains of this event ("cendres"), "progressing" through a traumatic past ("cicatrices"): "L'homme accroupi sur ses cendres infidèles a progressé / par cicatrices." And yet, it is precisely at the moment the poem seems on the point of effecting this movement, rising back through the past to rediscover a previous state of wholeness ("à travers le filtre feint de son dépaysement"), that the voice erupts in a condemnation of the present "filth" still surrounding the poetic subject:

> Sera-ce toujours tout bénéfice au conservateur du phare
>   le calendrier mis en pièces après quelque naufrage
>   hilarant
> L'homme accroupi sur ses cendres infidèles a progressé
>   par cicatrices et monté la somme de ses pas à travers
>   le filtre feint de son dépaysement
> Crasse !

The process of investment, observed in the preceding analyses, is even more apparent here. The exclamatory force of the final term is not derived from its semantic connotations and punctuation alone, but from its phonetic structure as well; a sequence that, heightened by accentuation, violently expulses the voice—from the friction of the back consonants [kR], into the central [a], releasing from the front of the mouth in the prolonged sibilance of [s] (recalling Baudelaire's "<u>cra</u>`ch<u>e</u>r," analyzed on pp. 57–58 of chapter 1): "<u>Cra</u>sse !" Furthermore, the force of this exclamation, which seems to arise spontaneously out of the poet's frustrated monologue, has in fact accumulated in the preceding lines, building up from the "crouching man," and eventually pulsating against the obstruction placed before it (`ƒi`ltre `ƒe`int):

> L'homme a*ccr*oupi *sur ses* cen*dr*es in*f*idèles a p*rogr*essé
>   par c*icatr*ices et monté la *s*omme de *s*es pa*s* à *tr*avers
>   le `*f*i*ltr*e `*f*eint de *s*on dépay*s*ement
> `*Cr*asse !

And yet, despite the significant investment of force in this term, the carefully placed projectile of the poet's language cannot displace the accumulated matter, it would seem, and must be re-iterated:

> [...] le `*f*i*ltr*e `*f*eint de *s*on dépay*s*ement
> `*Cr*asse !
> **Q**ue la *ch*ambre des ma*ch*ines se *c*ou*ch*e à tes pieds
> `*Cr*asse ! (106–7).

The poet himself would appear to acknowledge, in the following lines, that the "chance" of producing an enduring "victory" for his voice through such an aggressive force, with its continual "pile of unemployed prey," is minimal. All that will remain, as we arrive at the cul-de-sac of the poem ("la rue de notre perdition"), are the fragments of what encased a brief surge of intensity:

> J'ai crié une chance de se recouvrer en victoire longue et aplanissante
> Telle que ton bras s'étendant se perpétuerait en toit
> Rouge d'un tas de proies inemployées.
> Achevés nous voici arrivés à la rue de notre perdition
> Bris de coquilles vigueur (107).

These lines in fact serve to highlight the inherent conflict within Char's creative process at this stage of his career. In order that a crucial transition take place in his work, he will need to somehow resolve the conflict between his desire for a continuous intensity in the poetic enunciation, and his insistence that the material of the latter not obscure, or be mistaken for the essence of such intensity—its vital and ephemeral core.

Another poem in the collection, "L'Essentiel intelligible," further suggests that Char is aware of the "comic ugliness" that inevitably accompanies what is most dynamic in his own voice, and that he is attempting to navigate this problematic in the process of composition. The opening line of the penultimate section, "Je suis interdit," can be read in two ways—the writing subject is at once alienated by language, and continually immersed *in* it, unable to extricate himself ("inter-dit"):

> Je suis interdit
> Distingué j'ai élu
> Ce fut paille d'un bruit acné d'un éclair
> Présent à l'ancre où vais-je égarer cette fortune d'excréments
> Qui m'escorte comme une lampe
> Verbiage d'architecte [...] (110).

The poetic event is immediately displaced by the dessicated stalk ("paille") and lesions ("acné") that remain, the poet's ability to briefly illuminate the night ("éclair") negated. If there is light here, it is indeed negative—a heightened lucidity from which he cannot escape. Most significantly, the "fortune of excrement" is no longer the discourse of a despised *other*, as elsewhere in *Dehors*, but of the poet himself. In the lines that follow, Char in fact seems to be seeking a way for his poetry to transcend this sterile economy, as a positive, "beautiful" presence is invoked – an idealized feminine figure that would hover above the poet's "refuse": "Belle dont je me prive plane sur mes déchets stériles" – and the hope of a new, unified state of being is held out: "Mais tout coïncidera à nouveau." Yet once again, in a progression (or more accurately, *regression*, as suggested earlier) now familiar from the preceding analyses, the poet proposes an ideal state, only to follow it with a violent expulsion of, and against language, punctuating the close of the text. The fragile state of continuity evoked in the penultimate line is effaced by what immediately follows, the awkward exclamation of the final terms heightened by the mid-line insertion of "lumière," unpunctuated (highlighted with backward slashes below); an illumination that jolts the reader, unexpected:

> La frêle attardée des pistes se dirigeait sur la rosée fanée
> Tandis que tu berçais\lumière***égoïs**tement ta `**cra**sse.

This conflict within the young poet's creative process becomes so *pronounced* in *Dehors*, that it takes the form of a dialogue in one of the last poems ("Remise"), the voice of poethical conscience entering in to arrest the movement toward an apparent moment of sovereignty and lyrical effusion:

> Laissez filer les guides maintenant c'est la plaine
> ....

> Des êtres bienveillants se porteront vers nous
> La main à votre front sera froide d'étoiles
> Et pas un souvenir de couteau sur les herbes
>
> Non le bruit de l'oubli là serait tel
> Qu'il corromprait la vertu du sang et de la cendre
> Ligués à mon chevet contre la pauvreté
> Qui n'entend que son pas n'admire que sa vue
> Dans l'eau morte de son ombre (122).

Even as his writing involves a process of reflection on, and censorship of tendencies to material excess, however – not only in an exterior other, but in his own activity as a poet – Char appears unable to entirely disengage from these tendencies. Throughout *Dehors*, that which is decried for its recurring, obstructive presence is invoked for these very qualities: in the repeated expulsion of *crasse*, resistant matter serves as a source for the production of dynamics in the voice—literally, as we have observed, in the guttural articulations demanded by the text. Such figures are of limited use, ultimately, both because they are in conflict with the ideal of progress (whether in society or the poet's own creative process) valorized in these poems, and because, on a more immediate, aesthetic level, they do not afford the type of sustained expressive force that will distinguish Char's mature work. In the poems published immediately after *Dehors*, we will find that the transition into such a mode of expression has been effected, not simply in the resolution of a problematic relation to language, but through a new ability to negotiate conflicts within the process of composition. Similarly to Césaire's *Cahier*, *Seuls demeurent* reveals a writer who, having succeeded in reproducing a certain event or presence – whether positive or negative, past or present – is capable of letting go of what has been expressed, allowing a new force to seemingly surge up of its own accord from the progression of the poem.

Seuls demeurent: New Remains

> La terre est ainsi comprise comme lieu d'une immanence qui est déjà une transcendance, lieu où toute notion d'avoir se transmue en sentiment d'être et, ainsi, récuse et déthrône la possibilité même de l'échec, de la perte.
> BISHOP ("L'avenir" 132).

The optimistic "Jeunesse" directly references this transitional moment in Char's life and writing, in the form – interestingly enough – of another dialogue. The poem would indeed seem to take up again the conflict introduced in "Remise," analyzed above—though with significantly different results. While the earlier text reflected a desire to move beyond the limited discursive structure organizing most of the poems in *Dehors* – an alienated subject speaking *about* or *at* an objectified other – the conversational form here demonstrates a new ability to remain aware of, and actually mediate conflicts within the writing psyche—where much of the struggle depicted in the poet's earlier work was actually taking place, as we observed. Char's new relation to, and acceptance of his own writing is expressed in the simplicity of a single line, which rings out of the space separating it from the surrounding text:

> Éloge, nous nous sommes acceptés (132).[8]

The simple element of spacing here is actually quite significant, as the sense of intimacy in these new poems depends, paradoxically, upon a certain detachment within the writing process—an ability to distance the instant of enunciation from the past, both lived and written. In the final lines of the text, following an extended exclamation of regret, by a second voice (distinguished by *guillemets*: "« si l'éclair m'avait ouvert sa grille, si tes nuits m'avaient pardonné… »"), the voice that opened the poem returns to interrupt:

> Regard, verger d'étoiles, les genêts, la solitude sont distincts de vous ! Le chant finit l'exil. La brise des agneaux ramène la vie neuve.

At its close, the poem itself thus enacts the central figure of the opening lines —the fountain, which continually "gives birth to [it]self," despite its inevitable falling:

> Loin de l'embuscade des tuiles et de l'aumône des calvaires, vous vous donnez naissance, otages des oiseaux, fontaines.

Where Char's earlier work *insisted* on the inexorable processes of entropy and condensation, despite the poet's supposed resistance to these forces, the poetic enunciation justifies itself here, rising up out of the remains of an unresolved past. "Song finishes the exile" the poet had imposed upon himself.

---

8 For other analyses of this line, and the poem in general, see Raybaud (144) and Dupouy (193).

It is important to note, however, that this new, affirmative impulse in Char's writing does not appear independently of the lucidity observed in the earlier poems. Similar to what we observed in Césaire's transformative work, the authenticity of the lyrical *élan* that now appears in Char's poetry depends on an acknowledgement of those forces that have worked, and would continue to work against this "birth" of a new voice. The appearance of the fountain, in the above poem, for instance, is immediately followed by a declaration that includes figures and qualities encountered in our reading of *Dehors* ("nausée," "cendres," "vindicative"):

> La pente de l'homme faite de la nausée de ses cendres, de l'homme en lutte avec sa providence vindicative, ne suffit pas à vous désenchanter.

While this passage includes the strong presence of self-censorship ("la nausée de ses cendres") observed in the preceding collection, it nonetheless differs significantly, both in the degree of self-awareness demonstrated – the abstract, often politicized *other* of the earlier poems replaced by the autobiographical "man" – and more importantly, in the way this awareness is now utilized, more effectively, in new acts of creation. The confident surge of affirmation in this and other poems of the later period arises in inverse relation to the restrictive forces imposed upon the subject by *conscience*—here, the downward propensity ("la pente") of introspection.

We find a very similar structure in "Allègement," where a self-reflexive process of composition is no longer burdened by its perceived imperfections, but able to incorporate and transform them. As the principal voice of "Jeunesse" brought the lyric enunciation back up from, *against* the gravity of the past, the voice that opens this poem (also in *guillemets*) "declines the refuge" of past suffering, instead choosing to inhabit a dynamic space of indeterminacy:

> « J'errais dans l'or du vent, déclinant le refuge des villages où m'avaient connu des crève-cœur extrêmes » (134).

Whether or not the poet is referring specifically to the experience of convalescence depicted in "Confins," analyzed above, this line suggests he is in any case aware of, and reacting to problematic *textual* phenomena in that poem, and in *Dehors* more generally. Not only do the "crève-cœur extrêmes" here suggest, in the context of this enclosed "refuge/village," the angst depicted in the earlier poem, but the articulation of this figure recalls that text's key, expressive term, redeploying a similar, if muted, affective charge: "<u>Cr</u>a<u>s</u>se ! / [...] / <u>Cr</u>a<u>s</u>se !" => "<u>cr</u>è<u>v</u>e-<u>c</u>œu<u>r</u> e<u>xtr</u>êmes." Having attained a degree of distance from such experiences, however, observing these "villages" from outside, the poet no longer employs phonetic structures in order to lash out, but is able to merely evoke "extreme" moments, detached.

This has a significant effect on the continued development of the text. While the subject of "Confins" could only hope his exclamations would somehow lead to a "victory," composed of the defeated's bloody carcasses, for instance ("J'ai crié une chance de se recouvrer en victoire longue et aplanissante / Telle que ton bras s'étendant se perpétuerait en toit / Rouge d'un tas de proies inemployées"), the success of the present text *is* actually granted, in an "unraveling" of beauty. Where the convalescent's brief moment of respite ("un bien limpide à l'instant de la pause") only led to a greater sense of his confinement and degradation, the detached lucidity of the matured poet allows him to "extract" a sense of reassurance from this arrested moment—a sort of intimated, angelic presence which – unlike the similar figure from "L'Essentiel intelligible," analyzed on p. 160 – believed in, blossoms subtly into reality:

> « Du torrent épars de la vie arrêtée, j'avais extrait la signification loyale d'Irène. La beauté déferlait de sa gaine fantasque, donnait des roses aux fontaines ».[9]

The undulations of this unraveling, furthermore, are actually allowed to take place in the fabric of the text itself, in a way the anti-lyrical, avant-garde poetics of Char's earlier work would have prohibited. As the composition expands, repetitions begin to appear and resonate, one texture passing into the next. Whatever meaning the poet may have actually "extracted" from his "extreme" states, the latter are transformed, *poetically*, in the course of these few lines, as they pass from one echo to the next, propulsing the text ("extrêmes => Irène => gaine => fontaines"):

> « J'errais dans *l'or* du *v*ent,\ dé*cl*inant *le refuge* des *v*i*ll*ages où m'avaient *c*onnu des *c*rève-*cœur* e*x*`*tr*êmes.\ Du *t*orren*t* épars de la *v*ie arrê*t*ée,\ j'avais e*xt*rait *la* signi*fic*a*t*ion *l*oyale *d*'I*`r*ène.\ *L*a beau*t*é *d*é*f*er*l*ait *d*e sa *g*a*i*ne *f*an*t*asque,\ *d*onnait *d*es *r*oses aux *f*on`*t*aines.\ »

The poet's new-found control of the writing process is most evident, however, in the way he now handles the inevitable end of this unraveling, and what remains—the textual matter that always exceeds any ephemeral flashes of insight produced. In contrast to the preceding collection, in which the

---

9 This feminine presence probably corresponds, at least in part, to an actual individual—Irène Hamoir, with whom Char was briefly involved in the fall of 1937 (Leclair 100).

insistence on these remains seemed forced, burdening the text ("Bris de coquilles vigueur / [...] des loques de secousses," "mes déchets stériles"), Char is now able to incorporate this moment of lucidity into the transformative process developed throughout the text. As in "Jeunesse," the state of detachment attained by the writer is reflected in the plurality of the poetic voice—in this instance, where the first person narrative (in *guillemets*) is suddenly replaced by the third person; as if the poetic subject were observing himself from outside, an *other*: "j'avais extrait la signification loyale d'Irène. [...] La neige *le* surprit". While Char would have at one time fetishized this definitive moment of reification, he now focuses, not on the dead form rendered by "winter," but on the task of somehow preserving what was once vital in that form, despite its current absence. In drawing the essence of this enigmatic *rencontre* into himself ("Il en but à longs traits"), he is able to leave the site of the poem behind; not forcibly, but, through an admirable formulation, "carried" by his insistent belief, *despite* reality ("superstition")—a controlled "wave" that is felt in new, as well as returning rhythms and resonances ("*signification*" => "*superstition*"; "*villages*" => "*la neige*," "*visage*"; "*fontaines*" => "*laine*"):

> La neige le surprit.\ Il se pencha sur le visage anéanti,\ en but à longs traits la superstition.\ Puis il s'éloigna,\ porté par la persévérance de cette houle,\ de cette 'laine.

The permanent form of the text no longer encumbers the transitory event it presents, but allows the latter to appear and disappear as if organically. Furthermore, it is as if the poetic processing of this event allows the sense of presence experienced to somehow continue on, resonating at a profound level of the poet's being, drawing him out of the past and into the future.

The poem that most fully demonstrates the transition in Char's creative process at this point, however, is surely "Calendrier"—the first section of which is cited below in its entirety:

> J'ai lié les unes aux autres mes convictions et agrandi ta Présence. J'ai octroyé un cours nouveau à mes jours en les adossant à cette force spacieuse. J'ai congédié la violence qui limitait mon ascendant. J'ai pris sans éclat le poignet de l'équinoxe. L'oracle ne me vassalise plus. J'entre : j'éprouve ou non la grâce (133).

As in the poems analyzed above, this first half of the text reveals a writing process that is highly self-reflexive, figuring problematic elements of past work in order to move beyond them—in fact deriving a certain force from this letting go: "J'ai congédié la violence qui limitait mon ascendant." But even more convincing, this particular text unabashedly effects the lyrical *anabasis*—a tendency toward ascension that was often present in the earlier poems, only to be "grounded" ("Présent à l'ancre"): "mon ascendant"; "le poignet de l'équinoxe." The poet has seemingly found a way to pull himself up (or to *be pulled* up) out of the continual conflict between the forces of day and night that became problematic in the preceding collection.

Furthermore, this new sense of resolution and affirmation is articulated, even more noticeably than in those poems analyzed above, in the material structures of the text. The first phrase immediately enacts the dynamic, generative event recounted, through its phonetic and prosodic structures. The methodical "binding" ("J'ai lié les unes aux autres") is sensed in the halting series of monosyllabic terms leading up to the enclosed (by bookend back articulations) "/**convic*ti*ons**\"; a tension that is then released in the expansion of "presence," with the forward movement of the articulated series in "ag*ran*d**i**," and the sibilance of the final term itself:

> *J*'ai *lié l*es\unes\au*x*\aut*r*es\mes **convic*ti*ons**\ et ag*ran*d**i** ta **P**r**é**`sence.

This movement now continues into the following phrase, as the pattern is repeated, reconfigured. With the transformation of "convictions" into "presence," Char can "render a new course" for his voice by redeploying these controlled kinetic forces ("**convic*ti*ons** [...] **P**r**é**`sence" => "oc*tr*oyé [...] s**p**a`*cieu*se"), the final sense of expansion in the fricatives again heightened by the contrasting density of back phonemes in the first half of the line:

> *J*'ai oc*tr*oyé un **cou***r*s nou*v*eau à mes *jou*rs en les a**d**ossant à ce**tt**e *f*orce s**p**a`*cieu*se.

The poet's new optimism in life, and ability to generate morale, are mirrored in this willingness to cultivate potentials for cohesion and resonance in the material of textual production.

Perhaps the most striking aspect of the poem, however, is to be found in the continuing elaboration of these textural configurations, producing a degree of regularity that was resisted in the earlier work, while allowing the poem to move beyond itself, bypassing the production of unwanted accumulations. Instead of attempting to violently rupture an existing discourse, as in earlier work ("`**C***r*asse !"), the poet forces his language into increasing concision, eliminating the "piles of prey" ("des tas de proies inemployées") accumulated to sustain the voice in its nocturnal voyage:

L'Oracle ne me vassalise plus. J'entre : j'éprouve ou non la grâce.

And as the text enacts this renunciation of excess, with its increasingly succinct phrases, the forward, ascensional movement out of the past is continually assured through resonance with key dynamic terms that preceded. In relinquishing his proclivity for textual violence, the poet simultaneously grounds the enunciation in the extant matter of the poem ("agrandi," "Présence," "adossant"), and allows it to rise up—the elimination of the sibilant in "violence" cutting short the final term, while emphasizing its verticality: "violence" => "ascendant\":

J'ai con*g*é*di*é la *vio*lence qui limi*t*ait m*o*n a*s*cen*d*ant\.

While sacrificing the high degree of intensity that had oriented his work ("J'ai pris sans éclat"), the poet nonetheless actively elevates and refines the poetic enunciation, as the source of the poem reappears within more open, and discrete articulated textures ("<u>c</u>onvi<u>c</u>tions" => "équi<u>n</u>o<u>x</u>e"), the vertical "taking" of this "wrist" echoing the generative structures found in each of the preceding lines ("*J*'ai l*i*é," "*J*'ai octro*y*é," "*J*'ai con*g*é*di*é"):

J'ai <u>p</u>ris *l*e <u>p</u>oi*gn*et de *l*'équi*n*o<u>x</u>e.

And when the abrupt announcement of "entering" (cited above) definitively ends the series of past acts, bringing the text into the present, the poet nonetheless allows this acceptance of vulnerability to resonate with preceding elements of openness in the poem ("Présence," "spacieu*s*e," "l'équino*x*e" => "grâce"):

J'en<u>t</u>re\ : *J*'é<u>p</u>rou*v*e ou *n*on *l*a gr**â**ce =>.

While the poem could effectively end here, it continues into a second section—a choice that would initially appear to undermine the controlled tension achieved up to this point, since it immediately involves the poet's return, yet again, to a problematic past. More than any of the texts analyzed thus far, however, these lines in fact demonstrate the degree to which Char has become cognizant of the pitfalls arising in his creative process. The "shattered calendar" of *Dehors* can be redeemed by the present poem ("Calendrier"), only if the poet's capacity to bind his convictions into a new future also allows him to dissolve past conglomerations. And indeed, following the opening statement of this second section – that the past "menace" has been "smoothed out" ("La menace s'est polie") – the language of the poem performs just such an operation. The awkward density of the following articulations no longer suggests self-indulgent pleasure, in hypocritical condemnation (the "irrésistibles gourmandises d'ordures," observed earlier), but reflects an ability to use productively the expressive forces of language. The text is progressively liberated from the "regressive legends" that once cluttered the landscape of the poet's imagination, as the heavy darkness and choke of back articulations ("**b**ras **l**ou**r**ds") are gradually incorporated into the fluid, brisk, and evenly paced undulations of the front series—as if the latter's clear sibilance was literally dissolving the obstructive matter of language:

> La menace s'est polie. La plage qui chaque hiver
> s'encombra**i**t de *régress***i***ves l***é***gen*des, de s**i**b**y***lles* aux
> **b**ras *l*ou**r**ds d'or**t***i*es, se **p**ré**p**a**r**e aux ê**t**res à se**c**ou**r**ir. *Je*
> sais **q**ue la **c**ons**c***i*en**c**e **q**u**i** se **r***i*s**q**ue n'a *ri*en à re**d**ou**t**er
> **d**e *l*a `*plane* =>.

This mastery of compositional process is remarkable for the way it corresponds to changes within the poet himself. For the ability to *write through* subjective memory, detaching himself from the obsessive tendency to fetishize this past in language, coincides with a profound existential and ethical transformation of the writing subject: a "conscience," significantly enough (given this chapter's opening remarks), that in "risking itself," is poised to recognize, and even help other beings. His vision of regeneration is not perhaps any more definitively consummated in reality, as a result; the poet no less vulnerable to the alienating attraction of his own language than in the poems of struggle that precede this work. But the coordinates for a path have been established— a potential way through the linguistic conglomerations that must be acknowledged each time René Char begins the work of writing a poem. A revolution, if endless, beyond revolting.

Conclusion

The revolt that comes to define much of French poetry in the modern era thus undergoes a number of significant transformations, as poets are forced to reflect on the limits, as well as the inherent possibilities in this new paradigm for expression. As Baudelaire discovers that brute expressive force can be accessed, not only in imagery and vocabulary, but in the very *body* of language – previously constrained or ignored, according to aesthetic conventions – this recognition subsequently calls for another, more self-reflective approach on the part of those who follow. Whatever level of lucidity Lautréamont might demonstrate or claim, while amplifying and "exaggerating" the dark Romanticism of an earlier generation, he cannot help indulging in comparable excesses in his own meta-genre, however innovative, unable to control a liberating process of composition that originates, to a great degree, in the psychosomatic drives of the writing subject. By attaining a higher level of self-awareness in – or more accurately, *through* – the writing process, Césaire and Char are able to recognize their own participation in the production of excess and corruption they critique, discovering ways of controlling and rechanneling the forces of revolt for the sake of affirmation.

The conclusion to such a study would not be satisfactory, particularly given the time elapsed since the later of those publications treated, without considering the legacy of this evolving "tradition." Do elements of the revolting poetics, that is to say, from any of the stages identified here – whether transgressive or redemptive – continue to define, or even figure in the work of succeeding poets? The answer would seem to be an unequivocal yes, when considering the most prominent post-war poets directly following in the path of Char, generally associated with the journal *L'Éphémère*—Yves Bonnefoy and Jacques Dupin, in particular. For both men, an authentic poetic event can only take place, in the wake of what has preceded (both in the poetic tradition, and historically in general), where the coherence and integrity of its expression is contested from within; where the intensity of the lyric is not simply defused in detached nihilism, but survives in a more austere, and patient form of creative energy, surviving the ruins the poet must acknowledge and incorporate. In his *Hier régnant désert,* Bonnefoy proclaims an (anti-)aesthetic that could just as easily be attributed to Dupin (and indeed, to a good number of contemporary poets)—"La Cime de l'imperfection" (the poem's title) that the modern poet should strive to reach:

> Il y avait qu'il fallait détruire et détruire et détruire,
> Il y avait que le salut n'est qu'à ce prix
> Ruiner la face nue qui monte dans le marbre,
> Marteler toute forme toute beauté.
> Aimer la perfection parce qu'elle est le seuil,
> Mais la nier sitôt connue, l'oublier morte (152).

And just as significant, we can perceive this drive to imperfection in the sound and articulation of Bonnefoy's language—effects that we immediately recognize at this point. The enigmatic, violently metamorphosed body at the center of his most famous work, *Du Mouvement et de l'immobilité de Douve*, is the body of the text itself, in fact. A "strange music" indeed arises from the ruptured and decomposing matter of the lines below; the compressed forces of "musique saugrenue" – enclosed by the labialized [y] and back articulations – are released, after circulating outward on the semantic level of the text ("dans les mains, dans les genoux"), in the cracked open head—site of reasoning thought and subjective identity:

> La /mus**i**que s*au*g*r*enue\ commen*c*e dans les ma*i*ns,\ dans les *g*enoux,\ p*ui*s *c*'est la t*ê*te\qu**i**\`c*r*aque\ (52).[1]

Like the complex textures observed in the preceding chapters, such effects are not the result of a single, salient phonetic series alone ("t*ê*te\qu**i**\c*r*aque\"), but arise in the course of a carefully structured passage. In a similar sound-image, from the same work, as invasive roots slowly shatter this body – the latter condensing at the end of the first line ("dans\son\co*r*ps\") – this rupturing then "radiates" outward, transformed into the discrete, "strident" sounds of insects—as if, in articulating this precise, percussive series, the reader him- or herself were biting through the subject *matter* of the poem:

> [...] où des racines trouvent leur chemin dans\son\co*r*ps\ – elle *r*ayonn*e* une *joie* st*r***i**dent*e*\ *d*'insec*t*es,\ **U**ne m**U**s**i**que a`*ff*re**u**se (56).

The expressive intensity sought by the poet is not realized through the imagery or general tone of the enunciation alone, but physically *enacted*, "flaming out" of the straining body of the text:

---

1 The slashes around "/musique saugrenue\" are intended to denote the generally enclosed, contracted state of the buccal cavity throughout this articulation—an effect that is not completely conveyed through the highlighting of particular phonemes. As in preceding analyses, the front [y] is annotated based on its participation in this enclosed texture.

Ce **bras** que tu *soul*èves *s*oudain `*s*'ou*v*re,\ *s*'en`*flam*me (50).

Conflict and rupture are even more central to the poetry of Dupin. A protégé of Char (who helped him to publish his first collection of poems, *Cendrier du voyage*, in 1950), he has clearly embraced the revolting poetics inherited – and modified, as I have suggested – by the older poet. In elements of "La Trêve," from his *Suite basaltique*, we can indeed identify *all* of the different individuals and phases in the history traversed by the preceding chapters—in both the violent, agonistic scene at the work's origin ("Je l'ai [...] combattu pied à pied"),[2] and the regenerative function of such violence, when its enactment is oriented by self-reflection ("Le temps rectifiera la trace de nos luttes" => "[J'ai] [e]nfanté à chaque rupture"):

> Le temps rectifiera la trace de nos luttes,
> Donnant une raison, un toit, à mes poussées de fièvre.
> Je l'ai débusqué, combattu pied à pied,
> Étranglé dans chaque nœud,
> Enfanté à chaque rupture.
> Aujourd'hui nous faisons route ensemble
> Comme le fleuve et le rideau de peupliers.
> Les chiens qui dorment dans ma voix
> Sont toujours des chiens enragés (30).[3]

And similarly, in "La Patience," from *À l'aplomb* ("tandis que ma fureur et mon dénuement luttaient" => "je naissais"):

> Au tremblement de la rose et du fer, à l'étincelle de la forge, tandis que ma fureur et mon dénuement luttaient et s'anéantissaient devant la force de l'unique amour, je naissais... Le rocher, où finit la route et où commence le voyage, devint ce dieu abrupt et fendu auquel se mesure le souffle (71).

---

2 One thinks particularly of Baudelaire's "Duellum" and "La Mort des artistes," and of *Maldoror* in general.

3 Elsewhere, in *Moraines*, Dupin situates himself more directly in relation to the poetic tradition: "Rompre et ressaisir, et ainsi renouer. Dans la forêt nous sommes plus près du bûcheron que du promeneur solitaire. Pas de contemplation innocente. Plus de hautes futaies traversées de rayons et de chants d'oiseaux mais des stères de bois en puissance. Tout nous est donné, mais pour être forcé, pour être entamé, en quelque façon pour être détruit,—et nous détruire" (165). Pagination for all of the following citations of Dupin corresponds to the major collection of his work (1963–1982), *Le corps clairvoyant*.

If Dupin has learned to contain and preserve the intensity of his voice – the "rabid dogs" who "sleep" there – the pulsional, *textural* forces that distinguish the revolting poetics, far from dormant, are even more pronounced than in the writing of Bonnefoy. Such forces are indeed frequently deployed, calling attention to the willed "imperfection" of poetic language as a transparent and stable conduit for full signification, and disrupting any illusion of repose achieved by the poem—as in the closing lines of *Saccades*:

<u>P</u>a*r*ole <u>d</u>é*ch*Ique`<u>t</u>ée,\
*Fi*en<u>t</u>e\d**U** *f*eu <u>p</u>er<u>p</u>é<u>t</u>uel (96).

Dupin's continual struggle with this more volatile mode of expression demands a greater presence in the text as well—an exertion that, involving the body of the writing subject (not arising from some unlocalizable site of thought alone) must manifest itself in the body of language (again, from *Saccades*):

Mon co*r***ps** [...]
. . . .
 Comme un *s*ang*li*e*r* empê<u>t</u>*r*é <u>d</u>ans *l*es `**b**asses `**b**ran*ch*es
 <u>T</u>U *t*ré`<u>p</u>i*g*nes,\ <u>t</u>U\<u>t</u>e\<u>d</u>é`<u>b</u>ats (94).

And yet, like Césaire and Char, Dupin is also able to distance himself from such forces at the very moment he participates in their "detonation"—as in "La déesse par excellence" (*À l'aplomb*):

*J*e n'ai plus la *voix sèche* des ado*l*es*c*ents <u>q</u>u**i** gue<u>tt</u>ent *l*es <u>d</u>é<u>t</u>ona`*t*i*o*ns\ (72).

Such intensive structures in Dupin's work are not limited to individual lines, or passages, furthermore, but can be found extended over the course of an entire poem, as observed in work treated in the preceding chapters. In "Le point du jour," for instance, from the original *Le Corps clairvoyant* (the first section of *L'Embrasure*), the initial "scraping of shovels" anticipates a surging presence, producing it *now* in the text ("**ra**<u>c</u>*l*ement" => "**J'é**<u>c</u>**r**i*r*ai"), while continuing to anchor the voice in the dark matter of the "tomb" it leaves behind on the semantic level ("Passé [...] [l]es **tombeaux**")[4]—elements

---

4 As annotated in similar passages, the [y] of "**gu**<u>tt</u>**U**ra*l*e" is in bold, as well as larger font (for its front articulation), due to the back velars encasing it ([g], [R]), the general closure of the buccal cavity, and the semantic connotations of the term itself.

that are intertwined throughout the succeeding texture, producing a *torsion* within the voice, also familiar to us by now ("*la* p*o*r*t*e\d*u**t*o*ri*l" "*ro*c\ et *t*o*r*peu*r*"):

> P*a*ssé *le* r*a*c*l*ement des p*e*l*l*es
> Et *l'*éc*u*me *d*es *t*om*b*eaux,\
> *J'*éc*r*i*r*ai c*o*mme e*lle* j*a*i*ll*it,\
>
> Ve*r*t*i*g*i*neu*s*e, g*u*tt*u*r*al*e,
>
> D*e*b*o*ut cont*r*e *ce* b*o*i*s* qui *s*e `*f*end,\
> Ma *t*ab*l*e *r*en*v*er*s*ée, *la* p*o*r*t*e\d*u**t*o*ri*l.
> . . . .
> P*r*o*l*onge*a*nt *l'*â*c*re *j*ou*i*ss*a*nce
> De me *v*oir naî*t*re et demeu*r*er
> *F*ou*r*che et de*v*in,\ `*ro*c\ et *t*o*r*`peu*r* (105).

While the revolting poetics clearly maintains a vital presence in the work of these post-war poets, however, its legacy appears less certain when considering more recent writing. In his *Adieux au poème*, poet and critic Jean-Michel Maulpoix confronts any remaining readers of poetry with a bleak diagnosis. Increasingly entrenched in the consciousness of this tradition, the disabused, critical perspective of the first post-Romantic poets becomes less a source of generative force, than of entropy, "exhausting" ("tout ce qui mine") what was once the most affective form of literary expression:

> La poésie française de ce temps s'est nourrie, jusqu'à l'étouffement, de tout ce qui mine, empêche et paralyse le chant. Ayant pris acte du désastre, elle n'en finit plus de répéter la fracture, le défaut et l'évidement. [...] Étrangère, hostile à ses anciens rêves, fatiguée de son impuissance, honteuse de ce qu'est devenu le monde, la poésie voudrait en finir avec sa propre histoire (10).

The conflicted nihilism of a Lautréamont is no longer rendered in *song* (*Les Chants de Maldoror*), with a dynamic, cadenced linguistic texture – however grotesque – but is instead "blanched" of any salient musicality; an "object," the materiality of which is a curse, and no longer a cause for celebration:

> Voilà bien des années pourtant que les modernes s'efforcent de *blanchir* le poème de ses fautes en le délivrant de la musique et des images. Amaigri, appauvri, interdit de Chant, le voici devenu un rude et sobre objet de langue (Ibid. 11).

And indeed, in the lucid perspective exemplified by Deguy's "(I Git)," cited below, the most appropriate response to the encroaching "night" that threatens to engulf any remnants of meaning in human experience, is an expression of equal starkness; not resisting, but facilitating the "only progression" possible, ultimately, into oblivion:

> La seule progression que nous viv-
> Ons cette poussée vers le seuil au-delà-i
> Ci seul cas de possession : par la mort alentie
>
> – Rampe dans le tunnel haut de ton épaisseur
> Desquame Efface « toi »
> La tranchée de nuit te hale vers la nuit – (*Poèmes II* 99).

When the language of contemporary poetry *is* animated by repetition and modulation, it is often not in order to communicate an affective experience, positive or negative ("[…] je / ne dis pas le monde est bain de fiel je ne dis pas voici des yeux / et des merveilles," in the passage from Roubaud's *E*, cited below), but to insist on the impossibility of the poetic event as such. A continually mundane state of existence can no longer be agitated out of ennui through the expression of desire—whether for beauty or violence:

> Je vis sans hivers sans lieux nul lieu nul temps n'est plus qu'un
> autre j'ai cessé d'entendre le bruit que fait l'eau aujourd'hui je
> ne dis pas le monde est bain de fiel je ne dis pas voici des yeux
> et des merveilles je suis soir et neutre (15).

Indeed, given the crucial relationship we have identified in the revolting poetics, between expression and the body, it is significant that with Roubaud's "neutering" of the poetic subject, the final silencing of the voice later in the same work follows a negation, not only of the senses, but of the most central source of vitality (the "warm" and "beating" heart)—a death sentence that revokes the subject's very "right" to live:

> je vais m'arrêter dans le noir dans le noir
> je n'ai plus d'œil je n'ai plus de cœur chaud

CONCLUSION 175

> j'ai perdu le droit d'être un cœur et de battre
> ....
> ne parle pas [...]
> ....
> va et la nuit bientôt te pèsera moins
> que tes jours reçurent (78).

While the changing perception of humanity's relation to the cosmos produced a significant re-orientation of poetic expression in the wake of Romanticism, as discussed in my Introduction, the discrediting of a meaningful, theocentric universe no longer stokes the fires of proud and indignant anarchy, but results in a detached view of violence and chaos. "Even Satan," the patron saint of much of Romantic and post-Romantic poetry, refuses to sing, in Réda's "L'heure douce":

> Or le monde en effet module, mais proteste
> Contre son propre goût de s'ébattre sans but :
> Incartades, fureurs, et même Belzébuth
> A déserté ce chœur sans demander son reste (51).[5]

In Dantzig's "L'Arc du corps," from *Les Nageurs,* even the ultimate, most physically experienced (positive) intensity, orgasm (expressed here, interestingly, through the very "intensive" structures observed in the preceding readings, language straining against its own density) –

> Ten*d*U pa*r* un o*r*a*g*e int*érieur*
> Le *c*a*rq*uoi *l*a*r*gue un o*r*a*g*e *l*ai*t*eux
> Qui tombe en `*l*ou*r*des `goutt*es* (34)

– is immediately recognized as a "defeat," in the perspective of the contemporary poet:

---

5   The irony of the revolting poets, it should be noted, is still quite present here (if relatively muted), as in much of contemporary poetry—Alain Bosquet's penetrating view of the overanalytical smugness of postmodern consciousness, "Lucidité," for instance: "Est-il plus pure joie que de s'interroger / sur son siècle incertain, dans cette bousculade / entre le vide et le néant ? Est-il amour / plus insensé que de comprendre où vont l'espace // et l'azur et le doute et le vieux désespoir ? / [...] / Est-il destin plus juste, entre tant de mystère, // que de mener sur soi, comme sur un serpent, / l'autopsie du bonheur [...]?" (*Sonnets pour une fin de siècle,* in *PC* 425–26).

> [...] hourra de la victoire aussitôt défaite
> Dont l'homme une virgule en œuf sous l'œil
> Tente en vain de garder le souvenir captif (Ibid.).

As Meschonnic insists, in *Et la terre coule*, to cry out – again, whether for or against, in ecstasy or condemnation – only leads to a form of silence, as it merely drowns out (or is drowned out by) another cry in an endless series. Whatever we may presume to illuminate by speaking, it is "night," in the end, that "speaks us":

> et les cris font du silence
> puisqu'un cri
> étouffe un cri
> et les paroles
> maintenant
> sont du sang qui sort des bouches
> et quand on veut parler jour
> c'est de la nuit qui nous parle (8).

In a universe that will continue to exist beyond humanity's end, and without our attempts to invest it with something more than brute being, the poet should limit herself to the simplest of pleasures, viewed against the backdrop of mortality, according to Bancquart, in "Imprécatrice, non !"—a humble attention to the untranscendent thingness of the world, that demands austerity of expression:

> On ne pleure pas
> sur le sacré.
> On n'amplifie pas
> en criant
> la voix des vagues.
> ....
> Ce qui me reste : l'âpre et courte délectation
> d'une pierre aux contours inattendus
> ....
> la certitude
> que la mort me prendra bientôt (92).

Caws has gone so far as to suggest, following recent catastrophic events of the new millennium (writing from New York, "cette grande ville que nous sentons universelle à présent, en grande partie à cause de nos catastrophes," 95), that the only French poets now worthy of the contemporary reader, "companions," are those who have fully incorporated the experience of death into their work —Deguy and Roubaud, for instance, following the passing of their wives: "Pour qu'un poème, une pensée poétique, puisse nous parler aujourd'hui, pour que nous l'entendions, il faudra absolument que le vide soit compris là-dedans : compris, au sens d'entendement, et compris, entouré, avalé, regardé en face" (95).

Admittedly, these are not the only responses to the reality facing the contemporary poet. Long before the current state of the world, certain French poets have found in the experience of mourning and doubt, for instance, neither an incitement to elegiac effusion, nor a cause for resignation and silence, but a site of possibility—for the individual who is willing to fully inhabit it. As Thélot suggests, in his reflection on the function of prayer in a universe "without gods," it is precisely the *precarity* of modern poetry (beginning, in this context, with Vigny), that provides the source of this genre's unique *potential*, allowing it to move beyond – in an entirely different way than that offered by revolt – the limitations of existing forms, and even language itself: "c'est dans la mesure où le poème est précaire – sans dieux – qu'il sort de soi par la question, qu'il outrepasse le seul plan de sa forme et tend au dehors de ses mots" (*PP* 129). And indeed, for Bonnefoy, one of the more recent poets treated in Thélot's study, the disruption of plenitude and unity is not a purely negative gesture,[6] for the sake of textural intensity, as my analysis of this work at the beginning of the present chapter might suggest. As the poet states, in his own reflections on mortality, *Les Tombeaux de Ravenne*, published the same year as *Douve* (1953), the broken and sullied state of the real is in fact, paradoxically, the poet's "salvation":

> c'est ce fragment de l'arbre sombre, cette feuille cassée du lierre. La feuille entière, bâtissant son essence immuable de toutes ses nervures, serait déjà le concept. Mais cette feuille brisée, verte et noire, salie, cettte feuille qui montre dans sa blessure toute la profondeur de ce qui est, cette feuille infinie est présence pure, et par conséquent mon salut (36).[7]

Even as the capacity for language to somehow access presence becomes increasingly improbable (the title, in fact, of the poet's 1959 publication), if not impossible, in the Bonnefidian universe – the longer, pulsing lines of *Douve*,

---

6 In the sense of this term (negative) utilized by Friedrich, cited in note #5, p. 3, of my Introduction.

7 Published with *Douve*, in the Gallimard edition cited for the present study.

observed above, replaced by the fragmented phrases of *Dans le leurre du seuil* ("Nous, la voix que refoule / Le vent des mots. / Nous, l'œuvre que déchire / Leur tourbillon," 29) – this rarefied atmosphere somehow enables the poet to wait and hope. As Née observes, contrasting Bonnefoy's stance with that of Rimbaud—a poet who similarly held out for a lost plenitude of existence, though never long enough to withstand the overwhelming forces of irony and deception ("mais le retour au réel désacralisé, comme du poème haschish, en refusera brutalement la séduction," *RP* 57): "Yves Bonnefoy dédie ses propres litanies incantatoires à ce qui *paraît* être la perte, ou l'absence actuelle de ce qui fut (et fut cru) pleine présence ; mais qui, en tant que signes de la présence antérieure des dieux, reste porteur d'espoir de leur *rémanence*" (Ibid. 57).

Another poet who has continued to remain relevant since the post-war years, and who is far from being overtaken by pessimism in his approach to language and the world, is Philippe Jaccottet. As Bishop has observed, if he too acutely feels the "awful pull between silence and speech, derision and celebration" (*CPF* 58), this experience is always counteracted by his inherent desire to somehow commune with the world, whatever it may present: "the energy to reverse the negative thrust [...] comes perhaps primarily from the poet's constantly experienced and very real need to question, but above all embrace: 'accueillir le monde et même ses plus choquants secrets.' Writing thus involves a going forth to meet the world; it is a gesture of committed immanence" (Ibid.); "Language thus challenges the void, the nothingness of our experiential, sensory and indeed, coldly intellectual being, in an effort to 'transmute' and 'decant' it, as Reverdy has proposed, better, to *re-convert* it into a *something* that it *is* only potentially, without humankind" (Ibid. 61).

Bishop has in fact continued to track this type of gesture in French and Francophone poetry more generally, reminding us that a number of contemporary poets insist on inhabiting the space of precarity, receptive to a world they might somehow "decant," as expressed in the above formulation. As he acknowledges, in his recent study of sixteen such writers, *Dystopie et poïein, agnose et reconnaissance*, the "drama" of modern existence is, for the lucid poet: "ce que l'on peut voir comme la lutte d'une agnose – d'une troublante incertitude face à ce que Gérard Titus-Carmel appelle notre 'présence au monde' – qui risque de noyer intuitions et instincts, viscéraux et psychiques" (7). And nevertheless, he confirms (in language that recalls the "revolution" observed in the second section of the present study, in the case of Char in particular) that the writing subject can still manage to endure this state of conflict and doubt with grace, able to accept that which exceeds his or her ability to master it: "[...] là peut intervenir l'urgence de ce qu'on peut nommer la reconnaissance face à tout ce qui excède nos catégories et même nos signes" (Ibid.).

Presenting the reader with a number of examples – both the canonized and marginalized, women (Béatrice Bonhomme, Esther Tellermann) as well as men – he is able to assert that a fundamental, affirmative gesture of the lyric is indeed still possible, and takes place, within the "dimensions" of poetic activity: "Au cœur de ses dimensions, parfois apparemment tragiques, persiste cela qui exulte" (Ibid. 8).

If we are conscientious in recognizing the multiplicity of responses to the existential/creative crisis confronting the contemporary poet, we must also acknowledge other work by Maulpoix, quite different in tone and outlook than the reflections cited earlier. In *Une histoire de bleu,* and *L'Instinct de ciel* (cited below), he is also able to locate a source of stability in the unstable, a groundedness in the groundlessness that otherwise haunts modern consciousness, "taking root" and purifying that consciousness of the "smallness" it clings to:

> Pourquoi demeurent-ils si longtemps devant le bleu, sinon pour faire face à ce qui fut là avant eux et qui restera toujours après eux : cette question muette, à jamais posée ?... S'ils y pouvaient prendre racine, ils deviendraient troncs et feuillages, délivrés de leurs petitesses, leurs envies, leurs calculs mesquins et leurs jalousies. Plantés, non dans le sol, mais dans l'énigme de toutes choses. Leur vie, une inquiétude, mais solide, enracinée dans ce qu'elle ignore mieux que dans toute croyance (15–16).

The poet, in any case, *must* write in uncertainty, rebinding – like Char, his "calendar" – the scattered "notes" of significant experience ("Écrire renoue la mélodie. Entre nous, tant de notes éparses," Ibid. 97):

> Geste irréductible à des causes et qui somme toute ne se poursuit que pour tenter de mieux connaître ses raisons d'être. Geste d'eau ou de sable, qui recouvre lui-même ses propres traces à mesure qu'elles s'impriment. Ce geste nous est nécessaire en ce qu'il maintient la coulure, seul apaisement possible de la grande soif inextinguible. Cette coulure nous tient lieu de larmes. Ce que nul ne peut boire, il le pleure (Ibid. 97–98).

Furthermore, the present state of poetry is not necessarily as dire as some would have it. For a number of poets and individuals who read and think about poetic language, the latter need not be reduced to a stance of receptivity and hopefulness, as discussed above, anymore than it should be pronounced defunct. Rather, poetry can continue to facilitate a communion with the natural world, through its own substantiality and affective potentials. Much as I, in elaborating the methodology of the present study, have questioned conceptual tendencies that limit our understanding of poetic expressivity, Collot has insisted that we must find a way of moving beyond the binary oppositions and polemics that sterilize poetry in the end, taking us away from the "matter" of language, and what actually *happens* in the poetic event:[8]

> Dresser l'objet contre le sujet, le corps contre l'esprit, la lettre contre la signification, c'est manquer l'essentiel, et le plus difficile à penser, qui est leur implication réciproque. La poésie moderne nous impose de dépasser toutes ces dichotomies, pour tenter de comprendre comment le sujet lyrique ne peut se constituer que dans son rapport à l'objet, qui passe notamment par le corps et par les sens, mais qui fait sens et nous émeut à travers la matière du monde et des mots (116–17).

Drawing on the thought of phenomenologist philosopher Merleau-Ponty, Collot proposes that certain ideas of the young Rimbaud are more than mystical yearnings. A loss of self – or rather, access to the *other* within the self ("Je est un autre")[9] – is in fact possible, to a certain degree, allowing one to re-establish a lost connection with reality, through (resonating, again, with the terms of the present study) the "physics"/"physicality" of speech: "Or pour donner la parole à cet autre en lui qui procède du dérèglement de tous les sens, le poète doit recharger de sensorialité le langage, « trouver une langue » « résumant tout, parfum, sons, couleurs ». C'est en mobilisant toute une physique de la parole qu'il parviendra à donner corps à la pensée" (Ibid. 118). The poetry of Ponge, for instance – another poet we must account for in the present reflections – can be read in a very different light, in this regard, he proposes. If a certain form of lyric subjectivity is famously absent in Ponge's work, according to a number of critics and the poet himself,[10] it is precisely the enhanced attention of *object-ivity* resulting from this stance – toward language, as well as the "thing" under observation[11] – that allows the writer to establish and communicate a very subjective experience of the world. Discussing the influence of

---

8 In the polemic in question, which occupied a number of French poetry scholars in the 90's, a subjective, lyrical mode of expression was pitted against an objective, text-based process of composition: "Rien de plus narcissique à certains égards que l'antilyrisme contemporain, dont le sujet se complaît parfois dans la délectation morose, n'en finit plus de contempler sa propre défection au miroir d'une écriture qui ne cesse de revenir sur elle-même" (Collot 125). See also Harrow, mentioned below.

9 From Rimbaud's famous "Lettre du voyant" (*Œuvres* 349).

10 See Harrow's overview and nuanced perspective on this important topic in Ponge scholarship (Chapter 3).

11 The poet's most famous work, the reader hardly needs reminding, is *Le Parti pris des choses*.

CONCLUSION

painters on Ponge, and the poet's attention to the material of his own medium ("matériau verbal," 123), Collot insists that these thing-poems cannot be reduced to a clever "play" with language, but demonstrate a highly innovative mode of communing with the natural world:

> Le libre jeu des signifiants permet d'écarter les significations établies pour en créer de nouvelles. Il s'agit pour Ponge de rendre cette matière « expressive », de faire des mots ces « objets émouvants », dont les « sons significatifs » « nous servent *à la fois* à nommer les objets de la nature et à exprimer nos sentiments ». La notion pongienne *d'objet* fait du poème un « objet transitionnel », au sens de Winnicott, qui réalise, grâce au *jeu* de mots, une transaction entre le *je* du poète et « *l'objet* de (son) émotion » (Ibid. 124).

Not unlike the Eastern practices of Zen and Haiku, a focused attention on the simplest objects of everyday life distinguishes the work of a handful of poets who continue to receive attention, among the "lay," as much as the critical readership—Follain and Guillevic, most notably, in addition to Ponge. In many ways, these poets, and their inheritors, would seem to have the best chances of surviving the forces menacing modern poetry, with their inherent awareness of the limitations of language and their modesty of expression; attributes that do not however prevent them – and their readers – from appreciating a world that is still here, if often lost to touch. A recognition/gratitude, that the single French term employed by Bishop so wonderfully conveys (*reconnaissance*). Even the work of a poet whose high degree of lucidity would seem to preempt any such communion with the world continues to draw the attention of readers, maintaining this connection. As Frénaud himself observes – in terms that resonate with observations of the present work – in the complex event that is the creation of a poem, a volatile "energy" arises, which the poet then embodies in language, "perpetuating" it for others:

> Cette énergie, il en est saisi quand il élève son chant. En lui donnant la parole, il lui assure chaque fois une apparition nouvelle et imprévisible qu'il perpétue dans l'objet qu'il forme. Et c'est avec sa voix qu'il l'incarne, si changée qu'il ne la reconnaît pas d'abord […]. Car le violent va-et-vient unificateur qu'opère le bouillonnement de la source, c'est avec ses moyens d'expression habituels que le poète agit pour en reproduire l'action tant qu'il l'éprouve (*IPP* 238).

Something significant can still take place at the intersection of poet, world, and text. No amount of disillusionment, it would seem, can entirely extinguish a certain *enthousiasme* that distinguished the lyric at its origin, and that continues to "erupt":

> Je ris aux mots j'aime quand ça démarre,
> Qu'ils s'agglutinent et je les déglutis
> Comme cent cris de grenouilles en frai ("L'irruption des mots," SF 78).[12]

・・・

We could not conclude, however, without confirming that active pockets of dissension *do* in fact continue to exist in the present state of poetry as well—more in the open, actually, than the controlled forces deployed by Bonnefoy and Dupin, analyzed earlier. There are yet poets who find the greatest source of linguistic conglomerations ("ils s'agglutinent") – language that, substantial, can still sustain the modern subject ("je les déglutis") – in the *revolting* poetics. Poets who are not concerned with reversing the dystopian tendency of human existence, since the loss of connection between the word and the sacred is not only not to be mourned, in its inconsequence, but is precisely that which enables poetry to draw freely upon the most vigorous, uncivilized elements of linguistic expression. In the first of Denis Roche's "Douze textes," from *Le Mécrit*, for instance, we recognize the "economy of *crasse*" identified in the preceding studies—a linguistic body that takes form (and is *trans*formed, mutating), in the accumulating matter of articulated language, as well as the text's figurative sequences, one "breath" leading to another ("*fesses* [...] en*flés*" => "Le poumon en*flé*"):

> *c*r*a*paud d'un mi*lli*er de *f*esses [...] en*fl*és [...] => Le *p*oumon en*fl*é du *c*an*a*rd *f*ait la *fl*aque du *seuil* n*o*ir [...] => *l*'é*lo*ge monst*rUeu*x du *p*ays de *G*a*ll*es **gra**ndit à *l*'excès *le v*a*gı*n g*lUa*nt ou*v*ert sur *le f*aut*e*uil (PI 551).

And the viral quality of such articulations in Roche's "monstrous panegyrics" is not so much unchecked, as it is embraced. In his "Après Saint-Just, les F," also published in *Le Mécrit*, it is as if, having reached a state of self-awareness similar to that identified in the work of Césaire and Char, he abandons any pretensions to renewed purpose or fought-for significance, questioning the semantic value of an initial, absurdly violent image – "Félin écartelé entre un

---

12 See Broome's analysis of this text and Frénaud's sensitivity to the palpable qualities of language more generally (AF 140). Debreuille also discusses the poem, in his study of the poet's own reflections on poetic process, "L'autocommentaire."

temple et un sanctuaire / Qu'est-ce que cela veut bien pouvoir dire?" (573) – only to follow this with an equally, if not more absurd (for its mock seriousness) explanation, which derives "something" – if not gold – from the vilest of matter:[13]

> [...] A croire qu'à aligner des mer-
> des sans suite il va en sortir un début d'intestin
> Prêt à toutes les roulures rhétoriciennes. Flooop.
> Sans chronologie. Purée d'asticots à l'assaut du
> Mot nuisance. Il va sans dire qu'à ce rythme il
> Finit bien par se passer quelque chose [...]
> ....
> A vomir une berline goudronnée – je veux dire une
> Pleine goudronnée. Ici un peu de balbutiement, ça
> Met du baume au cœur (Ibid.).

The development of such a text does not so much satisfy the reader's innate desire to arrive at some ostensible new level of meaning, as yet unrevealed, as it serves as a conduit for, cathecting the psychosomatic drives that *do* in fact exist, trapped in the body of the writing/speaking subject—a "stuttering" that serves, beyond all reasoning, as "balm for the heart."[14]

If there is one contemporary poet who has consistently and systematically deployed this most aggressive form of revolting poetics, it is Christian Prigent. Since the late 1960's, he has based the act of composition (if such a term is appropriate here) on the belief that poetic expression should first and foremost involve a radical form of disruption, confronting the reader with the fundamental, unbridgeable distance that exists between language and the

---

13 The ludic textural structures here, and in the following citations, are so dense and complex – and so recognizable to the present reader at this point – that they have not been annotated.

14 Roche develops a very different form of textual disruption in his innovative *Notre Antéfixe*. Bypassing the *textural* forces utilized in the revolting tradition, he splices together lines of – non-literary as well as literary – text, something in the manner of a collage, based on an aesthetic theory of the photographic still: "un appareil photographique ne crée pas une situation ou un geste ou un objet donnés, mais, les « cadrant », il les oblige, comme lors d'une répétition, à exister à nouveau et, ce faisant, de dire sans doute quelque chose de nettement différent de ce qu'ils disaient avant l'irruption *d'en face* de l'appareil capteur" (24).

real.[15] In a passage that explicitly enacts the revolutionary poetic gesture identified by Kristeva (a significant influence on the poet, along with Lacan), the "unknown" is summoned up from the depths of the writer, truly em*bodied* in the text, *semiotic*:[16]

> Summant l'insu d'en dessous de s'exhiber dessus, d'imbiber les tissus, de pisser son poissé dans l'air, d'envahir l'atmosphère. Pour s'extraire, soi, cracra, de son propre pochon, en vessie pétée d'cochon. Bavant, s'encrassant. [...] Vivant sa stature comme un collage de provisoires épluchures. Pas bien sûr de son écorce, corsant les forces pour en éclater l'os (*Commencement* 18).

And as in the above citation of Roche, this volatilized gathering of forces is not (re)performed unreflectively, but would seem to involve a level of self-awareness similar to that observed maturing in the preceding studies, as Prigent acknowledges the potential limitations of such a creative/destructive process. Through a dialogical structure that recalls Char's "Jeunesse" (analyzed on pp. 162–63 of the present work), he inserts a second, more cautious voice into the text, whose questioning makes possible the determined volition of the principal voice:

> Et t'as pas peur de tout casser ? – On casse jamais que l'encrassé, mais qui le sait, j'essaie, j'essaie, je ne sais rien, je trace mon petit chemin, je cherche un frais, tout juste un frais, même pas un vrai (Ibid. 20).

Having traced the evolution of the revolting poetics, however, reflecting critically on its purported capacity for novelty and liberation, one must question whether such writing, however lucid, continues to constitute a form of progress in this "tradition." The linguistic play observed above becomes suspect from our perspective—due, not merely to the "crass" discursive register

---

15 "[...] traverser le mur de représentations mortes, de sens éreintés, de mots inadéquats à l'expérience réelle que le langage irrémédiablement maçonne autour de chacun des vivants que, malgré tout, malgré cela, nous sommes" ("L'Amour," *CQM* 125). Ironically (considering that such militant revolt against established concepts and forms of expression was at the heart of the older poet's own work), Prigent has written a scathing contestation of Char's canonization, as noted earlier, on p. 153 of the present work.

16 The passage in question appears, interestingly, in a section entitled: "*Premier matin* : Pantomime des mômes." Regarding the influence of Lacan and Kristeva, see Prigent's theoretical writings in the journal he co-founded in 1969, *TXT*—"L'organon de la révolution," for instance, recently republished in *La Langue et ses monstres* (55–68).

that predominates ("pisser," "c[r]ac[r]a," "pétée," "s'encrassant"), but to the insistent terminal [e] that punctuates the entire second passage ("casser," "encrassé" etc.), both modulating and flattening out the poetic prose of the text, an interior *rime "plate."* However revolutionary at first appearance, such writing recycles what is an ultimately limited mode of expression, as we have observed, promptly inciting a constant *need* for disruption, insufficiently "fresh" ("je cherche un frais"). Whatever industry and wit are reflected in the continual rupturing of surfaces, the condensations of language that inevitably result – in both the subject, and phonetic *matter* – come to define a discourse that, for many readers, amounts to little more than a sophisticated form of potty humor:

> Pour avoir mal et pour entrer dans la propre peau déchirée de soi quand elle se cire du sang d'une autre peau qu'on a blessée. Pour faire son trou dans une boue instillée dans des blessures sales aux genoux. Pour boire par l'anus la nuit du fond du pré. Pour se sentir tas (Ibid. 18).

Later in the same text, the reader is indeed made to "feel [a] pile" – unable to accompany the poetic voice in its ostensible "deliverance" from the forces of entropy and reification – with the deposit, unexpected (even today, to a certain degree, in "literary" discourse), of *shit*: "Bravo, la délivrée ! [...] Exit l'ego nouveau [...]. Malaxé à mort ! Jeté ! dans l'herbe, comme une merde !" (Ibid. 192).

Advocating for the poetic devil, one might nonetheless propose that *this* group of poets – the latest generation in the revolting lineage – holds the greatest promise for ensuring the survival of poetry in the coming years; a world in which readers are perhaps less likely to be drawn into *reconnaissance* of the natural world – in written, poetic form at least – much less amenable to the lucidity and patience required to endure the precarity of the "threshold" occupied by Bonnefoy and others. Or are *all* stages in the French poetic tradition – including the affirmative thing-poems and expressions of communion, noted above, as much as the Romantic and Parnassian, etc. – merely passing tendencies in a larger *revolution* (again, in the original sense of this term)— a progression that is ongoing, but cyclical, returning to points along a continuum that will never lead beyond itself? Surely we are not, in any case, witnessing a point of no return, as Maulpoix prognosticates in the work initially cited in this chapter (*Adieux au poème*)—where future poets will *have to* choose the path of the *poète maudit*, truly damned, without novelty or the redemption of catharsis, limited to repeating what was already a repetition. Not merely gnashing his or her own teeth, but *gnawing* on the matter of expression, as Baudelaire his "**I**rrépara**b**le":

> Ne peut-il être que violent, moqueur et désespéré : iconoclaste témoin de la fin d'un monde qu'il aurait tout à fait renoncé à rendre plus lisible ? Difficile après Rimbaud Lautréamont Bataille Beckett ou Artaud, de faire entendre encore *la voix qui espère*. Depuis que l'écriture a su faire face au Mal et à l'informe pour les dire avec force, il semble que seule la voie du négatif lui demeure ouverte, et qu'elle ne puisse combattre les laideurs de l'Époque qu'en les répétant violemment (14–15).

With the same writer's indomitable "instinct for sky," cited earlier – an instinct shared by a number of the faithful, the present author included – such an apocalypse would seem improbable. The gleefully defiant exclamations of Jean-Pierre Verheggen, friend and collaborator of Prigent, on the other hand, would appear to confirm such a scenario, as he hyperbolically and repeatedly insists on the equivalence between expression and failure, in his "Entre Saint Antoine et San Antonio (Manifeste cochon)," from *Ridiculum vitae*: "Tout dire ! Tout parler ! Oser ! Tout écrire ! Tout sembler réussir pour mieux finir par tout rater ! Tout échouer et en rire ! Tout oser !" (90). He in fact goes so far as to counsel his young readers to "flee" poetry in general, leaving behind the degenerating corpus that his predecessors and contemporaries have either acknowledged or ignored, contributing to its decomposition either way, ultimately: "Tout pue, jeunes gens !" (Ibid.). Poetry is little more than "ridiculous" babbling, that the discerning reader should leave behind, once the present poem has been finished, however amusing: "Fuyez ces mammouths ! Fuyez leurs mamours ! Fuyez leurs moumoutes ! En avant toutes !" (Ibid.).

And yet, however tongue-in-cheek (Verheggen probably doesn't want his readers to walk away from *all* poetry—at least, not his own!), such commands point to two key elements of the revolting poetics that may in fact help to ensure the survival, not only of this particular "strain," but of poetry in general. For it is by desecrating the honey-tongued idols of the past, as Baudelaire once dumped on Musset ("Croque-mort langoureux,"), and Ducasse on Lamartine ("la Cigogne-Larmoyante"),[17] that the revolting poet points, however obliquely, to an ostensible essence of poetry just beyond the *marécages* he cultivates, luring asocial young readers of future generations into "unexplored lands." And such gestures will likely continue to be effective, as long as the very material of the revolting discourse challenges palates accustomed to the otherwise unremarkable articulations in conventional expression. Where such contortions of the poetic body actually lead is, in the end, for each of these readers to decide.

---

17 *OC* II 234, and *Poésies* 340, respectively.

Bibliography

Almeida, Lilian Pestre de. *Aimé Césaire : Cahier d'un retour au pays natal*. Paris: L'Harmattan, 2008.

Artuk, Simone Luise. *Une descente aux enfers : Images de la mort et de la destruction dans « Les Chants de Maldoror » de Lautréamont*. Bern: Peter Lang, 1995.

Babuts, Nicolae. *Baudelaire: At the Limits and Beyond*. Newark: University of Delaware Press, 1997.

Bachelard, Gaston. *Lautréamont*. Paris: José Corti, 1956.

Bancquart, Marie-Claire. *Terre énergumène*. Bordeaux: Le Castor Astral, 2009.

Barney, Tom. "Phonetics and the Empirical Study of Poetry." *Empirical Approaches to Literature and Aesthetics*. Eds. Roger J. Kreuz and Mary Sue MacNealy. Norwood (NJ): Ablex Publishing Corporation, 1996. 309–28.

Barthes, Roland. *Le Plaisir du texte*. Paris: Éditions du Seuil, 1973.

Bataille, Georges. *Œuvres complètes*. Vol. 5. Paris: Gallimard, 1973.

———. *La Littérature et le mal*. Paris: Gallimard, 1957.

Baudelaire, Charles. *Œuvres complètes*. Tome I. Ed. Claude Pichois. Paris: Gallimard, 1975.

———. *Œuvres complètes*. Tome II. Ed. Claude Pichois. Paris: Gallimard, 1976.

———. *Correspondance*. Tome II. Eds. Claude Pichois and Jean Ziegler. Paris: Gallimard, 1973.

Beaujour, Michel. *Terreur et rhétorique*. Paris: Éditions Jean-Michel Place, 1999.

Bellec, Dominique. *René Char, le poète et le maquis*. Preface Georges-Louis Roux. Paris: Passager clandestin, 2007.

Benveniste, Émile. *Baudelaire*. Presentation and Transcription Cloé Laplantine. Limoges: Éditions Lambert-Lucas, 2011.

Bersani, Leo. *A Future for Astyanax*. New York: Columbia University Press, 1984.

Bibliothèque nationale de France. *René Char*. Ed. Antoine Coron. Paris: Gallimard, 2007.

Bishop, Michael. *Dystopie et poïein, agnose et reconnaissance. Seize études sur la poésie française et francophone contemporaine*. Amsterdam: Rodopi, 2014.

———. « L'avenir du passé : les différences du même chez Char ». *Autour de René Char : Fureur et mystère, les Matinaux* : actes de la Journée René Char du 10 mars 1990. Paris: Presses de l'École Normale Supérieure, 1991. 129–37.

———. *The Contemporary Poetry of France. Eight Studies*. Amsterdam: Rodopi, 1985.

Blanchot, Maurice. *Lautréamont et Sade*. Paris: Éditions de Minuit, 1963.

———. "Lautréamont, ou l'espérance d'une tête." *Sur Lautréamont*. Maurice Blanchot, Julien Gracq, J.M.G. Le Clézio. Bruxelles: Éditions Complexe, 1987. 41–64.

Blin, Georges. *Le sadisme de Baudelaire*. Paris: José Corti, 1948.

Blood, Susan. *Baudelaire and the Aesthetics of Bad Faith*. Redwood City: Stanford University Press, 1997.

Bonnefis, Philippe. *Mesures de l'ombre*. Lille: Presses Universitaires de Lille, 1987.

Bonnefoy, Yves. *Du mouvement et de l'immobilité de Douve,* suivi de *Hier régnant désert*. Paris: Gallimard, 1979.

———. *Dans le leurre du seuil*. Paris: Mercure de France, 1975.

———. *L'Improbable*. Paris: Mercure de France, 1959.

Bosquet, Alain. *Je ne suis pas un poète d'eau douce. Poésies complètes (1945–1994)*. Paris: Gallimard, 1996.

Bosquet, Jacques. *Les Thèmes du rêve dans la littérature romantique*. Paris: Didier, 1964.

Bourdon, Bernard. *Expression des émotions et des tendances dans le langage*. Paris: Alcon, 1892.

Breton, André. *Œuvres complètes*. Tome I. Ed. Marguerite Bonnet. Paris: Gallimard, 1988.

Brillat-Savarin, Jean Anthelme. *Physiologie du goût*. Paris: Hermann, 1975.

Broome, Peter. *Baudelaire's Poetic Patterns: The Secret Language of* Les Fleurs du mal. Amsterdam: Rodopi 1999.

———. *André Frénaud*. Amsterdam: Rodopi, 1986.

Brunel, Pierre. *Charles Baudelaire, Les Fleurs du mal : Entre « fleurir » et « défleurir »*. Nantes: Éditions du temps, 1998.

Catani, Damian. "Notions of Evil in Baudelaire." *The Modern Language Review*. 102.4 (2007): 990–1007.

Caws, Mary-Ann. "Qu'est-ce que la poésie en France peut nous dire en ce moment ?" *Sens et présence du sujet poétique : la poésie de la France et du monde francophone depuis 1980*. Eds. Michael Brophy and Mary Gallagher. Amsterdam: Rodopi, 2006. 89–95.

Césaire, Aimé. *Cahier d'un retour au pays natal*. Paris: Présence Africaine, 1983.

———. *Cadastre*. Paris: Éditions du Seuil, 1961.

———. *Et les chiens se taisaient (Tragédie)*. Paris: Présence Africaine, 1956.

Chambers, Angela. "Prophets and Heroes: Ideology and Aesthetics in Aimé Césaire's Poetic." *Heroism and Passion in Literature: Studies in Honour of Maya Longstaffe*. Ed. Graham Gargett. Amsterdam: Rodopi, 2004. 221–32.

Char, René. *Œuvres complètes*. Intro. Jacques Roudaut. Paris: Gallimard, 1983.

Chesters, Graham. *Baudelaire and the Poetics of Craft*. Cambridge: Cambridge University Press, 1988.

Coates, Carrol. "Phonemic Structuration and the Reading of the Poem: Rimbaud's 'Le Châtiment de Tartufe' and 'Cocher ivre.'" *Understanding French Poetry: Essays for a New Millennium*. Ed. and Intro. Stamos Metzidakis. New York: Garland, 1994. 87–97.

Collot, Michel. *La Matière-émotion*. Paris: Presses Universitaires de France, 1997.

Crouzet, François. *Contre René Char*. Paris: Les Belles Lettres, 1992.

Dantzig, Charles. *Les Nageurs*. Bernard Grasset, 2010.

Dash, Michael. "Introduction to Edouard Glissant." *Carribean Discourse: Selected Essays*. Edouard Glissant. Charlottesville: Virginia UP, 1989. xi-xlv.

———. "Le cri du Morne : La Poétique du paysage césairien et la littérature antillaise." *Soleil éclaté : mélanges offerts à Aimé Césaire à l'occasion de son soixante-dixième anniversaire par une équipe internationale d'artistes et de chercheurs*. Ed. Jacqueline Leiner. Tübingen: Narr, 1984. 101–10.

Davis, Gregson. *Aimé Césaire*. Cambridge: Cambridge University Press, 1997.

———. "'Homecomings without Home': representations of (post)colonial *nostos* (homecoming) in the lyric of Aimé Césaire and Derek Walcott." Homer in the Twentieth Century: between World Literature and the Western Canon. Eds. Emily Greenwood and Barbara Graziosi. Oxford: Oxford University Press, 2007. 191–209.

Debreuille, Jean-Yves. "L'autocommentaire." *André Frénaud, « La négation exigeante », Colloque de Cérisy 2000*. Ed. Marie-Claire Bancquart. 265–81.

Deguy, Michel. *Poèmes II*. Paris: Gallimard, 1986.

Delbouille, Paul. *Poésie et sonorités*. Paris: Société d'Édition « Les Belles Lettres », 1961.

Depierris, Jean-Louis. *Tradition et insoumission dans la poésie française*. Nancy: Presses Universitaires de Nancy, 1992.

Dessons, Gérard. « Une manière bizarre ». *Lautréamont : Retour au texte*. Ed. and Preface Henri Scepi and Jean-Luc Steinmetz. Poitiers: UFR Langues Littératures, Université de Poitiers, 2001. 85–98.

Diop, Papa Samba. *La Poésie d'Aimé Césaire*. Paris: Honoré Champion, 2010.

Dobelbower, Nicolas. "Pushing the Limits of the Modern Subject: Lautréamont's *Les Chants de Maldoror*." *Literature and Cruelty: proceedings of the Sixth Annual Graduate Student Conference in French, Francophone and Comparative Literature, Columbia University, March 1, 1996*. Ed. Vincent Desroches. 14–24.

Ducasse, Isidore, le Comte de Lautréamont. *Les Chants de Maldoror, Poésies I et II*. Ed. Jean-Luc Steinmetz. Paris: Flammarion, 1990.

Dupin, Jacques. *Le Corps clairvoyant*. Paris: Gallimard, 1999.

———. "Dehors la nuit est gouvernée." *L'Arc* 22 (1963): 64–68.

Dupouy, Christine. *René Char*. Paris: Pierre Belfond, 1987.

Durante, Daniel Castillo. "De Sade à Lautréamont : L'Altérité et le problème du mal." *Le Mal dans l'imaginaire littéraire français*. Ed. and Intro. Myriam Watthee-Delmotte and Metka Zupancic. Paris: L'Harmattan, 1998. 37–49.

Eliot, T.S. "The Lesson of Baudelaire." *The Tyro*. No. 1 (Spring 1921): 4.

Evans, David. "Baudelaire and Irresolvable Poetic Tension." *Visions/Revisions: Essays on Nineteenth-Century French Culture*. Bern: Peter Lang, 2003. 241–60.

Ferdinand, Malik. "« La Force de l'écorce en dessous crie... » : La Négritude comme esthétique antillaise de la révolte chez Aimé Césaire et Reinaldo Arenas." *Negritude:*

legacy and present relevance. Eds. Isabelle Constant and Kahiudi C. Mabana. Newcastle upon Tyne: Cambridge Scholars Publishing, 2009. 241–55.

Fisher, Andreas. "What, if Anything, is Phonological Iconicity?" *Form Miming Meaning: Iconicity in Language and Literature*. Eds. Max Nänny and Olga Fischer. Philadelphia: John Benjamins Publishing Company, 1999. 123–34.

Fónagy, Ivan. *La vive voix, Essais de psycho-phonétique*. Paris: Éditions Payot, 1991.

——. "Communication in Poetry." *Word* 17 (1961): 194–218.

Frénaud, André. *La Sainte Face*. Paris: Gallimard, 1968.

——. *Il n'y a pas de paradis*. Paris: Gallimard, 1967.

Friedrich, Hugo. *The Structure of Modern Poetry*. Evanston: Northwestern University Press, 1974.

Galibert, Thierry. *Le Poète et la modernité*. Paris: Éditions L'Harmattan, 1998.

Gauthier, Théophile. Préface, *Mademoiselle de Maupin*. Paris: Garnier Frères, 1966.

Gendre, André. *Évolution du sonnet français*. Paris: Presses Universitaires de France, 1996.

Giusto, Jean-Pierre. "*Les Chants de Maldoror* ou Le Triomphe du miroir." *Sur Lautréamont*. Valenciennes: Presses Universitaires de Valenciennes, 1994. 79-127.

Golston, Michael. *Rhythm and Race in Modernist Poetry and Science*. New York: Columbia University Press, 2008.

Gonsalves, Joshua. "Byron – In-Between Sade, Lautréamont, and Foucault: Situating the Canon of 'Evil' in the Nineteenth Century." *Romanticism on the Net* 43 (August 2006).

Goraj, Sylviane. "Henri Michaux, lecteur de Lautréamont ou l'aventure d'une dépossession." *Le Mal dans l'imaginaire littéraire français*. Ed. and Intro. Myriam Watthee-Delmotte and Metka Zupancic. Paris: L'Harmattan, 1998. 77–89.

Gourio, Anne. "Aux sources de la nuit, Char et Dupin : genèse d'un imaginaire." *René Char 2, poètes et philosophes : de la fraternité selon Char*. Eds. Danièle Leclair and Patrick Née. Caen: Lettres modernes Minard, 2007. 145–72.

Gracq, Julien. "Lautréamont toujours." *Sur Lautréamont*. Maurice Blanchot, Julien Gracq, J.M.G. Le Clézio. Bruxelles: Éditions Complexe, 1987. 9–39.

Grammont, Maurice. *Petit traité de versification française*. Paris: Armand Colin, 1965.

——. *Le vers français*. Paris: Delgrave, 1937.

Guermazi, Jamel. "Les procédés de la discontinuité dans *Les Chants de Maldoror*." *Poétiques de la discontinuité, de 1870 à nos jours*. Ed. Isabelle Chol. Clermont- Ferrand: Presses Universitaires Blaise Pascal, 2004. 189–203.

Guermès, Sophie. *La Poésie moderne*. Paris: L'Harmattan, 1999.

Guitard, Bruno. "La séduction du lecteur." *Malédiction ou révolution poétique*. Colloque de Cerisy-la-Salle, 15–22 juillet 1989. Valenciennes: Presses Universitaires de Valenciennes, 1990. 45–54.

Hara, Taichi. "Évocation créatrice : une lecture des *Chants de Maldoror*." *La Licorne* 57 (2001): 168–81.

Harrow, Susan. *The Material, the Real, and the Fractured Self: Subjectivity and Representation from Rimbaud to Réda*. Toronto: University of Toronto Press, 2004.

Hénane, René. "Le Lexique d'Aimé Césaire... pourquoi ?" *Aimé Césaire à l'œuvre*. Eds. Marc Cheymol and Philippe Ollé-Laprune. Paris: Éditions des archives contemporaines, 2010. 87–94.

———. *Césaire & Lautréamont, bestiaire & métamorphose*. Paris: L'Harmattan, 2006.

———. *Aimé Césaire, le chant blessé : biologie et poétique*. Paris: Éditions Jean-Michel Place, 1999.

Hrushovski, Benjamin. "The Meaning of Sound Patterns in Poetry: An Interaction Theory." *Poetics Today*. 2:1a (1980): 39–56.

Igou, Anna. "Dangerous Appetites: Violent Consumption in the Works of Flaubert, Baudelaire, and Césaire." Diss. Emory University, 2013.

Jackson, John E. "The Devil Doesn't Only Wear Prada: Dialectics of Evil in Baudelaire." *After Satan*. Eds. Kirsten Stirling and Martine Hennard Dutheil de la Rochère. Newcastle upon Tyne: Cambridge Scholars Publishing, 2010. 155–64.

———. *Baudelaire sans fin*. Paris: José Corti, 2005.

Jakobson, Roman and Linda R. Waugh. *The Sound Shape of Language*. Berlin: Mouton de Gruyter, 1987.

———. *Six Lectures on Sound and Meaning*. Trans. John Mepham. Cambridge: The MIT Press, 1978.

———. *Child Language, Aphasia, and Phonological Universals*. The Hague: Mouton, 1968.

Jameson, Frederic. "Baudelaire as Modernist and Postmodernist: The Dissolution of the Referent and the Artificial 'Sublime.'" *Lyric Poetry: Beyond New Criticism*. Eds. Chaviva Hošek and Patricia Parker. Ithaca: Cornell University Press, 1985. 247-63.

Jenny, Laurent. *La Terreur et les signes*. Paris: Gallimard, 1982.

Johnson, Barbara. *Défigurations du langage poétique*. Paris: Flammarion, 1979.

Kaddour, Hédi. "Les Élégiaques et la canaille." *Baudelaire : nouveaux chantiers*. Lille: Presses Universitaires du Septentrion, 1995. 19–25.

Kayser, Wolfgang. *Das sprachliche Kunstwerk*. Berne: Francke, 1951.

Keats, John. *John Keats*. Ed. Susan J. Wolfson. New York: Pearson, 2007.

Kesteloot, Lilyan. *Aimé Césaire*. Paris: Pierre Seghers, 1962.

Kirkegaard, Søren. *The Present Age*. Trans. Alexander Dru. Intro. Walter Kaufman. New York: Harper & Row, 1962.

Kouassi, Germain. *La Poésie de Césaire par la langue et le style : l'exemple du "Cahier d'un retour au pays natal."* Paris: Éditions Publibook, 2006.

Kristeva, Julia. *Sens et non-sens de la révolte*. Paris: Librairie Arthème Fayard, 1996.

———. *La révolution du langage poétique*. Paris: Éditions du Seuil, 1985.

Kubayanda, J.B. *The Poet's Africa: Africanness in the Poetry of Nicolàs Guillén and Aimé Césaire*. New York: Greenwood, 1990.

Labarthe, Patrick. *Baudelaire et la tradition de l'allégorie*. Genève: Droz, 1999.
Lamartine, Alphonse de. *Méditations poétiques*. Paris: Gallimard, 1981.
Launay, Claude. *Les Fleurs du mal de Charles Baudelaire*. Paris: Gallimard, 1995.
Lawlor, Patricia. *Le Fonctionnement de la métaphore dans* Les Chants de Maldoror. University, Miss.: Romance Monographs, 1984.
———. "Lautréamont's Outrageous Text; Language as Weapon and Victim in the Chants de Maldoror." *Chimères*. XVII.2 (1984): 3–13.
Lecercle, Jean-Jacques. *The Violence of Language*. New York: Routledge, 1990.
Leclair, Danièle. *René Char : Là où brûle la poésie*. Croissy-Beaubourg: Éditions Aden, 2007.
Le Clézio, J.M.G. "Le Rêve de Maldoror." *Sur Lautréamont*. Maurice Blanchot, Julien Gracq, J.M.G. Le Clézio. Bruxelles: Éditions Complexe, 1987. 65–134.
Lindsay, Cecile. "Tearing the Body: Modern Self and Postmodern Corporality in *Les Chants de Maldoror*." *Nineteenth Century French Studies*. 22.1–2 (1993–94): 150–71.
Mallarmé, Stéphane. "Crise de vers." *Divagations. Œuvres complètes* II. Ed. Bertand Marchal. Bibliothèque de la Pléiade. Paris: Gallimard, 2003.
———. *Œuvres complètes*. Eds. Henri Mondor and G. Jean-Aubry. Bibliothèque de la Pléiade. Paris: Gallimard, 1945.
Marder, Elissa. *Dead Time: Temporal Disorders in the Wake of Modernity (Baudelaire and Flaubert)*. Redwood City: Stanford Univeristy Press, 2001.
Mathieu, Jean-Claude. *La poésie de René Char, ou Le sel de la splendeur, II. Poésie et résistance*. Paris: José Corti, 1988.
Maulpoix, Jean-Michel. *Adieux au poème*. Paris: José Corti, 2005.
———. *L'Instinct de ciel*. Paris: Mercure de France, 2000.
———. *Une histoire de bleu*. Paris: Mercure de France, 1992.
Merlin, Irène. *Poètes de la révolte : de Baudelaire à Michaux, alchimie de l'être et du verbe*. Paris: Éditions de l'École, 1971.
Meschonnic, Henri. *Et la terre coule*. Mesnil-sur-l'Estrée (France): Éditions Arfuyen, 2006.
Michel, Laure. *René Char : Le poème et l'histoire, 1939–1950*. Paris: Honoré Champion, 2007.
Molino, Jean and Joëlle Gardes-Tamine. *Introduction à l'analyse de la poésie, II*. Paris: Presses Universitaires de France, 1988.
Murphy, Steve. "À Propos de quelques rimes et vents." *L'Année Baudelaire*. Paris: Éditions Champion, 2007. 231–51.
Nathan, Michel. *Lautréamont : feuilletoniste autophage*. Seyssel: Éditions Champ Vallon 1992.
Née, Patrick. *Rhétorique profonde d'Yves Bonnefoy*. Paris: Hermann, 2004.
———. "Amont, mythe de compromis." *René Char 10 ans après*. Ed. Paule Plouvier. Paris: L'Harmattan, 2000. 155–79.

Nesselroth, Peter. "Suicider l'autre : Maldoror et la colonne de la place Vendôme." *L'Infini.* 109 (Winter 2010): 72–81.

———. *Lautréamont's Imagery: A Stylistic Approach.* Geneva: Librairie Droz, 1969.

Newman, Stanley. "Further Experiments in Phonetic Symbolism." *American Journal of Psychology.* 45 (1933): 53–75.

Onyeoziri. Gloria Nne. *La Parole poétique d'Aimé Césaire : Essai de sémantique littéraire.* Paris: L'Harmattan, 1992.

Paviot, Christian. *Césaire autrement : Le mysticisme du Cahier d'un retour au pays natal.* Paris: L'Harmattan, 2009.

Philip, Michel. *Lectures de Lautréamont.* Paris: Librairie Armand Colin, 1971.

Pichois, Claude. *Baudelaire, Études et Témoignages.* Neuchâtel: La Baconnière, 1967.

Pickering, Robert. *Lautréamont/Ducasse : thématique et écriture.* Paris: Minard, 1988.

Pierre-Quint, Léon. *Le Comte de Lautréamont et Dieu.* Marseille: Les Cahiers du sud, 1929.

Pierssens, Michel. *Ducasse et Lautréamont : l'envers et l'endroit.* Saint-Denis: Presses Universitaires de Vincennes, 2005.

Plato. *Cratylus.* Trans. C.D.C. Reeve. *Plato, Complete Works.* Ed. J.M. Cooper. Indianapolis and Cambridge: Hackett, 1997.

Pleynet, Marcelin. "Situation : Lautréamont." *L'Infini.* 109 (Winter 2010): 58–61.

———. *Lautréamont par lui-même.* Paris: Éditions du Seuil, 1967.

Pluth, Ed. "An Adventure in the Order of Things: Jean-Claude Milner on lalangue and Lacan's Incomplete Materialism. *S: Journal of The Jan Van Eyck Circle for Lacanian Ideology Critique.* 3 (2010): 178–90.

Poe, Edgar Allen. "The Poetic Principle." *Edgar Allen Poe, Critical Theory: The Major Documents.* Ed. and Intro. Stuart Levine and Susan F. Levine. Urbana: University of Illinois, 2009.

Ponge, Francis. *Le Parti pris des choses.* Paris: Gallimard, 1982.

Poulet, Georges. "Exploding Poetry." *Charles Baudelaire.* Ed. Harold Bloom. New York: Chelsea House Publishers, 1987. 63–79.

———. *Exploding Poetry: Baudelaire/Rimbaud.* Trans. Françoise Meltzer. Chicago: University of Chicago Press, 1980.

Prigent, Christian. *La Langue et ses monstres.* Paris: P.O.L., 2014.

———. *Ceux qui merdRent.* Paris: P.O.L., 1991.

———. *Commencement.* Paris: P.O.L., 1989.

Raybaud, Antoine. "Sous l'angle fusant de la rencontre." *Autour de René Char : Fureur et mystère, les Matinaux* : actes de la Journée René Char du 10 mars 1990. Paris: Presses de l'École Normale Supérieure, 1991. 139–49.

Réda, Jacques. *L'adoption du système métrique.* Paris: Gallimard, 2004.

Richter, Mario. *Baudelaire : Les Fleurs du mal.* Genève: Éditions Slatkine, 2001.

Riley, Denise and Jean-Jacques Lecercle. *The Force of Language*. New York: Palgrave Macmillan, 2004.

Rimbaud, Arthur. *Œuvres*. Eds. Suzanne Bernard and André Guyaux. Paris: Garnier, 1983.

Roche, Denis. *La Poésie est inadmissible*. Paris: Éditions du Seuil, Coll. Fiction & Cie, 1995.

——— . *Notre Antéfixe*. Paris: Flammarion, 1978.

Roubaud, Jacques. *E*. Paris: Gallimard, 1967.

Sanyal, Debarati. *The Violence of Modernity: Baudelaire, Irony, and the Politics of Form*. Baltimore: The Johns Hopkins University Press, 2006.

Sanz, Teo. "Un refuge redoutable : la nature chez Lautréamont." *L'Esprit Créateur*. 46.2 (2006): 42–55.

Sartre, Jean-Paul. *Baudelaire*. Paris: Gallimard, 1988.

Saussure, Ferdinand de. *Cours de linguistique générale*. Paris: Payot, 1995.

Schulz, Michael. *René Char : du texte au discours*. Paris: L'Harmattan, 2004.

Shinabargar, Scott. "Unexorcised Conscience: The Byronic Complex of *Maldoror*." *Intertexts*. 17:2 (Fall 2013): 113–28.

——— . "René Char and the Matter of Language." *French Forum*. 37:3 (Fall 2012): 81–97.

——— . "Disarming Transgressions: Maldoror, Michaux and Beyond." *Dalhousie French Studies*. 96 (Fall 2011): 63–72.

——— . "L'Esthétique du mal : La violence des œuvres de d'Aubigné et de Baudelaire." *Papers on French Seventeenth-Century Literature*. 33:62 (Spring 2005): 125–42.

Soulier, Jean-Pierre. *Lautréamont, génie ou maladie mentale ?* Genève: Droz, 1964.

Spackman, Barbara. *Decadent Genealogies: The Rhetoric of Sickness from Baudelaire to D'Annunzio*. Ithaca: Cornell University Press, 1989.

Spire, André. *Plaisir poétique et plaisir musculaire*. Paris: Librairie José Corti, 1986.

Steinmetz, Jean-Luc. "Isidore Ducasse et le langage des sciences." *Lautréamont : Retour au texte*. Eds. Henri Scepi et Jean-Luc Steinmetz. Poitiers: La Licorne, 2001. 151–65.

——— . "Une Affaire spirituellement ténébreuse." *Sur Lautréamont*. Valenciennes: Presses Universitaires de Valenciennes, 1994. 139–79.

Stevens, Wallace. *The Palm at the End of the Mind*. New York: Vintage Books, 1990.

Sunderland, Luke. "The Art of Revolt: Rebellion in the Works of Bertran de Born and Julia Kristeva." *Comparative Literature*. 62:1 (2010): 22–40.

Thélot, Jérôme. *La poésie précaire*. Paris: Presses Universitaires de France, 1997.

——— . "La Prière selon Baudelaire." *Baudelaire : Nouveaux chantiers*. Lille: Presses Universitaires du Septentrion, 1995. 85–96.

——— . *Baudelaire / Violence et poésie*. Paris: Gallimard, 1993.

Thomas, Andrea S. *Lautréamont, Subject to Interpretation*. Amsterdam: Rodopi, 2015.

Thut, Martin. *Le Simulacre de l'énonciation: Stratégies persuasives dans* Les Chants de Maldoror *de Lautréamont*. Bern: Peter Lang, 1989.

Tsur, Reuven. *Toward a Theory of Cognitive Poetics*. Eastbourne: Sussex Academic Press, 2008.

———. *What Makes Sound Patterns Expressive?* Durham: Duke University Press, 1992.

Turgenev, Ivan. *Fathers and Sons*. Trans., Ed., Intro. and Notes Richard Freeborn. Oxford: Oxford University Press, 2008.

Van Rogger Andreucci, Christine. *René Char sous sa casquette amarante... René Char 10 ans après*. Paris: L'Harmattan, 2000.

Verheggen, Jean-Pierre. *Ridiculum Vitae* précédé de *Artaud Rimbur*. Paris: Gallimard, 2001.

Vivès, Vincent. *La Beauté et sa part maudite*. Aix-en-Provence: Publications de l'Université de Provence, 2005.

Vivier, Robert. *L'Originalité de Baudelaire*. Bruxelles: Palais des Académies, 1989.

Voellmy, Jean. "La Fureur de René Char ou 'Genus irritabile vatum.'" *Lettres Romanes*. 53:3–4 (1999): 349–72.

Watthee-Delmotte, Myriam and Metka Zupancic. *Le Mal dans l'imaginaire littéraire français*. Paris: L'Harmattan, 1998.

Winspur, Steven. "Ethics, Change, and Lautréamont." *L'Esprit Créateur*. XXVII.2 (1987): 82–91.

Zanker, G. "Enargeia in the Ancient Criticism of Poetry." *Rheinisches Museum für Philologie*. Neu Folge, 124. Bd., H. ¾ (1981). 297–310.

Electronic Resources

<http://slingmoore.blogspot.com/>
<http://www.slinging.org>

Index

Almeida, Lilian Pestre de   132, 133n7, 139n12
Aragon, Louis   76n
Artaud, Antonin   186
Aubigné, Théodore Agrippa d'   93n

Bachelard, Gaston   76, 80, 82, 84n10, 89n18, 95n23
Balzac, Honoré de   84n11
Bancquart, Marie-Claire   176
Barney, Tom   6
Bataille, Georges   1, 36n8, 73n, 186
Beaujour, Michel   23
Beckett, Samuel   186
Bellec, Dominique   153
Benveniste, Émile   38-39
Bersani, Leo   79, 82, 87
Bianchon, Horace   59
Bishop, Michaël   161, 178, 181
Blanchot, Maurice   79n, 81, 100, 103, 117, 121
Blin, Georges   34
Blood, Susan   33n1, 190
Bonhomme, Béatrice   179
Bonnefis, Philippe   42, 66n41, 72n
Bonnefoy, Yves   169-170, 172, 177-178, 182, 185
Bosquet, Alain   175n
Bosquet, Jacques   95n24
Breton, André   23, 40, 127, 138n11, 139n12
Brillat-Savarin, Jean Anthelme   150n
Broome, Peter   40-42, 46n, 51n, 69n44, 182n
Brunel, Pierre   42n
Brunetière, Ferdinand   33n1
Byron, George Gordon   75, 80, 88n

Cain   59, 60n
Catani, Damian   34, 36n8, 69n45, 71n46
Caws, Mary-Ann   176
Chastaing, Maxime   12
Chateaubriand, François-René   36
Chenu, Jean-Charles   104, 109
Chesters, Graham   39-40, 65n40
Christ   57
Coates, Carrol   7
Collot, Michel   180-181
Crouzet, François   153

Dante   59n31, 139n12
Dantzig, Charles   175
Darwin, Charles   14
Dash, Michael   128n, 134n, 139n13, 141n
Davis, Gregson   132, 139n12, 143n, 148
Debreuille, Jean-Yves   182n
Deguy, Michel   174, 177
Delbouille, Paul   7, 15n
Denys d'Halicarnasse   12
Depierris, Jean Louis   2n2
Dessons, Gérard   81
Dionysius of Halicarnassus   86n15
Diop, Papa Samba   128, 130, 137n, 140n, 142
Dobelbower, Nicolas   77, 108n
Dupin, Jacques   153n4, 169, 171-172, 182
Dupouy, Christine   162n
Durante, Daniel Castillo   80n

Eliot, T. S.   59n31
Evans, David   35, 39, 64n37

Ferdinand, Malik   129
Fischer-Jorgensen, Eli   13
Fisher, Andreas   6
Flaubert, Gustav   4, 19, 80
Follain, Jean   181
Fónagy, Ivan   10, 12, 14, 16n22, 19-20, 81, 98n
Frénaud, André   181-182
Friedrich, Hugo   3-4, 21, 27n33, 177n6

Galibert, Thierry   2
Gardes-Tamine, Joëlle   35
Gauthier, Théophile   2n3, 16, 18, 42n
Golston, Michael   17n24
Gonsalves, Joshua   80
Goraj, Sylviane   82
Gourio, Anne   153n4
Goya, Francisco   52
Gracq, Julien   117
Grammont, Maurice   9-11, 15n-17
Guermazi, Jamel   192
Guermès, Sophie   3
Guillevic, Eugène   181
Guitard, Bruno   192

INDEX

Harrow, Susan   180n8
Hénane, René   95-96, 128, 130n, 136, 140n
Homer   139n12
Hrushovski, Benjamin   6
Hugo, Victor   2-3, 127

Igou, Anna   150n
Ionesco, Eugène   98n

Jaccottet, Philippe   178
Jackson, John E.   36-37, 39, 57n, 69n44
Jacobi, Friedrich Heinrich   2n4
Jakobson, Roman   6n8, 12-13, 27n34
Jameson, Frederic   33n1
Jean, Marcel   76n, 79n
Jenny, Laurent   23
Jespersen, Otto   6n8
Johnson, Barbara   35n6

Kaddour, Hédi   35n5
Kayser, Wolfgang   7
Kesteloot, Lilyan   127n
Kierkegaard   2n4
Kouassi, Germain   136n
Kristeva, Julia   19-22, 25, 77, 81-82, 184
Kubayanda, J.B.   134n

Labarthe, Patrick   58n
Lacan, Jacques   20, 25n31, 184
Laclos, Pierre Choderlos   36n8
Lamartine, Alphonse de   17, 53, 60, 88n, 186
Launay, Claude   60n
Lawlor, Patricia   77-78, 89n18
Lecercle, Jean-Jacques   24-26
Leclair, Danièle   154n6, 156n, 164n
Le Clézio, J. M. G.   84n10, 122n45
Lindsay, Cecile   117n41
Louis XIV   118n
Louverture, Toussaint   137

Macdermott, M. M.   16n22
Maistre, Joseph de   34
Malécot, André   13
Mallarmé, Stéphane   3, 11-12, 19-21, 38, 75, 82, 128
Marder, Elissa   xii
Mathieu, Jean-Claude   151-153n2-4, 155-156n

Maulpoix, Jean-Michel   173, 179, 185
Merleau-Ponty, Maurice   180
Merlin, Irène   2n2
Meschonnic, Henri   176
Michel, Laure   153n2, 173, 189-191, 193-195
Mickiewickz, Adam   75
Milner, Jean-Claude   25n31
Milton, John   75
Molino, Jean   35
Murphy, Steve   65n40
Musset, Alfred de   75, 186

Napoléon   118n
Nathan, Michel   112n
Née, Patrick   153, 178
Nesselroth, Peter   78, 85n12, 86n14
Newman, Stanley   6
Nietzsche, Friedrich   2

Onyeoziri, Gloria Nne   136n
Orpheus   43

Paviot, Christian   139n12
Philip, Michel   77n3, 79n
Pichois, Claude   33, 189, 195
Pickering, Robert   81, 92n20, 100n27
Pierre-Quint, Léon   80
Pierssens, Michel   81
Plato   6
Pleynet, Marcelin   75n1, 77, 81, 83n
Poe, Edgar Allen   33-34, 53n
Ponge, Francis   28, 180-181
Poulet, Georges   34, 54n, 75n2
Poulet-Malassis, August   75n2
Pound, Ezra   17n24
Prigent, Christian   153, 183-184, 186

Raybaud, Antoine   162n
Réda, Jacques   175
Richter, Mario   58n, 65n40
Riley, Denise   24
Rimbaud, Arthur   7, 22n30, 75, 178, 180, 186
Roche, Denis   182-184
Ronsard, Pierre   12
Roubaud, Jacques   174, 177
Rousselot, Jean-Pierre   17

Sade, Marquis de   34, 69n45, 80, 84n11

Sanyal, Debarati   36n8
Sartre, Jean-Paul   127
Saussure, Ferdinand de   6, 11
Schneider, Michel   25
Schulz, Michael   153n2
Sisyphus   70
Sollers, Philip   77
Soulier, Jean-Pierre   79n
Spackman, Barbara   43n
Spire, André   17-18, 56
Steinmetz, Jean-Luc   75n2, 84, 104n, 106n31-107n, 109n, 114n37
Stevens, Wallace   93n
Stravinsky, Igor   4, 21-22
Sunderland, Luke   22n29

Tellermann, Esther   179
Thélot, Jérôme   58n, 177

Thomas, Andrea S.   78n5
Tsur, Reuven   7-12, 15-16
Turgenev, Ivan   2n4

Van Rogger Andreucci, Christine   153
Vautrin   59
Verheggen, Jean-Pierre   186
Verlaine, Paul   75
Vigny, Alfred de   3, 177
Vivier, Robert   39, 41
Voellmy, Jean   152
Vossius   12

Walker, Keith Louis   129, 139n13-140n
Winspur, Steven   77

Zanker, G   86n15

Printed in the United States
By Bookmasters